Real Success Without a Real Job

Real Success Without
a Real Job

There Is No Life Like It!

Ernie J. Zelinski

TEN SPEED PRESS
Berkeley | Toronto

Published by Visions International Publishing in
association with Ten Speed Press.

Ten Speed Press
P.O. Box 7123
Berkeley, California 94707
www.tenspeed.com

Cover design by Bella Totino and Verne Busby,
Totino Busby Design, www.totino.com

Cover image by Joshua Blake, purchased from
www.istockphoto.com

FOREIGN EDITIONS:

Published in Spanish by Planeta (Amat Editorial),
Barcelona
Published in Russian by Gayatri Publishing, Moscow

Library of Congress Cataloguing-in-Publication Data
Zelinski, Ernie J. (Ernie John), 1949–
Real success without a real job : there is no life like it /
Ernie J. Zelinski.
p. cm.
  ISBN-13: 978-1-58008-800-8 (alk. paper)
  ISBN-10: 1-58008-800-7 (alk. paper)
1. Career development. 2. Success. I. Title.
  HF5381.Z34 2006
  650.1—dc22

                                        2006011003

Printed and bound in Canada by Friesens
  1 2 3 4 5 6 7 8 9 10 — 12 11 10 09 08 07 06

Contents

Chapter 8: It's All in How You Play the Game, Isn't It? 203

Preface

The idea for this book came to me shortly after a friend announced that it was seven years since he started his government job. This surprised me — I didn't realize it had been so long. We had met in a coffee shop more than a decade ago when he was unemployed and I was just starting my publishing and writing career.

Moments after my friend mentioned how long he had worked for the government, I realized that in October of that year it would be twenty-five years since I was fired from my engineering job at a public utility for taking two months of unapproved vacation. Better still, I realized that it would be twenty-five years since I had a real job.

Talk about real success — to me anyway! That called for a grand celebration with my paying the entire bill. I even felt compelled to locate the manager who fired me so I could thank him and invite him to the celebration. I had not seen the man since he liberated me from corporate life.

> A career is a job that has gone on too long.
> — Jeff MacNelly

Alas, although I did contact him through a former colleague, my ex-boss had already made other plans for the evening of my celebration. Ironically, a few years back I had run into his successor, who told me — with a mischievous smile on his face — that he had bought my ex-boss a copy of my book *The Joy of Not Working* for a retirement gift.

Let's jump back to the fateful day that I was terminated from my engineering job. I was quite flabbergasted, indeed, close to being traumatized. I should have known at the time, however, that I was destined for much greater heights. A few years later I realized that, from a career perspective, my firing was the best thing that ever happened to me.

What's more, getting fired was great for other aspects of my life, including my mental and physical health. As I tell my friends, "The two best things I ever did for my well-being were to quit smoking and to get axed from my last real job, never to return to another."

The fact that I spent a princely sum to celebrate my not having worked as an engineer after having been fired twenty-five years earlier will surprise many people — particularly engineers. Not all engineers, however, given that there are many who would love to exit the field. Like a significant number of workers in all professions, a lot of engineers don't like how they earn their living and despise corporate life. Their personal lives may appear just fine to onlookers, but they suffer their jobs badly and with silent indignity. Indeed, there are many so-called successful people — engineers, lawyers, executives, and even doctors — in this sad and bleak situation who would like a more joyful career.

> Yet it is in our idleness, in our dreams, that the submerged truth sometimes comes to the top.
>
> — Virginia Woolf

Regardless of what profession you are in, you may also want to leave your line of work for something better. Particularly if you were intensely drawn to this book, a corporation is likely not the best place for you to hang out for the rest of your work life. The purpose of this book is to inspire people like you to reclaim their creativity, their freedom, and their lives.

In short, *Real Success Without a Real Job* is for individuals who:

- ◆ Are heavily committed to having "fun" in their work and want more freedom in their lives
- ◆ Want a more relaxed work environment
- ◆ Want no set hours and a lot of latitude in how their work gets done
- ◆ Want to avoid becoming just another cog who works for a faceless giant
- ◆ Want to find their own important mission, true calling, or passionate pursuit
- ◆ Know — without any doubt in their minds — that they are organizationally averse
- ◆ Believe that having two or three real friends and the time to spend with them is more important than making a lot of money
- ◆ Want to work at a dream job or run an unconventional business
- ◆ Want to gain courage to leave the corporate world forever
- ◆ Want to live an extraordinary life that is the envy of the corporate world

> I don't dream at night, I dream all day. I dream for a living.
>
> — Steven Spielberg

This is largely an inspirational book; it does not provide a specific road map for choosing your perfect unconventional career and making a million dollars at it in the next several years. Plain and simple, this book can't because a massive amount of detail the equivalent of many encyclopedias would be required. I include many recommendations for further reading throughout, however, that will provide more valuable information on how you can attain real success without a real job in your own special way.

The success principles emphasized in this book are the ones I have followed to make a decent living as an author and self-publisher by working only four or five hours a day. What a great profession! Why work at a real job when I can get away with doing what I have been doing for so long? No doubt some people will say I am lucky. True, but I am lucky in the sense that I had the courage to do what had to be done to get where I am today.

Others will point out that not everyone can do what I am doing. True again, but I didn't allow my mind to make up this flimsy excuse for not doing it. Neither did Abraham Lincoln, Bill Clinton, or George W. Bush make up the excuse that not everyone can be president of the United States. Otherwise, they would never have become president themselves.

Besides, not everyone can work in a real job. If we use an excuse, we should use it in a positive way to better our position in life, and not in a negative way to justify an unpleasant situation. Since not everyone can have a conventional job, why not be one of the prosperous individuals with an unconventional job similar to mine? This way you will find success, prosperity, and happiness on your own terms.

Throughout the book I use the term "unreal job," which is loosely defined as anything you joyfully do for a living with a lot of flexibility in your working hours, rather than a traditional job, which requires you to work in a rigid corporate environment with fixed hours. I also talk about starting an "unconventional business," which is out of the ordinary because it requires few or no employees, has low start-up costs, and does not demand that you work the long hours that traditional businesses require.

I can sing the praises of the success principles in this book because these principles have worked for me. I believe that these same principles can work for millions of other people in hundreds of other occupations in addition to mine. Indeed, you will read about several people in much different

What advice would you give to someone just starting a new job in a large corporation?

Never let your boss know that you exist!

> I believe you are your work. Don't trade the stuff of your life, time, for nothing more than dollars. That's a rotten bargain.
>
> — Rita Mae Brown

fields than mine who have left the corporate world for good. The great news is they are living lifestyles that are about as good as anyone can imagine.

No doubt the principles in this book will not work for everyone. One reason is that many people apparently don't want freedom; they would rather be imprisoned by organizations that tell them what to do, when to do it, how to do it. As Lord Boyd-Orr once said, "If people have to choose between freedom and sandwiches, they will take sandwiches."

If you are one of those mundane people who would select sandwiches over personal freedom, real success without a real job is definitely not for you. On the other hand, if you are trapped in the corporate world as the majority is, but would like to be liberated, then the success principles herein can inspire and help you to create a much more rewarding lifestyle for yourself.

You will have to re-do your thinking, however. Totally! Money, material possessions, secure jobs, and free stuff don't make the world go around for truly successful individuals. What does? Purpose! Family! Friends! Challenging projects! Creative satisfaction! Job gratification! Spiritual fulfillment! And, above all, personal freedom!

This leads us into a major premise of this book, which is that you can't be genuinely prosperous unless you have personal freedom. You will have attained true freedom in this world when you can get up in the morning when you want to get up; go to sleep when you want to go to sleep; and in the interval, work and play at the things you want to work and play at — all at your own pace. The great news is that not having a real job — and creating your own unreal job instead — allows you the opportunity to attain this freedom.

If you are still not in the least way dissuaded from reading further, you already have enough presence to recognize that real success and happiness are possible without having a real job. Obviously your aim is much higher than simply working at a conventional job, and you believe in being paid for your creative results rather than actual time spent in a cubicle or office. Keep reading — this gets much better.

1

Life Without a Real Job Will Set You Free

Corporate Employment Is So Last Year!

Imagine that you are at your high-school reunion where former classmates are bragging about how successful they are or are about to become. Brock, the science graduate, talks about the mining company he manages and how he got a $120,000 bonus last year in addition to the Porsche Boxster. Bella, who has been focusing her energy on international development projects with the government, is about to spend $58,000 on tuition for a two-year MBA program that she thinks will increase her income from $95,000 to over $200,000 a year.

After listening to several people boast about their careers and how much their mansions are worth, you realize that either only the jet-setting moneyed class goes to reunions, or there is a lot of lying going on. Eventually the group curiously looks at you, wearing your T-shirt that says "Organizationally Averse." Someone asks, "What do you do now and where do you live?"

You smile and say, "Actually, to millions of us, corporate employment is so last year! I don't like working for corporations and like to work only when I want. Although I dropped out of university, I live in Vancouver half the time and spend the six coldest months of the year in Costa Rica."

"So, how can you do this?" someone else quips. "Did you inherit a couple million or win it in a lottery?"

With a wry look of amusement, you answer, "No, I have never had any rich relatives and I never buy lottery tickets. So I have to work for a living, but I am a

> Men go fishing all their lives without knowing that it is not fish they are after.
>
> — Henry David Thoreau

5

one-person show specializing in the information business. This allows me to work on my own schedule — sometimes two hours a day and sometimes seven, other times on a whim taking three or four days off. I love a lifestyle without much pressure and with the freedom to do things on my own without the hassle of partners, colleagues, or employees."

> Every day I get up and look through the *Forbes* list of the richest people in America. If I'm not there, I go to work.
>
> — Robert Orben

"Sounds like a dream job," retorts Henry, a hugely successful dentist who lives in California and has just purchased a house worth three million dollars. "What about money? Can you make a decent living doing this? I read somewhere that many people who are self-employed live a pauper's life."

"Some do, many don't," you reply. "The fact that a person doesn't have a university degree and is self-employed doesn't mean that he or she can't make a decent living. Although I don't make as much as some of you do — not yet, anyway — I do make a much better income than the average person. More important, however, is the fact that I love what I do and I have my freedom. To me this is priceless, given that I am not the corporate type."

Is this starting to sound like too much of an unattainable fantasy to you? It shouldn't. If it is, you are likely too programmed with society's meaning of traditional success and need to experience a paradigm shift to realize that you can escape the corporate world and still make a good living. Better still, life without a real job will set you free.

Perhaps you took the fast track to life. Since high school, heck, maybe since junior high, you had a plan. You visited colleges and applied for scholarships. You graduated with honors from high school, won more scholarships when you took your undergraduate program, and then attended graduate school, maybe even earned your doctorate.

When you entered the world of work, you couldn't help thinking that the words "My future's so bright, I gotta wear shades" from some obscure song applied to you. You began your career life exactly as planned. Everything went according to schedule and every year virtually every item on your career itinerary became a reality.

> Success has made failures of many men.
>
> — Cindy Adams

Today you have a decent paying job, the bigger than normal cubicle — maybe even an expensively furnished office with a great view — and are peacefully coexisting with others in your office. There is one major problem, however: You are not happy in your work environment. Put another way, the thrill is gone — if it was ever there to begin with!

Perhaps you're questioning yourself and your place in this world more than ever before. Perhaps you are troubling yourself with intense self-interrogation. Perhaps you are filled with anxiety and fear. And maybe you believe you are the only one in your age group who feels so dissatisfied. Believe me, regardless of your age group, you are not.

> What is it that you like doing? If you don't like it, get out of it, because you'll be lousy at it.
>
> — Lee Iacocca

A lot of evidence exists that many workers in North America are terribly dissatisfied. For instance, a recent survey by *The Globe and Mail* asked its readers "Are you suffering from career inertia?" The results:

- 33 percent answered, "Yes, I can barely drag myself into the office."
- 23 percent chose, "Yes, but I can't be bothered to look for another job."
- 25 percent selected, "No, I find ways to stay engaged with my work."
- 19 percent picked, "No, career inertia is just an excuse to be lazy."

What makes these results particularly fascinating is that most of the readers of *The Globe and Mail* are highly educated, are well-paid, and work in prestigious jobs. Yet at least 56 percent of the readers are suffering from career inertia. No doubt the figure is much higher for employees as a whole in North America. Indeed, several career consultants claim that up to 70 percent of all Canadian and American employees would escape the confines of the corporation if they found something they loved to do and knew how to pursue it.

Perhaps the people suffering from career inertia are the most likely to show up at school or university class reunions, so they get to tell others how much "success" they have attained, at least in the traditional sense of the word. The question here is to what end are these people trying to achieve all those things that define success? Another question: How much are these

> Oh, you hate your job? Why didn't you say so? There's a support group for that. It's called Everybody, and they meet at the bar.
>
> — Drew Carey

people deluding others and, even more importantly, themselves?

Apparently not everyone deludes themselves. In a book called *The Great Divide* (Avon Books, 1989) by the legendary Studs Terkel, American worker Isabelle Kuprin talked about her job: "I'm a copywriter for an ad agency. It involves being a total asshole. I do it for the money, it's easy and horrible. I do nothing good for society." No doubt there are millions of people just as dejected about their jobs in today's corporate world, particularly if they work just for the money.

Clearly, one of life's biggest traps today is working hard for money, clinging to the illusion of job security, looking forward to retirement to make life a lot better. Sadly, fear — the fear of not paying bills, the fear of not being able to work for themselves, and the fear of not having enough money for retirement — keeps most people working at their corporate jobs. The darkest side of this fear is that it keeps employees in the vicious cycle of commute, work, commute, sleep, commute, work, commute, sleep, and so on.

Nine to five — what a way to make a living! We should pay heed to the song "Nine to Five" by Dolly Parton that was featured in the 1980s comedy film of the same name. In the film Parton and her two co-workers, played by Jane Fonda and Lily Tomlin, teach their jerk-of-a-boss a lesson. The song, however, reminds us that the daily grind of a regular job can suck big time.

Regular media reports indicate that many workers, including well-paid professionals and executives, are experiencing low morale, burnout, and a diminished quality of life. Indeed, every year brings another new study concluding that people are more stressed out and less satisfied than they were the year before.

What fascinates me most about this field of business is how we stay awake all day conducting it.

In the midst of it all, good news awaits, however. Perhaps you have seen the movie *The Great Escape*. There is an even greater escape you can make — the escape from corporate life. The reasons to do so are many. The typical workplace is demeaning to the human soul, particularly to the creative and independent soul. So is looking for a job, everything from drafting up résumés, sending out résumés, not getting replies, the interview process itself, and the formalities that come with starting a new job.

Of course, after working at a job for a year or two things don't necessarily get any better. This comes from the Idler website: "With very few exceptions the world of jobs is characterized by stifling boredom, grinding tedium, poverty, petty jealousies, sexual harassment, loneliness, deranged co-workers, bullying bosses, seething resentment, illness, exploitation, stress, helplessness, hellish commutes, humiliation, depression, appalling ethics, physical fatigue and mental exhaustion."

The typical work environment — a world without career satisfaction and personal fulfillment — is likely not a place you want to be. Maybe you have a job and are looking for a better one. You will discover that when you apply for a job that appears better than yours, a thousand other people have already applied. When the thrill of their jobs is long gone, many people look for a new one. They think that a new work environment will actually make them happier. Most often it doesn't.

> Dear, never forget one little point. It's my business. You just work here.
>
> — Elizabeth Arden

Then there are those who think that freedom is achieved by being promoted to a management position. Wish them luck. The promotion-in-waiting more often than not is trouble-in-waiting. In this regard, it is worth pondering the words of Robert Frost: "By working faithfully eight hours a day you may eventually get to be a boss and work twelve hours a day."

Perhaps the answer is to find some way to like the job that you presently have. Good luck to you as well. It will just take you a lot longer to realize that you and your job were not a match made in heaven. Even if you trick yourself into liking your job, you are likely to encounter situations such as your office mate bathes only whenever there is a full moon, your boss expects an immediate response to his weekend e-mails, and you don't get a raise even after your creative breakthrough saves your company a million dollars or two.

In this day and age, if you want an office with a great view, I suggest that you make the great escape. Become self-employed like I am and perform most of your work on a laptop in various coffee hangouts. This way you can have many different interesting views and not just be confined to one. Of course, there are hundreds of other alternatives for escaping the corporate world other than what I have done to make my great escape.

> I've been promoted to middle management. I never thought I'd sink so low.
>
> — Tim Gould

Best of all, there are many fantastic reasons not to have a real job! Many reasons will be given throughout the book; for now here are the ones that initially made my top-ten list:

Top Ten Reasons to Have an Unconventional Job

1. Although they will never admit it, your ex-boss and former co-workers will be green with envy.
2. You can get up at the "crack of noon" every day instead of the "crack of dawn."
3. After you get up, you can wear a T-shirt that says "Too Prosperous to Do Mornings."
4. When you don't have a real job, "multitasking" takes on a new meaning, such as working happily and leisurely on your laptop at Starbucks and watching attractive members of the opposite sex at the same time.
5. When someone new asks what your real job is, you can say, "I am too prosperous to have a real job; I have an unreal job instead."
6. Not having a real job will really irk all your relatives (and, better still, your in-laws too).
7. *Late Night with David Letterman* can be the first TV program you watch in the evening instead of the last.
8. You won't waste time reading the Dilbert cartoon every day because you won't relate to it anymore.
9. You no longer have to witness the turkeys escape the corporate ax while the eagles either leave or get fired.
10. On your death bed, regardless of your age, your last words will be: "Hey, I don't want to go just yet. The thing I enjoy most about life is working at my unreal job!"

I have to admit that the typical workplace is not a total waste of time if you are willing to stoop to its level. After twenty-five years of happily and successfully being without a real job, I am not. An unreal job such as the one I have created for myself really rocks.

> You don't resign from these jobs; you escape from them.
>
> — Dawn Steel

In my view, 95 percent of traditional jobs can't even come close to providing the freedom I enjoy. The good news is that you can also create an unreal job that you love and that provides you with a good measure of freedom.

Ordinary Career Success Is a Real Good Job; Real Career Success Is a Real Good Life

A miserable work environment is often discussed by co-workers in the same manner as bad weather: Nearly everybody complains but few people do anything about it. Of course, the best way to experience a better work environment is no different than the best way to experience better weather. Don't try to change either — instead, find a funkier place to hang out!

Like me, many people do find a funkier place to hang out than the corporate world. Take, for example, Eartha Haines of Oceanside, California. Eartha wrote to me at the time I was writing this book. Receiving her letter was synchronistic because I was looking for a great example to start this topic. Here is the complete content of the letter that Eartha sent to me:

> Kill my boss? Do I dare live out the American Dream?
>
> — Homer Simpson

Dear Ernie:

I purchased your book *The Joy of Not Working* over a year ago. I used to have a full-time job as a web developer working in downtown San Diego. I was a commuter and caught the train to and from work, an hour each way, so I read your book fairly quickly on the train rides. Since then, I have read it two more times.

I worked at my previous job for five years and was completely burned out and frustrated. However, I was a good employee and I brought my frustrations to my employer. He agreed to let me work from home a couple times a week but it did not solve the stress and demands of my job. After reading *The Joy of Not Working* I would daydream about being free from the daily commute and boredom of my current job. All I knew is that I no longer wanted to commute and whatever job I'd take next would be less stressful.

In March I turned in my resignation letter and agreed to stay on for three weeks so that they could find a replacement and so I could get them up to speed in my duties. I decided to start my own Web company but as I quickly discovered, it was difficult to get clients. As word got out that I quit my job, former co-workers, who also quit to pursue their dreams, began to contact me for freelance projects. I no longer have a Web company, but I am a happy freelancer, which turned out to be even better because I do not have to deal with landing clients or with any of the office politics.

I now wake up when I feel like it and my commute has been shortened to my office located right next to my bedroom! I am making a decent income and I can come and go as I please. I am finally living my dream because I took your advice and dared to make the first move toward a less stressful and happier life. I will continue freelancing for as long as it supports my needs. Even if I end up acquiring another job, I will be wiser in my choice. It will be much closer to home and something part-time. With the free time I have, I've also become a partner of an online store and it is taking off. Thanks for writing a great book. It will remain one of my favorites.

Sincerely,

Eartha Haines

> Sometimes you wonder how you got on this mountain. But sometimes you wonder, "How will I get off?"
> — Joan Manley

Obviously Eartha escaped corporate life because she was prepared to think differently and more creatively than the majority in North American society. She had a dream about how she could be successful in her own way. Then she did what she had to do to make her dream of personal success come true.

One of the keys to escaping a miserable work environment is to take a close look at what success really means to you. Although this is a success book, it is not a self-help manual on how to attain "success" in the traditional sense of word. It is an inspirational book on how you can attain a good measure of success, but you have to define success in a way that is different from any other person's on earth.

The biggest mistake that people make is adopting the

traditional paradigm of success instead of defining success differently. If all individuals had their own specific definition of success, they could achieve success a lot easier and experience a lot more of it. They could also escape corporate life. What an incredible liberation that can be!

More of us don't escape corporate life because money seems to be the bottom line in our fast-paced, overly materialistic Western society. Advertisers, the media, career consultants, and society in general place a lot of value on money and the things that money can buy, which are in themselves associated with success. Humans strive for a high-paying job so that they can have power, status, expensive SUVs, big houses, exotic vacations, and trendy clothes. These elements of success are supposed to make all of us feel successful, fulfilled, and happy.

There is a problem, however, even if people eventually attain the traditional model of success. When they do, many find that they still don't feel good about themselves. Now they are in serious trouble, because they cannot delude themselves anymore. On second thought, most people still can and actually do delude themselves, but it gets more and more difficult with time.

If you have adopted the traditional model of success, but want to attain success outside the corporation, it's wise to create your own model. When defining success, we should go beyond the normal parameters and look at what real success is to us individually. I would imagine that if we asked a million individuals, we would get a million different answers. Every one of us would have our unique version of what we would like to achieve in our lives.

There would be some elements of success that the majority would have in common, however. All of us want health and happiness. Most, perhaps all, of us want at least a measure of financial independence so that we don't have any money problems and the stress that accompanies these problems. Financial independence is often construed as enough money to do what we want, when we want to do it. For over 90 percent of us, having more money than we have today would be required before we achieve real success.

Of course, given that most of us would want to continue working even if we were financially independent, enjoying our work would be an important ingredient in our recipe for success. The sad truth is the vast

> Success for some people depends on becoming well-known; for others it depends on never being found out.
>
> — Ashleigh Brilliant

majority of people today, whether Americans, Canadians, or Europeans, don't stand a chance of achieving this element of real success if they remain in their present jobs.

What else would we have in common in our definitions of real success? Particularly for independently-minded individuals, freedom would be high on the list. Surveys of the new generation of employees entering the workforce, for instance, indicate its members value freedom highly. According to a recent survey by the international consultancy Watson Wyatt, new graduates entering the workforce tend to be less committed to their first jobs. Most seem to want flexible work arrangements, with some preferring a home-based office.

At this point it is worth asking, "What does success look like to you?" Besides the general elements of health, happiness, financial independence, job satisfaction, and freedom, what other specific ingredients would you add to your recipe for real success? These should be elements that have not been programmed into you by your parents, advertisers, the media, and society as a whole.

> Success is doing what you like and making a living at it.
>
> — Greek proverb

To help you get started on your model of success, I will share what success means to me. A good portion of my success paradigm was first introduced in *The Lazy Person's Guide to Success*, but this definition has changed somewhat since I wrote the book, and no doubt will continue to change to some extent over time.

One of the most important elements of real life success to me is having the freedom and independence to make choices in what I do with my life. Success means doing what I want at the time I choose. Corporate life, of course, would interfere with the freedom I enjoy.

Here is a sample of the freedom I have: After I get up — sometimes at the crack of noon — my first priority is to exercise one to two hours to maintain my physical health. Then I have a shower, which I truly experience in a leisurely and meditative state, followed by putting on my official work attire — most often a pair of jeans, sandals, and a T-shirt with something such as "I Am Big in Europe" written on it.

Unlike the majority of people, I fit in my work whenever I can, usually writing on my laptop in one of my favorite coffee bars. I don't know whether the owners of the coffee bars where I hang out consider me a coffee house phenomenon or a coffee house nuisance — I consider myself the writer in residence, which adds to my experience of success.

Most days I start working about 3:30 in the afternoon and put in only four or five hours a day, sometimes a little less, sometimes a little more. The odd time I don't start work until 4:30 in the afternoon, at which time I chuckle to myself because government workers are already going home after having put in eight hours of regimented work.

> If you get to be thirty-five and your job still involves wearing a name tag, you've probably made a serious vocational error.
>
> — Dennis Miller

Although I don't make as much money as I could by working more hours each day, I live comfortably and freely. I certainly wouldn't trade my present lifestyle for a boring or stressful job that pays a million dollars a year, not even for one year. This was even the case several years ago when I was struggling financially, $30,000 in debt, and sometimes not knowing where my next month's rent was going to come from. Real life success to me does not entail being worth a million dollars or two, although I would certainly get satisfaction from attaining this status through my creative efforts — particularly without a real job.

In financial terms, real success to me is handling money wisely so that I don't have financial problems. Financial success means earning the money to buy the necessities of life and having a little extra to buy some luxuries, such as going out to a great restaurant two or three times a week. Financial success is also the sense of freedom that comes from having saved a nice little nest egg. This can come in handy in the event I want to do nothing but play for a year or if my income drops for some reason.

Success to me is having not only the time, but also the ability to enjoy a lot of leisure activities. It is also the wise use of leisure time. Maintaining optimum health at any age must be a priority. This can only be attained by allocating some leisure time for adequate exercise and meditation each and every day.

Given the important role friendship plays in our lives, success to me is also being able to spend plenty of my leisure time chatting, wining, and dining with friends at a small bistro instead of going to a big state dinner, which, of course, is fortunate because I am never invited to any. In chapter 7, I will discuss why finding and maintaining real friends is a big part of achieving real success without a real job.

Career success to me, above all, is having a worthwhile purpose to pursue. My purpose is to help people develop their potential, make progress toward attaining some of their dreams, and have a great work/life balance. Like many authors, I receive a great deal of feedback from readers, such as the aforementioned letter from Eartha Haines. There is no greater satisfaction than receiving a handwritten letter, e-mail, or phone call from someone who has benefited greatly from reading my books.

Another ingredient of career success is having my own attainable dreams, regardless of how old I get. One of my goals is to have one of my books appear on the *New York Times* bestseller list. Indeed, it would be nice if this one did. Although achieving this goal is not essential to my happiness, I would get great satisfaction from doing so. This is one of my career dreams that motivates me and brings me smaller career successes along the way.

> Ask yourself the secret to your success. Listen to your answer, and practice it.
>
> — Richard Bach

That is more than enough about what success means to me. Now you should take the time to think about and write down the things that really matter to you in order that you can establish your own paradigm of success. With no personal definition of success, you will have no distinct personal goals and career dreams to pursue. Your definition of success may be similar to someone else's, but surely it should not be identical.

Sample Elements for Your Success Paradigm

- Create and work at a job I love
- Own my own home business
- Maintain optimum mental, physical, and spiritual health
- Earn an income that is in top 10 percent of wage earners
- Have at least three real friends
- Have plenty of time for friends
- Attain financial independence with $500,000 in savings
- Be able to take a one-year sabbatical every five years
- Write three books in the next five years
- Create something artistic of lasting value
- Learn a subject thoroughly and expand its frontiers
- Help make other people's lives better

Although the two are related, it may be worthwhile to create your own separate definitions for both career success and overall life success. To attain overall success in life it's important to have attained success in one's career simply because work takes up so much of our lives. Thus, your elements of career success may include

> There is only one success —
> to be able to spend your life
> in your own way.
> — Christopher Morley

job satisfaction, a healthy working environment, and some sense of control in your job.

But career success in itself does not mean that we have attained overall life success. As many of us already know, having a good job does not necessarily lead to our feeling successful, experiencing freedom, and enjoying prosperity and happiness. The way I see it, ordinary career success is a real good job; real career success is a real good life.

Once you have established your success paradigm, it's important to determine which elements are most important for your happiness. Then you must set your priorities accordingly. You must be reasonable in which elements in your success paradigm you want to attain. How achievable the elements in your success paradigm are will eventually determine how successful you become and how successful you feel.

Here is a warning: For some of us the biggest obstacle to attaining and experiencing success is expecting too much. Avoid placing equal importance on driving a Ferrari, becoming a renowned entrepreneur, getting a Ph.D. in Comparative Literature, learning twenty languages, becoming friends with both Donald Trump and Richard Branson, having a loving family, writing ten business books, and owning a twenty-four room mansion as well as a vacation home in Monte Carlo. Anyone who tries to attain this much or more will likely wind up being a total failure at everything.

Clearly, each and every one of us wants to win at the game called success. Above all, real success is being able to work and live in your own special way. Don't be a pig about it, however. Refrain from going overboard and feeling that you have to achieve all that the most ambitious of megalomaniacs wants to achieve. Excessive endeavor has been known to cause premature hair loss, nervous twitching, high blood pressure, and even insanity.

Summing up, if you can define what career success and overall life success mean to you in clear and compelling detail, you will have a much better idea if you, in fact, want to escape corporate

> Success is simple. Do what's right, the right way, at the right time.
>
> — Arnold H. Glasow

life. Career success in the corporate world is having a good job, one that either pays very well or has a lot of status. Career success for purposes of this book, however, is having gratifying work that is both personally and financially rewarding. If you can create a job that brings you freedom and creative satisfaction — a job that you feel good about and not just one that brings a good paycheck — career success can be yours in your own special way.

Don't Work Solely to Make a Lot of Money and You Will Likely End Up Making a Lot of Money

If you don't jump out of bed every work day when the alarm goes off eager to do some work, you are likely not all that enthusiastic about your job. Perhaps you complain, roll over, and contemplate whether you can get away with calling in sick for the third time this month. In this case, it is quite clear that you need to find something more challenging and satisfying.

Perhaps you work at a job that not only has good pay but also has a lot of status. Although your vocation is rated as highly desirable in career guides, you still feel that you made a terrible mistake and feel sick just thinking about most aspects of your work. Even if you are a lawyer, a dentist, or a chartered accountant, so what? You are not the only professional to regularly look out the window at work and ask, "Is this all there is to life?"

If you are presently grossly dissatisfied with your work, it doesn't necessarily have to be this way. The key is to find out what you really want to do. Imagine how much better life would be if you liked your work as much as you like your most enjoyable leisure activities. Put another way, you would be willing to do your work even if you weren't paid for it.

> People who think money can do anything may very well be suspected of doing anything for money.
>
> — Mary Pettibone Pool

Truth be known, for most people, regardless of their occupation, work is a gross inconvenience or necessary evil they have to put up with in order to earn enough money to survive for the time they aren't at work. Even people who occasionally get some satisfaction from completing a heavy workload or a challenging project constantly wish they were someplace other than the workplace. This is why most people feel they would have chosen a different career if they had their work life to live all over again.

> You are what you do. If you do boring, stupid, monotonous work, chances are you'll end up boring, stupid, and monotonous.
>
> — Bob Black

A lot of people work in jobs they don't like simply because they don't even know what they really want to do. One research study indicated that 40 percent of workers drifted into their jobs without giving much consideration to what they truly like and don't like about work.

Believe it or not, 37 percent of Canadian employees can't even give an accurate explanation of what their company does. I would venture to say that just as many employees throughout the corporate world, including Europe and the United States, can't give an accurate account either. If employees don't even know exactly what their company does, there is not much chance that they have a higher purpose or mission associated with their work.

Weirdly, both new employees entering the workplace for the first time and seasoned employees looking for a better job don't give much thought to what type of work would really turn them on. This is the case even though the average person will spend at least forty-five years of his or her life working forty hours a week. This works out to 90,000 hours or the equivalent of 3,750 twenty-four-hour days that a lot of people will spend in misery, wishing they were somewhere else.

One of the biggest reasons people end up in jobs they hate is that they choose careers which offer the most opportunity for making the most money. Pick up the career section of a major newspaper and you are likely to find a feature story about the best careers to pursue this year. The article will list all the hot fields as well as the fields that have moderate and limited opportunity. How much money you can expect to earn in any of the occupations will likely be a highlight in a sidebar or within the article itself. Alas, there will be no mention of whether the people working in these fields actually enjoy the work they do.

Whether you choose to remain in corporate life or leave it altogether, above all, you want to make sure that you end up working at something that you love instead of working just for the money. Working at something just for the money is something fearful people do. It is a sign of their lack of self-confidence in their ability, talent, and creativity to earn money doing something they enjoy.

> People first, then money, then things.
>
> — Suze Orman

If you feel that work is just a job, a way to make money, you are wasting forty or more hours a week of your life. You are stealing life from yourself by spending time on routine and drudgery instead of spending time doing something that you really enjoy. Working strictly for the money usually leads to one or more of the following negative outcomes:

Consequences of Working Solely for the Money

- Feelings of disillusionment, dissatisfaction, and unhappiness
- Feeling continually stressed, which impacts one's health as well as relationships with family and friends
- Feeling underpaid regardless of how much money one earns
- Feeling unprepared or unable to accept a job that pays less money
- Compromising one's integrity by working for a company that is unethical
- Winding up in debt due to constantly buying oneself material goods as a reward for working at a lousy job
- A lack of creative fulfillment
- A feeling of imprisonment while at the workplace
- A lowered sense of overall self-worth
- A lack of self-confidence to pursue a much more enjoyable career

Clearly, money is important in the areas of life where it is important and useless in areas of life where it is not important. This will be discussed in a little more detail in chapter 6. For now, the main point is that, sadly, too many people believe that money is everything and end up with the above consequences.

There can be no doubt that getting trapped into believing that money is the most important thing in a job increases your chances of being trapped in a miserable job for the rest of your life. Generally speaking, the more money you make at your job, the more you become dependent on that job to take care of you. This is particularly true if you can't handle money very well. Of course, most North Americans are not masters of money given that savings rates are at an all-time low — negative, in fact, for the first time in half a century.

Having a higher income allows you to buy more and more stuff on credit, putting you further and further into debt. Leaving corporate life becomes unimaginable when you have a mountain of debt that will take many years to pay off. Some desperate characters find a higher-paying job, which just locks them into corporate life even more because they buy more material goods on credit and the debt process repeats itself.

> If you make money your god, it will plague you like the devil.
>
> — Henry Fielding

The truth is that most people have been living with debt for so long that they are truly used to it. They can't imagine what their lives would be like without a high-ratio mortgaged house and a car that is 95 percent financed and furniture that won't be paid off for another five years, let alone a maxed-out Visa card. As columnist Leah MacLaren recently wrote in *The Globe and Mail*: "No one wants to talk about debt, but it comes home and roosts on your doorstep like a big, fat, clucking hen from hell."

The core of the matter is that common sense is in short supply when it comes to our accumulating more and more debt so that we can buy more "things." American humorist Will Rogers put it much more eloquently than I ever could: "Too many people spend money they haven't earned, to buy things they don't want, to impress people they don't like."

If something is missing in your life, it's likely not more stuff. How many more things do you have to you buy before you realize you have way too many? If you are like the average corporate worker, you are probably too afraid to admit that material possessions — regardless of how fancy and expensive — are not doing much for your fulfillment. More possessions just help dull the pain and emptiness inside you.

Fact is, addiction to material possessions can imprison us just as much as corporate life. I recently allowed an acquaintance named Denis to park his brand-new Harley Davidson in my rented garage while he went to work on the oil rigs for a three-week stint. While showing the motorcycle to my neighbor, he asked how much it cost. I replied, "Denis said he paid around $28,000 for it."

> We can create the ultimate job security by becoming less dependent on the organization for which we work and more dependent on our own resources.
>
> — Bo Bennett

Later as I was driving my 1974 MGB to one of my coffee hangouts, I laughed out loud when I realized that the total value of all my stuff — my clothing, three older cars, four bicycles, a laptop, and a bit of furniture — is around $18,000. That's right. Although I have money in the bank, the total value of all my material possessions is $10,000 less than what my friend Denis paid for a new Harley.

Do I feel deprived because I own so little in material goods? No, on the contrary — I feel extremely liberated! Unlike Denis, who feels compelled to work at a job that is not his dream job, just to make a lot of money to support his addiction to the latest commodities, I have been able to pursue something I enjoy and become a success at it. What's more, I now earn a decent living and am in a financial position to buy all sorts of things — even two or three new Harleys — for cash if I really want them.

Clearly, people living in debt and from paycheck to paycheck don't have freedom. What's more, they will never save a nice nest egg that can help them pursue freedom away from the corporation. Having a financial reserve could tide them over for a year or two if they wanted to pursue an unreal job or start an unconventional business at which they may not make that much money initially.

Speaking of freedom, one of the great paradoxes of North American life is the emphasis that is placed on freedom and how little freedom most people, in fact, have. Most North Americans are imprisoned by their jobs, by their material possessions, and by their financial debt. They could experience a lot more freedom if they worked for themselves, cut their spending on material goods, and attained financial independence.

My opinion is that the best way to attain personal freedom is not to work just for the money. It is a mistake to make your major purpose the attainment of money, whether you work in a corporate job, create an unreal job, or operate an unconventional business. The danger is that you will get so caught up in making money that you will forget to take time to enjoy life.

> When work is a pleasure, life is a joy! When work is a duty, life is slavery.
>
> — Maxim Gorky

Just as important, if your main focus is on earning a lot of money without having any major inner purpose to drive you, your chances of getting rich are not all that good. Trust me on this one: If you are not enough of an individual without a lot of money, you will not be much of an individual with it. Money can buy exotic vacations, fashionable clothing, expensive cars, and whatever else money can buy. Money can't fill the emptiness of a human soul, however.

If you aren't working at something you enjoy, you are settling for much less than you deserve. It is no secret that the happiest and most successful people at work have great affection for their selected vocation. Generally speaking, they are also the most successful in the long term, whether they work for corporations or for themselves.

> Some people think it's holding on that makes one strong; sometimes it's letting go.
> — Sylvia Robinson

What's more, focusing your life solely on earning money will take your attention away from what makes people wealthy. Wealth is a result of creating a product or a service that people value. If you concentrate on creating something that people value highly, the money will follow automatically as people reward you handsomely for it. Put another way, don't work solely to make a lot of money and you will likely end up making a lot of money.

In short, you will surprise yourself how intelligent you really are when you start doing work you enjoy. Working at something you love makes it so much easier to learn things you don't know. Of course, the more you learn, the greater your expertise, and the more money you will end up earning.

If You Recently Got Fired from Your Job, Your Good Luck Has Just Begun

Whenever friends or acquaintances tell me that they have either got fired or quit their conventional jobs, my response is, "Congratulations." After I said this to a friend who quit his job during an economic recession not so long ago, his face lit up, before he started laughing and remarked, "You are the only one who has said this to me. Everyone else is asking me things like 'How could you during a recession? Jobs are so hard to come by!' or 'How are you going to survive?' "

I congratulate people who have quit or lost their jobs because I know that for people who want real success in their lives, this is an opportunity for them to go on to something better. In fact, if you have been in the workforce for over twenty years and have never gotten fired, you are likely not a risk taker or all that creative.

Indeed, some of the most creative and famous people in the world have got fired. In 1978 Lee Iacocca was fired from his job as president of Ford Motor Company by Henry Ford II, who told Iacocca, "I just don't like you." Soon after, Iacocca became the chief of bankrupt Chrysler Corporation and made it profitable for years.

> Our disasters have been some of the best things that ever happened to us. And what we swore were blessings have been some of the worst.
>
> — Richard Bach

No doubt, getting fired can be distressing, as it was for me when I got axed from my engineering position over two and a half decades ago. But it wouldn't have been distressing at all if I had known at the time that I was destined for much greater things. Indeed, if I had known where I would be twenty-five years later — experiencing real success without a real job — I would have been profusely thanking my boss the second he fired me. What's more, I would have had a celebration that day as expensive and as big as I had twenty-five years later.

As an author and occasional professional speaker specializing in helping people be happy away from the traditional workplace, I have had an interest in good quotations about work and the workplace. It naturally follows that interesting anonymous comments about the workplace in the form of graffiti also get my attention. Thus, I put together a collection called *Graffiti for the Employee's Soul*. (It's free — just like all the other best things in life! You can download the e-book in PDF format at www.creative-e-books.com.) The following twelve items come from the e-book:

Workplace Graffiti to Remind You of the Typical Workplace

- Working here is a nightmare. You want to wake up and leave but you need the sleep.
- I owe. I owe. And off to work I go.
- The thought of suicide has helped me get through many days at work.
- Teamwork magically inspires our group to come up with solutions that are consistently and considerably dumber than any one of us.
- My job is a big secret. Even I don't know what I am doing.
- As long as we continue to work here, happiness is just an idea.
- Can I trade this job for what's behind door Number 2?
- I'm just working here till a good fast-food job opens up.
- Like to meet new people? Like a change? Like excitement? Like a new job? Then screw up just one more time!

- Around here, "progress" is everything getting worse at a slower rate than it used to.
- I just took a self-improvement course and discovered I no longer need to punish, deceive, or compromise myself — unless I want to keep my job.
- My work cubicle is just a padded cell without a door. I want my freedom and I want it now.

If you have just been fired from your job and are considering another job like it, the above comments may motivate you to consider something different that will lead to real career fulfillment. Whenever you catch yourself yearning for the benefits that your old job provided, it's best to look at the other side of the coin. It's like reminiscing about an old love affair. We tend to remember the good things much more so than the bad ones. So when you feel a little dejected because you miss the routine of your old job, consider all the things that you didn't like about the job.

The reality is that many hugely successful people have been fired at one time or another — sometimes several times — and gone on to better things. Most of these people admit that getting the ax placed them on a fast track toward career fulfillment. Indeed, it was the best thing that ever happened to them. For some, losing a job was the incentive they needed to open their own shop so that they didn't need to work at a job they hate ever again.

Years after working at an occupation that he hated, Leonard Lee, owner of Ottawa-based Lee Valley Tools and Algrove Publishing, told a reporter with *The Globe and Mail*, "No amount of money is worth doing a job you hate. It rots your soul. It destroys you." So why do so many work at a job they hate if it destroys their souls? Who knows? Perhaps they don't value their souls.

Many people do value their souls, however, and are not willing to sell out to the corporate world ever again once they get fired. Instead, they pass up even the most prestigious and high-paid positions, often for much less prestigious unreal jobs and lower pay, so that they can avoid working for a corporation.

Getting fired, as I found out, is the universe's way of telling you that you were in the wrong job in the first place. It is also the universe's way of testing you to see whether you can take advantage of adversity and create some opportunity out of it, such as starting your own business. Put another way,

> There's nothing wrong with being fired.
> — Ted Turner

> Unemployment is capitalism's way of getting you to plant a garden.
>
> — Orson Scott Card

unemployment is an opportunity to develop real character and true wealth.

If you are up to the universe's challenge, miracles will come your way. Money isn't as important as you may think it is. Many multimillion dollar businesses were started on kitchen tables. Passion, purpose, and dedication will take you places where money won't.

The reality is that great corporate jobs are hard to come by in today's world anyway. "The traditional admonition of one generation to the next, 'get a job,' has been replaced with a more complex mandate: 'Go out and create a job for yourself,' " George Gendron, editor of *Inc.* magazine, recently told *Publisher's Weekly.* Being fired is an opportunity to create a job for yourself instead of finding another corporation that has a ready-made job for you, from which you can be just as easily fired some time in the future.

A corporation can take away your job and your job title but it can't take away your talent and creativity. By firing you, the corporation may be doing you a great favor inasmuch as you now have an opportunity to fully utilize your creativity and talent. Getting fired is a great opportunity to rethink where you are, what your priorities are, what's important to you, and whether or not you are in the right career. Getting another corporate job may only result in treating the symptoms — damage control, in other words.

It has been my experience that the best way to fully utilize one's creativity and talent is to shun a real job and create one's own unreal job. If you can be successful at an unconventional job that involves self-employment, you won't get fired ever again because you are the boss. Above all, getting fired is a great opportunity to pursue the unreal job that you have dreamed about pursuing for some time.

> I was fired from my first three jobs, which in a funny way gave me the courage to go into business for myself.
>
> — Alfred Fuller

So again, don't look at being fired as all that bad of a thing. Your good luck may have just begun, particularly if you decide to make the great escape from the corporate world to pursue something totally unrelated to the field in which you were. You may feel that you have touched bottom, when, in fact, you are already headed upward. In the words of motivational speaker Zig Ziglar, "See you at the top."

Cool, Unusual Reasons to Quit Your Real Job

There is no point to working hard and spending time at things that are not important to us; yet this is exactly what many people are doing. Real passion for their work fled the scene a long time ago, if it was ever there to begin with. The result is that it becomes a huge mental struggle for these workers to haul themselves through the work week to the weekend, and the only thing they are looking forward to is watching a lot of bad TV.

Clearly, there are many so-called successful people in this sad and bleak situation. If you are one of them, one day, no matter how hard you try, you won't be able to accept the pretending that happens in the typical workplace. You will start wondering why so many workers blindly accept confinement to rigid work hours, waiting until they are in their sixties or seventies to be put out to pasture — either by layoff or poor health.

Joseph Conrad may have the answer. "It's extraordinary how we go through life with eyes half shut, with dull ears, with dormant thoughts," stated Conrad. "Perhaps it's just as well; and it may be that it is this very dullness that makes life to the incalculable majority so supportable and so welcome."

Given that you picked up this book, I would imagine dullness is not something you are searching for. After focusing on the negatives of the typical workplace long enough, you will start looking at alternatives. As is to be expected, the thought of life without a real job will appear highly promising. It will be easy to fantasize about the wonderful things that you can do by giving up traditional employment — take a real vacation at least two times a year, spend a lot more time with real friends, work at something that actually turns you on, or live and work at a dream job in Costa Rica for a year. If you have recently been having similar fantasies, perhaps it's time to tell your boss, "I'm outta here."

For the most part, it won't be easy to walk away from a traditional job. The important question you have to ask yourself is, if you had your career life to live all over again, would you choose the

> Never continue in a job you don't enjoy. If you're happy in what you're doing, you'll like yourself, you'll have inner peace. And if you have that, along with physical health, you'll have more success than you could possibly have imagined.
>
> — Roger Caras

> People don't choose their careers; they are engulfed by them.
>
> — John Dos Passos

career you are in now? If not, you are not alone — indeed, you are not a small minority either. A *Wall Street Journal/ABC News* poll found that about half of all American workers would opt for a different career if they had a second chance.

Why? A lot of it comes down to one simple word — freedom! Most people know that they will never realize their full potential working for a corporation in a job that doesn't test their creativity and doesn't incite their passions. No doubt most employees just dream about working for themselves and have no real plans of pursuing an unreal job or starting their own business. Nonetheless, many people are prepared to make the difficult and uncomfortable sacrifices in order to create an easier and more comfortable world for themselves. For example, John Grisham certainly wouldn't be an international best-selling author today if he hadn't been prepared to quit his lucrative law practice so that he could pursue his dream of writing legal thrillers.

If you don't like your job, particularly if you detest it, my advice to you is to quit while you are ahead — before they fire you! Luckily, there are many reasons to quit. If you can't think of your own, there are many to draw on. A recent survey of 250 Canadian advertising and marketing executives revealed that employees quit their jobs for the most unusual reasons. Here are some of them:

Cool and Unusual Reasons People Give for Chucking Their Jobs

- I don't like the smell of the office.
- I am making too much money and don't feel that I am worth it.
- I don't like to use a computer.
- The job isn't as glamorous as I thought.
- I don't like the lighting in the building.
- I am bored.
- I am over-employed.
- I can't get up in the morning.
- I don't want to work so hard.
- The location isn't exciting enough.
- I want to sunbathe on the beach in Europe.
- I want to train for a triathlon.
- I don't need the money; I am going to live on my trust fund.
- I am moving to Hollywood to be a movie star.

The most unusual quitter, according to one executive's opinion, was the employee who used the silent exit strategy. "He just walked out without a peep," sighed the executive. "Until this day we have no idea why he left, nor were we able to contact him."

If other people can quit their jobs for the flimsy excuses given above, certainly you can quit yours in order that you can escape corporate life to do contract work or start some small business. Of course, you must ensure that what you intend to pursue has some merit. There is a no more fatal blunder than to get excited about nothing, and then pursue it for the rest of your life. It will take all you have got just to keep up with the misfits of the world.

Some people may chastise you for quitting a job, particularly if you don't have another conventional job lined up for yourself. But so what? Quitting has always been cool according to American Evan Harris. "Our country was founded by quitters," the author of *The Art of Quitting* (Barron's Educational Series, 2004) recently told the *Detroit News*. "They left England and said, 'Forget this. We are so out of here. We are not putting up with this any more.'"

Quitting is not only cool; you can start living again. Whatever your gripe with your corporate job, you don't have to put up with it because there are so many other things you can be doing. You should have at least one passionate pursuit that you can make the cornerstone of a dream job and a new lifestyle. In chapter 2 you will find one hundred cool and unusual ways to make an exciting living without a real job.

If You Love Your Work, Keep on Rocking

Not so long ago Paul McCartney dismissed rumors he was planning to retire from music. He told www.billboard.com: "As far as retirement is concerned, I'd never consider it, although I'm getting up toward retirement age. I think someone falsified my birth certificate because I can't feel it. I don't want to retire. I love what I do. I always said if people don't come to the shows, I'll do this as a hobby."

"I have a vision of me at age ninety," continued McCartney, "being wheeled on stage very slowly, doing 'Yesterday.' At the moment, it's not like that. It's the opposite of that. We're loving it, the audiences are loving it, so while that's happening, I'm keeping on rocking."

> Work to learn. Don't work for money.
> — Robert Kiyosaki

If you are like Paul McCartney and love your work,

> All paid jobs absorb and
> degrade the mind.
>
> — Aristotle

congratulations. According to many studies you are in the minority. There is also the chance that your work situation may not be perfect, but you don't realize how good it is. It's all too easy in today's world to compare ourselves to others apparently more successful than us and think that we are missing out on something important, when, in fact, we aren't.

Take me, for example. Not so long ago I was feeling quite insecure about my financial position (oblivion is a better word), given that many people my age were quickly approaching the time when they could retire with a full pension. This got me thinking about the possibility of getting a real job, one with a great pension plan. Of course, I had my doubts that any employers would want to hire a character whose biggest accomplishment in the last fifteen years was writing a book called *The Joy of Not Working*.

Desperate times called for desperate measures so I checked out the French Foreign Legion, a military formation of about 8,500 men serving as a branch of the regular Armed Forces of France, which accepts foreigners from any country in the world. The good news was that after only fifteen years of service, I could get a full pension. The bad news, however, was that the minimum physical prerequisites for joining are being able to do thirty push-ups and fifty sit-ups, climb a twenty-foot rope without using your feet, and run eight kilometers with a twelve-kilogram rucksack in less than one hour. The most sobering news was the recommendation that people planning to join should prepare a last will and testament.

Even though the French Foreign Legion was out of the question, my thoughts about getting a real job with a great retirement plan continued for some time until I happened to read a career-planning article in *The Globe and Mail*. The article cited California lawyer Patrick Kelly, who advises that you ask yourself:

Three Important Questions to Help Recognize Your Career Strengths

1. What three accomplishments am I proudest of in my life?

2. What three things have other people praised me for doing?

3. What specific abilities allowed me to do all these things?

Just for the fun of it I decided to do Kelly's exercise. To the first question about the three accomplishments that I am proudest of in my life, I answered: (1) writing and self-publishing several books including my international best-selling *The Joy of Not Working*; (2) despite my fear of public speaking, having worked as a professional speaker and having taught courses part-time at two universities and two colleges; (3) making a living without a real job.

To the second question about what three things people have praised me for, I answered: (1) hundreds of readers have written to me to praise me for writing *The Joy of Not Working*; (2) my students in the university and college courses I taught always gave me great evaluations; (3) many people have acknowledged and envied me for making a decent living without a real job.

> To love what you do and feel that it matters — how could anything be more fun?
>
> — Katharine Graham

To the third question about what specific abilities allowed me to do all these things, I answered: (1) motivation to be creative and work on my own; (2) ability to take risks and handle rejection and failure; (3) willingness to be different from the masses.

After I completed this exercise, I immediately uttered, "Eureka!" I had experienced an incredible awakening. I realized I had reached the point of no return — I could no longer go back to the corporate world because my strongest abilities were not a good match with 99 percent of corporations. Besides, I have no desire to work for an organization — not even the French Foreign Legion with its great retirement plan. Most important, I realized that I love what I do and I would be crazy to give up writing and self-publishing, even for a traditional job that pays five times what I earn.

I suggest that you use the above checklist of three questions by Patrick Kelly to determine your career strengths and abilities. The answers may help you determine whether you are in the right line of work. If you are using your strongest abilities, and particularly if you love your work, keep on rocking, just like Paul McCartney. On the other hand, if you are not using your strongest abilities, and particularly if you don't love your work, it's probably time for a big change.

Keep in mind that to some degree, enjoying your work is a state of mind. Harvard psychologist Ellen Langer, author of *Mindfulness* (Addison Wesley, 1990) once conducted a study in which two groups of subjects were asked to perform the same tasks. One group was told the tasks were work and the other was told the tasks were play. "The 'work' group found the tasks tedious," claims

> The biggest mistake people make in life is not making a living doing what they most enjoy.
>
> — Malcolm S. Forbes

Langer, "but the 'play' group didn't, which suggests that we make evaluations based on our frame of mind."

The only problem with the tedious-work-is-fun approach is that it would be extremely difficult to convince oneself that digging ditches is play, particularly for more than a day or so. I don't know about you, but I would be hard pressed to develop a love for digging ditches. Toughing it out in the French Foreign Legion for fifteen years would likely be more satisfying and fulfilling than being a ditchdigger for the same length of time.

The important point here is that if you love your work, there are always ways to make it better. In most cases once a career is fouled up, however, anything done to improve it only makes it worse. And any time things appear to be getting better, you will have overlooked something. The good news is that it is never too late to give up a career you hate and pursue a much different career that you have fantasized and talked about for some time.

In his 2005 commencement address at Stanford University, Stephen Jobs, co-founder of Apple Corporation, advised, "Sometimes life hits you in the head with a brick. Don't lose faith. I'm convinced that the only thing that kept me going was that I loved what I did. You've got to find what you love. And that is as true for your work as it is for your lovers. Your work is going to fill a large part of your life, and the only way to be truly satisfied is to do what you believe is great work."

Jobs continued, "And the only way to do great work is to love what you do. If you haven't found it yet, keep looking. Don't settle. As with all matters of the heart, you'll know when you find it. And, like any great relationship, it just gets better and better as the years roll on. So keep looking until you find it. Don't settle."

Remember, Stephen Jobs along with Steve Wozniak started what today is the Apple Corporation in the Jobs family's garage. Obviously, both Jobs and Wozniak had to love building and marketing computers for them to become so successful.

Again, if you aren't working at something you enjoy, you are settling for much less than you deserve. It is no secret that the happiest and most successful people at work have great affection for their selected vocation. Generally speaking, they are also the most successful in the long term.

2

Unreal Jobs — So Many Worlds; What to Do?

The Best Time to Pursue Your Dream Career Is Twenty Years Ago and Today

Business Week magazine recently surveyed 500 American business executives about their job satisfaction. Surprisingly, almost three-quarters (72 percent) were not in their dream jobs. The first question that arises is: What would executives rather be doing? Many, in fact, named creative professions when asked about their fantasy careers. Here are the executives' top ten career choices with the first being highest on their list:

- Entertainment manager or events producer
- Winemaker or brewmaster
- Chef
- Restaurateur
- Pilot
- Golf pro
- Professional athlete
- Rock star
- Neurosurgeon
- Bed-and-breakfast-inn owner/operator

> Blessed is he who has found his work. Let him ask no other blessedness.
>
> — Thomas Carlyle

Of course, dream careers will depend on a number of factors, including the age of the people surveyed. For interest's sake, following are the top ten dream jobs chosen by Canadian youths:

- Entertainment reporter
- On-air personality
- Fashion designer
- Hair and makeup designer for film or music/video shoot
- Music-video director
- Big cheese at TV station MuchMusic
- Record producer
- Magazine editor
- Game designer
- Concert roadie

As is to be expected, most young people are not in their dream jobs because they have not had the time to establish themselves in their careers. This leads to the second important question: Why don't more executives move on to something better if they are not in their dream careers?

The apparent answer is that most executives are trapped in the corporate system and don't have the guts to do something different. Yet many ordinary people with fewer skills and financial resources than corporate executives have managed to leave corporate life to pursue dream careers. These ordinary people have become happier, wealthier, freer, and more satisfied in their lives.

> Never work just for money or for power. They won't save your soul or help you sleep at night.
> — Marian Wright Edelman

Estimates vary, but some career experts say that up to 90 percent of educated Americans don't like what they do for a living. There are several reasons why so many educated and intelligent people accept mediocre or lousy corporate jobs in the first place. One reason is that too many people go to college or university and major in the wrong field, which is usually recommended by someone else.

Take me, for example. I went into electrical engineering because my school principal recommended it. He felt I would make a good engineer because I was a whiz at physics and trigonometry. The truth is that I disliked engineering right from the start, but I had no idea what else I wanted to do. I also had no idea that people could make a great living outside corporations and actually enjoy their work.

Thus, I suffered through several years of taking engineering courses at a university and then another few years of working as an engineer. What made engineering even more unbearable was that I had to work in a corporate setting. Not so long ago a friend of mine, who was also in engineering at one time, found a course assignment that some engineering student had lost. Both of us couldn't believe that we had at one time actually done many variations of this type of assignment and allowed ourselves to be subjected to such severe punishment.

John Fletcher from Boston is another good example of someone who went into a profession that he hated right from the start. Fletcher shared his experience in a review he did of a career book on Amazon.com: "I was, until two years ago, a very successful lawyer," claimed Fletcher. "But, from the first day of law school, to the day I walked out the door for the last time, I hated every minute of it. What could be worse than spending every day dealing with lawyers? I spent years wrestling with the big question: What to do with my life? I knew I wanted to wake up with excitement rather than dread. I had no idea what that might be."

Despite not knowing what dream career to pursue, John Fletcher was able to eventually design a new career and leave law for good. In his words, "Now I wake up feeling like it is Christmas every day. What could be better?" Fletcher didn't say what new field he entered, but this is irrelevant. The point is that most lawyers end up hating their career choice, and a few manage to leave law behind for a much better life. John Grisham, for example, chucked his law career to write best-selling fiction.

Incidentally, John Fletcher attributed his success in designing an enjoyable career to his willingness and commitment to follow the advice of Nicholas Lore in his best-selling *The Pathfinder: How to Choose or Change Your Career for a Lifetime of Satisfaction and Success* (Fireside, 1998). Several career counselors have indicated that Lore's career book is by far the best one available anywhere. Just as telling, many of the best career advisors, coaches, and counselors use Lore's methods when working with their clients.

Another reason people wind up in wrong careers is that they do virtually no planning or soul-searching. Indeed, they just fall into their jobs. One person may find out from his friend about a job opening at the company the friend works for, seize on the so-called opportunity, and work there for years, hating every minute of it. Another person may look through the career opportunities of a newspaper, apply for a few jobs, be offered one, and

> The best augury of a man's success in his profession is that he thinks it the finest in the world.
>
> — George Eliot

go to work even though he knows absolutely nothing about the job and the company. A third character may choose to work as a welder because two of his motorcycle acquaintances are welders in a shop where they all can smoke cigarettes on the job.

It should be no surprise that so many workers feel unfulfilled, dissatisfied, underemployed, underutilized, or angry with the work they perform. If they were given better advice and support by parents, educational institutions, career centers, and corporations, many more people would be able to find or create pleasing work. Clearly, this is not about to happen anytime soon.

Of course, still another reason why so many individuals end up in distasteful work is the one we already briefly covered in chapter 1. Too many get caught up on the money side of careers. They see it as a choice between "love the work you do in poverty" or "hate the work you do in abundance." Sadly, they believe that you can't have your cake and eat it too.

Some of us know otherwise — we have gotten ourselves two cakes. This way, we get to keep our cake and eat it, too. Put another way, we have discovered work we love and still manage to earn a decent living in order that we can have abundance outside the workplace. Contrary to what some people believe, we have not had to give up all the comforts of modern life, move back to the country, sleep in the bush, and live on grass, berries, and an occasional squirrel. (On second thought, this may not be all that bad in comparison to some dysfunctional workplaces in which employees have to earn a living.)

Fact is, I know many people who have turned hobbies or favorite products into small businesses and have succeeded financially. Of course, they had to exchange a steady paycheck for their freedom and happiness, but their love for what they do was more important than the security of a regular paycheck.

At one time I thought I wanted to work at a dream job. It turns out that I just wanted decent paychecks to buy lots of beer.

Other people have traded the opportunity of a high-paying corporate position for an unreal job with less money but with much more freedom and much more enjoyment. Over the last few years my friend Andy has worked for a number of non-profit organizations. His income is only a third to a half of what he could make in the private sector. He considers his present position an unreal job, however. Besides enjoying his job more than most people enjoy theirs, Andy treasures the freedom of working at the time of day he chooses and not having a supervisor tell him what to do and what not to do.

As the executive director of an international film festival, Andy may have to work fairly hard for one to two months. Once the festival is over, he gets to work fewer hours a day than I work. The other day Andy told me that he regularly sleeps in until noon. Lucky guy! Andy, like me, also gets to take several days off anytime he wants without having to ask permission. In short, Andy would never trade the freedom he enjoys for an executive position that pays two to three times as much but imprisons him for eight to twelve hours a day.

Self-employment or having an unreal job, however, does not mean that your income has to have a limit on it. There are many people who leave the corporate world and actually earn much better money than they did in it. This can even happen to professionals who already are in the top 5 percent of wage earners.

Take, for example, Robin Sharma, who does not have a real job. Sharma was once an overworked and highly paid litigation lawyer tired of living without a central purpose or meaning to his life. His sense of emptiness and longing influenced him to search out the inspiration and wisdom of Og Mandino, Norman Vincent Peale, Gandhi, Albert Einstein, Nelson Mandela, and others. Within months of applying what he learned from his mentors, Sharma experienced profound positive changes in the quality of his thoughts, his energy level, and in the overall quality of his life.

Sharma chucked his career as a well-paid lawyer to become a writer and professional speaker instead. Today he has a lifestyle that's about as good as it gets. Sharma makes a great living, traveling around the world making motivational speeches in such places as Hawaii, Israel, and Europe. He has a great purpose to his life, he has his freedom, and he makes more money than he did as a high-paid lawyer.

Perhaps you presently feel like Robin Sharma felt at one time; you realize that you can lead a more meaningful, more fulfilling, and happier existence only if you make important changes in your life. All along, however, you have put off making a change because you are waiting for the perfect moment, with the right conditions. Clearly, there will never be a perfect moment. Waiting for things to get better will ensure that they don't

> Find a job you like and you add five days to every week.
>
> — H. Jackson Brown, Jr.

get better. Often, things get worse.

If you keep working in your job with the same resignation as if you had just swallowed a live toad, there is a way out when you are prepared to create it. The ideal is to have a dream job take up a good portion of your life instead of having your corporate job devour a good portion of your dream, along with your soul. To the extent we are not living our dreams, our circumstances have more control over us than we have over ourselves.

I am not saying that finding work you like is going to be easy. For sure, I don't expect that you will immediately go and find the work you love after reading this book or some of the other books that I recommend. You should get some wonderful insights about the possibilities that are available to you, however.

No doubt it would be nice to just resign yourself to the first job that comes along and end up being satisfied without any more effort. Most people, however, have to work at it. Determining what you want to really do with your life may be hard, but not extremely difficult. It does take getting rid of emotional baggage including programmed notions of what you are "supposed" to be doing, or "trained" to be doing.

> The miracle is not that we do this work, but that we are happy to do it.
>
> — Mother Teresa

Before you make the plunge to another line of work, you must do a great deal of soul-searching and planning. "If the world is really just a stage and we are all actors," asks Phil Humbert, "what kind of play are you writing with your life?"

Most people spend more time planning their next home purchase or next vacation than they do planning their careers and the rest of their lives. The more planning you do, the better the chances that you will succeed. Of course, you cannot plan forever. Sooner or later you must take action.

When you take action, you may not wind up where you want to go due to circumstances beyond your control. This can be a good thing, nonetheless. Even if you make the wrong decision, you still may not be disappointed. Many people have targeted a dream career, taken action to get there, and wound up with something even better.

I can give no better example than myself. I didn't have an incredible revelation one day after reading some insightful book that I wanted to make a living by writing books. In fact, I got to where I am today in an indirect way. My prime choice for an unreal job was to become a full-time instructor at a community college. I figured that I would like teaching students, thrive on having to teach only sixteen hours a week, and particularly enjoy the freedom that such a job offers.

After spending two-and-a-half years and substantial money to get an MBA, I found a part-time position at a private vocational institution teaching four courses each term. Later I taught only one course per term at two universities. When it became clear that I couldn't get a full-time position at a community college, I decided to become a professional speaker. To have at least some credibility as a speaker, it helps to have written at least one book. Thus, I self-published my first book, which helped me get speaking engagements for a while.

After I wrote and self-published my second book, I realized that I really liked writing and publishing books. Just as important, I could continue to pursue my purpose in life, which is to help people develop their potential and make progress toward attaining some of their dreams. I also felt at this point that I could make a living from the royalties from my books and didn't have to actively generate income through more speaking engagements.

Weirdly, by pursuing my goal to become a college instructor, which at one time seemed impossible to me, I actually attained this goal for a while, before winding up working at something much better. If I had made my goal merely to earn a living at some corporate job, I would likely have reached my goal, and remained miserable for a long time.

> Man's task is simple. He should cease letting his existence be a thoughtless accident.
>
> — Friedrich Nietzsche

Clearly, a corporate job is a goal much too small for many more people other than me. If you are not just a dreamer, but also a doer, a dream career does not have to be an unattainable fantasy. Michelangelo said it best: "The greatest danger for most of us is not that our aim is too high and we miss it, but that it is too low and we reach it."

If you are unhappy in your current job situation, isn't it time to take steps to change it? I believe that there is an old wise saying something like "If you always do what you have always done, you will always be what you have always been." It's seldom too late to discover and pursue an unreal job or unique vocation that will turn you on and contribute to a much better future. But it is better to do it sooner than later.

Chicago advertising executive Robert Cochrane warned Carl Laemmle with these words: "Don't be a salary slave! If you are going to do anything in this world, you must start before you are forty, before your period of initiative has ended. Do it now!"

Fortunately for Carl Laemmle, he took Cochrane's advice. Soon after, Laemmle quit his job as a clothing-store manager and eventually became a movie mogul who founded and headed Universal Pictures Corporation.

> I want to put a ding in the universe.
>
> — Stephen Jobs

Here's the bottom line: The best time to pursue your dream career is twenty years ago and today. If you eventually decide that the only way you can be happy in a job is to be doing something completely different, then no doubt it is important that you move on. You don't necessarily have to move on today. Indeed, it is wise not to jump straight into something immediately. But today is the day that you should start taking steps to discover some dream job that will turn you on much more than what you are presently doing.

It takes some strategy to find and pursue a new career. You are a unique individual with special abilities and interests that you should pinpoint when determining your dream job. The following strategy, according to many career practitioners, works best for finding a career that fits your personality.

Four Steps to Creating a Dream Career

Step 1: Inner Exploration — In this initial stage you look at what you enjoy doing, what motivates you, what you value, and what gives you a sense of fulfillment and meaning. You also assess what abilities, talent, and potential you possess besides the needs that you would like fulfilled in your work. When you decide on the skills you most want to use, what you are passionate about, the values that are the essence of your work, and the work environment that motivates you, you are then ready to explore possible options that fit your needs.

Step 2: Outer Exploration — In this stage you explore which unreal jobs or unconventional businesses would best suit you. Which would give you a sense of purpose or be conducive to your true calling in life? Identify existing jobs and create your own options that will match your requirements.

Step 3: Decision Making — When you get to this stage, you must use whatever decision-making ability you have. If you are not good at making decisions, you may have to enroll in a course to help you get better. Making a good decision depends on three factors: 1) knowing yourself well including what you truly want, 2) acquiring the right information about the work you would like to do, and 3) using an effective decision-making model (one model is given later in this chapter). Your choice should be the option that best matches your abilities, interests, and needs with an unreal job or unconventional business that allows you to make a contribution to others.

Step 4: Implementation — Once you make a decision, it's time to take action. This means having a plan to find or create the unreal job you want. Alternatively, you have to develop a plan and take the necessary steps for becoming self-employed or operating an unconventional business.

Stop Dreaming; Start Choosing

The late Buckminster Fuller, best known as the inventor of the geodesic dome, seriously contemplated suicide at the age of thirty-two as he stood on the edge of Lake Michigan. Fuller's first child had died; he was bankrupt, discredited, and jobless; and he had a wife and newborn daughter. Fortunately, Fuller stopped to ask himself whether he might be of value to the universe.

The spiritual answer that Fuller received — his existence was proof enough of his purpose for being — convinced him that he should continue living and make important contributions to humanity. He chose at that moment to embark on what he called "an experiment to discover what the little, penniless, unknown individual might be able to do effectively on behalf of all humanity."

To put it succinctly, Buckminster Fuller did not disappoint himself — or the world! He contributed to humanity not only as an inventor, but also as a writer, educator, philosopher, and poet, until he died at the age of eighty-eight. What's really cool is Fuller lived most of his adult life without a real job. Perhaps this amazing man would have indeed committed suicide if he had confined himself to a corporate job. The key to Fuller's

> At the age of six I wanted to be a cook. At seven I wanted to be Napoleon. And my ambition has been growing steadily ever since.
>
> — Salvador Dali

remarkable life was his overriding purpose to contribute to humanity and make the world a much better place.

Many people today could greatly enhance their work lives if they had some important meaning to their existence like Buckminster Fuller had. As is to be expected, the more people are tuned into some major purpose associated with their work, the easier it is for them to go to work. Without a major purpose, many employees regularly experience disillusionment or even depression. To be sure, an overriding purpose is a great antidote for depression; people feel useful and productive.

Constancy of purpose is the reason why some people such as Buckminster Fuller find their work fulfilling for many decades and don't stop working until the day they die. Of course, living a life of purpose is easy if you have one; but alas, not everyone has a purpose. I refer to purpose as an important mission, a true calling, or a passionate pursuit.

> The mark of the immature man is that he wants to die nobly for a cause, while the mark of the mature man is that he wants to live humbly for one.
> — Wilhelm Stekel

One of the keys to finding and eventually living a life of purpose is realizing that you, in fact, have no overarching purpose in your life. In this case, you must take steps to create a purpose. Unless you discover a career that you can pursue with passion, you will find it difficult to attain success without a real job.

Your purpose or calling is a much higher spiritual concept than a job that you do to create income for your bills and some extra to buy beer. Your purpose is something you do to make a real difference in people's lives. In the process you make the world a better place to live. The ideal is to be highly stimulated — even crazy or freaked out — about what you do for a living.

The major purpose to your job should be bigger than you and much, much bigger than money. Purpose leads to passion, that special fire in the heart that fuels successful people to pursue their dreams and helps them easily overcome obstacles that others think are insurmountable. When you end up passionate about what you do for a living, you will truly enjoy it. What's more, you will do it better and get a lot more done in less time.

Passion will get you in the flow of your work. You will not have to worry about what distasteful task is coming up next. Trying to get out of doing something will no longer be part of your agenda, and dreaming about taking a vacation to get away from your work will not be a daily occurrence.

Purpose involves pursuing activities that express our true selves. Clearly, it's not easy for everyone to discover a purpose that is their own. Ingrid Bacci, in her book *The Art of Effortless Living* (Perigee Trade, 2002), states, "For all our culture's so-called individualism, most people have very little true sense of themselves, or of a purpose to their lives that they can eagerly espouse. It is no wonder that, if we focus on externals and find our validation primarily in what we do and in what we get for what we do, we will never find ourselves."

Pursuing a dream career with a major purpose means traveling alone on your own path; this requires a great deal of courage because it is terrifying. A job with a purpose also requires more work and commitment initially than it takes to enter a corporate job where practically everything is laid out for us. The problem with following the most practical path for making a living is that it is not the most rewarding and fulfilling.

Many individuals — I use the term loosely in this case — don't have an important purpose because their focus has been on superficial pursuits, such as material possessions, status, competition, and wasteful consumption. They have been so programmed to work hard and earn a lot of money that they totally forgot who they are in the process. They don't recall what they deeply care about or what really turns them on. Ironically, some people have more than enough money to leave corporate life, but they are not quite sure what it is that they want to pursue.

You, too, may have allowed yourself to become so engrossed in the corporate world and in amassing material possessions that you have forgotten what makes you feel fulfilled and truly alive. Indeed, work and the pursuit of material things may have estranged you from who you really are. As is to be expected, discovering who you really are is essential because purpose is created from within.

It doesn't matter so much where you have been. The question is: Where would you like to go? The amount of time, money, and energy you have spent getting to where you are today is totally irrelevant if you are miserable doing the work you are presently doing.

Why not give it your best shot to

If you don't like driving cab, what would you rather be doing? In other words, what is your dream job?

There is only one thing that I can come up with — I want to rule the world!

> The great and glorious masterpiece of man is to know how to live to purpose.
>
> — Michel de Montaigne

pursue a higher avocation that is more in tune with the real you? If you have no idea what your true calling is, other than to ensure that you don't end up working at Wal-Mart or McDonald's, it's worthwhile to put in the time and effort to discover it, even if it takes years.

Miguel de Cervantes wrote, "Make it thy business to know thyself, which is the most difficult lesson in the world." Getting to know yourself, in other words, is not easy and takes effort. You must tune into and listen to your inner voice. It takes tuning out the other voices of the world to hear your true desires. Start by answering the following:

Soul-Searching Questions to Help Identify Your Life's Calling

1. What am I naturally curious about?
2. What is extremely important to me?
3. What makes me happy?
4. How have I trapped myself by pursuing traditional success?
5. What are my assumptions about money that may not be true?
6. What made me happy in my childhood and my teens that I would like to do again?
7. What made me happy in my career that I would like to continue doing?
8. What would make me a much happier person? (Becoming rich or famous does not count.)
9. What talents or skills am I most proud of?
10. What field of endeavor has a habit of continually challenging me in new and exciting ways?
11. What makes me feel most creative?
12. What special talent have I neglected due to my career?
13. What would I like to do that I have always wanted to do, but never got around to doing?
14. How would I like to make the world a better place in my own way?
15. What gift or legacy would I like to leave to the world?

Generating revealing answers to these fifteen questions will take time. Write these questions down in a notebook, leaving sufficient room for several answers for each question. Then take a few minutes to spontaneously record your answers to the questions without stopping to think about them. Keep going no matter what you write down. You don't want your rational mind to interfere with your answers. Remember, your rational mind has a habit of disguising the real you.

Carry this notebook of questions around for the next two to four weeks and add to your answers. Every day take fifteen minutes or so to contemplate the questions further without interruption from outside forces. Given enough time, you should eventually have sufficient information about your needs and wants to help you discover at least one important mission, true calling, or passionate pursuit. Some people will discover more than one.

If you are unable to find your true calling by utilizing the above fifteen questions, keep trying by utilizing other means. I won't walk you every step of the way until you create your dream career or unreal job. Quite frankly, I can't. Indeed, nobody can. Everyone's combination of experience, talent, and knowledge is unique.

There are a number of great books, however, that can help you rediscover who you are and the work you were born to do if you need more direction. One of the best career books is *Do What You Are* (Little Brown & Company, 2001) by Paul

> If you are going to ask yourself life-changing questions, be sure to do something with the answers.
>
> — Bo Bennett

D. Tieger and Barbara Barron-Tieger. Two others that come highly recommended are *The Career Guide for Creative and Unconventional People* (Ten Speed Press, 1999) by Carol Eikleberry and *Making a Living Without a Job: Winning Ways for Creating Work That You Love* (Bantam, 1993) by Barbara Winter.

A course or seminar on how to successfully change careers may also help you find your true calling. Check out the colleges and universities in your area to see whether they offer programs for people who want to ponder new careers, explore the changing world, and decide how they are going make a great living in it.

In addition to books and courses, individuals in a wide range of jobs, career stages, and income levels are utilizing the services of career coaches to help them change careers or leave corporate life altogether. "We're doing the same as an athletic coach would: helping talented, capable people problem solve and reach their goals," says renowned career coach Nicholas Lore. Incidentally,

Lore is founder of the renowned Rockport Institute (www.rockportinstitute.com) and has been a career consultant to several national and global leaders, CEOs of Fortune 500 companies, and people in nearly every field of endeavor.

Career coaches can help you in several ways. They can assess your job skills and personality traits to help you decide which dream career or unconventional business suits you. Better still, they can provide inspiration and motivation when you need it most. The number of career coaches is constantly growing so it shouldn't be hard to find a good one. Check out Kentucky-based The International Coach Federation (www.coachfederation.org), a nonprofit association for personal coaches which has over 8,000 members and over 132 chapters in 34 countries.

Whether you use books, seminars, or career coaches, with sufficient time and effort devoted to your self-discovery, you should be able to discover who you really are along with the nature of your important mission, true calling, or passionate pursuit. When you reach this point, it is definitely time to stop dreaming and to start choosing instead.

> Always suspect any job men willingly vacate for women.
> — Jill Tweedie

You want to find an unreal job that best matches your purpose in life. Once you know what your dream job is, try to find such a job. It could be contract work for a charity, an overseas assignment with a special-interest group, or a consulting project for the government. If you can't find a job exactly like this, find one close enough. Alternatively, you can try creating this job by becoming self-employed or starting your own unconventional business.

Later in this chapter there is a list of one hundred of the world's coolest jobs for making an unconventional living. Perhaps one or more of these jobs can be a match for your purpose or calling in life. Try meeting with people who are doing the types of jobs you are interested in or operating businesses similar to one that you would like to start.

Also think about someone who has a job that you would like to have. What is it about the job that appeals to you? Use this approach to find work activities about which you can feel truly "passionate." Those are the activities that will really turn you on and will make your job one that you would do for free.

At some point you may be afraid that you don't have the necessary skills to make a transition to your dream job, particularly if it is an unconventional career. You likely have a lot more relevant skills than you think you have. The key is to identify important transferable skills — honed in your present job, previous jobs, educational institutions, and life in general — that you can use in your dream job or business.

Many skills are highly usable in many careers. These include decision making, problem solving, time management, communication, organization, negotiation, creativity, and promotion skills. Following are four recommended steps for identifying the important skills that you already have and can apply to your dream job or business venture:

> Step 1: Identify Your Key Skills — List all the jobs you have had and jot down all the important skills you used in these jobs. Think about every important task you did. Don't undervalue any skill that you used.

> Step 2: Research Your Dream Job — Thoroughly research the field you intend to pursue. Read trade publications and association literature. Buy dinner for a practicing professional in the field you intend to pursue so that you gain a greater understanding of the field.

> Step 3: Look for Relationships — How do your background skills relate to your dream job or business venture? Think of each skill in terms of how transferable it is to what you want to do.

> Step 4: Emphasize the Most Important Skills — Summarize the most important transferable skills that you can use in your new venture. Your list should look quite impressive. What's more, you can always learn a lot of the important skills that you don't presently have.

Again, a true calling in an unreal job can fulfill your inner needs more than money or status can in a traditional job. You have to find a purpose that is bigger than you and bigger than money. Otherwise, you won't follow through with the action that is necessary for you to succeed.

You may have to think outside of the box to come up with some new job or business venture that matches your interests and deepest desires. Your new career may not appear as a logical one to others, but it will be

> I would have made a good Pope.
>
> — Richard M. Nixon

to you. The key — and challenge — is to find a career that you would want to wake up to every morning.

> Nothing contributes so much to tranquilize the mind as a steady purpose.
>
> — Mary Shelley

For some people, the idea of a dream career drops out of the blue one day, waiting to be acted on another day. This happened to Colin Brownlee who now lives in Puerto Viejo, Costa Rica. Colin sent me the following e-mail as I was writing this chapter.

Hi Ernie

I too have read *The Joy of Not Working* many times and referred it to many friends.

I decided to take a moment and let you in on my story. It might be a little different than ones I have read in your book. Nine years ago, I went on an adventure tour in Hawaii. It included meals and accommodation and each day it had these fun tours. It was all a lot of fun and I was very relaxed. I can remember vividly saying to myself "I want a job like that." That was the beginning. That experience and thought never left me.

Fast forward seven years: I was living in Vancouver with my Costa Rican partner and I was at the height of my career in an Internet marketing job at the age of forty-three. For sometime I really just felt like this was not the answer. I was making more money than I ever dreamed of and in fact even liked my job and living in Vancouver. But there was something big missing. I have always had a lust for adventure and where I was at in life, it all just seemed too predictable. I would buy nicer things, and take nicer vacations, etc., etc. But nothing big was going to happen unless I made it happen.

So I sold everything and reduced my whole life to four plastic storage boxes and packed what I could in suitcases and bought a sandy beachfront piece of property in the southern Caribbean town of Costa Rica called Puerto Viejo and built a beautiful open concept Caribbean style home. Now, I am busy on building a guest house where it is my plan to accommodate and host tours here in Costa Rica. It is my hope to also inspire people and make them seriously look at what they are doing in their lives.

It has been a lot of work, has taken a lot of courage, and has been anything but predictable. To do something like this you really have to learn to roll with the punches. But I have no regrets. It's been one year today since I landed here and I thought I should let you know how your book touched my life. It was really the tipping point to "just do it!"

If you or any of your readers want to know what that has been like, they can check out my blog at www.colinsito.blogs.com.

Cheers,

Colin Brownlee

When the idea for his dream job appeared, Colin Brownlee was ready for it. Although he did not act on it immediately, he recognized it as something that he definitely wanted to pursue sooner or later. Your purpose or passionate pursuit will also surface when you are ready for it. Paradoxically, some people find their true life's calling just when life appears to be going rapidly downhill — for instance, when they have been fired from their prestigious job. They then take a neglected hobby and turn it into a full-time passion, which eventually becomes a profitable business.

You may notice that Colin Brownlee made no mention of what sort of money he expected to earn in his new career. This leads to the ultimate test of the work for which you are most suited. If you can think of some unreal job that someone is paid to do, but you yourself would pay to be allowed to do if you were filthy rich, chances are that this is the dream job you should be pursuing.

Don't ever underestimate the power of having an overriding purpose, or several of them, if you want to enjoy life outside the corporation. A life without purpose can lead to dissociation from life, whereas a life with an interesting purpose can lead to an incredible love of life. As the following example indicates, people can ensure themselves a fulfilling life when they identify their passions and devote a good part of their waking hours to pursuing these passions.

George Bernard Shaw ended up enjoying his later years because he retained a great sense of purpose until he died at the age of ninety-six. Indeed,

> Hollywood held this double lure for me, tremendous sums of money for work that required no more effort than a game of pinochle.
>
> — Ben Hecht

he continued to write into his nineties. To the end, Shaw published brilliantly argued prefaces to his plays, flooded publishers with books, wrote numerous controversial articles, and regularly sent cantankerous letters to newspaper editors.

George Bernard Shaw exemplified why passion for one or more pursuits is a vital force for getting the most out of our work and out of life as a whole. Whether it's working to eradicate social problems, or trying to make it as an artist, or promoting your solar-energy project as a benefit to humanity, your passionate pursuit will enrich you much more than most corporate jobs ever could. Activities that support a major purpose will not only keep you mentally and physically active, they will also provide you with emotional and spiritual fulfillment

Why Not Work for the Best Boss in the World — Twenty Million Individuals Already Do!

Do you work in a corporate environment with all of the so-called great benefits that it brings, but still wonder why you are there? Should this be the case, it's likely because you don't feel listened to, your work is unappreciated, you are underpaid, and you have been overlooked for a promotion while someone less creative and productive has been awarded the job. At the same time you have become sick and tired of commuting to a job where you sit in a stupid cubicle all day.

Why do most of your friends continue to work at jobs they hate while you really enjoy yourself being self-employed?

They would rather stay in the corporate chicken coop instead of finding out if they can soar with the eagles.

If you are experiencing most of these things, along with yearning for new challenges because you are bored stiff with the same work you have been doing for years, you may be a prime candidate for working for the best boss in the world. Indeed, twenty million Americans already do. They have the best boss in the world because they are self-employed and the only boss they have is themselves.

Clearly, self-employment can be an enjoyable and rewarding way to slip out of corporate life — if you truly enjoy freedom and are prepared to earn it. You can end up working for yourself using the strategy that best suits you:

Three Basic Paths to Self-Employment

1. Get fired and be awakened to the fact that you don't ever want to return to the corporate world.
2. Plan to create an unreal job or start a business while you are in a real job in the corporate world and then take the plunge.
3. Accumulate enough funds so that you can semi-retire and then work or not work, as you please.

Following is an example of someone who took the path of being pushed into self-employment, the one that involves being fired. Adrian Chong from Melbourne, Australia, sent me a letter indicating that *The Joy of Not Working* and *How to Retire Happy, Wild, and Free* had helped him adapt to his new lifestyle. Here is a portion of the e-mail:

> I'd rather live precariously in my own office than comfortably in somebody else's.
>
> — Peter Mayle

Hi Ernie

Two years ago I got fired for being labeled "slow" and spending too much time chatting to my co-workers. This was in a job at an insurance company where I had worked for five years. But now I am doing contracting work. There's no office politics and life is great! I get to experience much more freedom being a contractor than in my former job. Like you, I am focusing more on life and less on work. Sometimes I go to coffee bars to have coffee or hot chocolate, walk in the park, visit friends, and engage in travel occasionally.

It's very unlikely I will go back to permanent work as I am trying to live life to the fullest. Being a contractor is enough for me to live on even though the income is not stable at times. At 32 years old, I am one happy man!

Regards,

Adrian

Like Adrian Chong, you will have much greater latitude to create a job environment that suits you if you become self-employed. The problem with looking to the corporate world for work you love is that over 95 percent of corporations don't allow employees to design their own jobs and control their own work areas. This means that finding the freedom and job happiness that Adrian Chong enjoys is highly unlikely in the corporate world.

The most important thing is that as long as you work for someone else, regardless of how much money you earn, you will never be truly free. You will be trapped forever in the corporate world, whether you have a big office with a great view or a dingy cubicle with absolutely no view at all. You may think that a regular paycheck means security, but what good is the security of a paycheck without freedom?

> My first six years in the business were hopeless. There are a lot of times when you sit and you say "Why am I doing this? I'll never make it. It's just not going to happen. I should go out and get a real job, and try to survive."
>
> — George Lucas

Interestingly, I recently came across a survey that indicated the majority of young people now think self-employment is more secure than a corporate job. One respondent to the survey said, "You're not secure in a regular job so why not trade that for self-employment?"

Of course, there are many advantages and just as many disadvantages to self-employment that you have to consider before you make a decision whether to make the great escape from corporate life. The following pros and cons come from various surveys done on the self-employed.

Advantages of Working for Yourself

- Flexibility to set your own work hours
- Opportunity to use special skills and talents
- Opportunity to be innovative and creative
- No boss to tell you what to do
- Convenience and cost-saving of not having to commute every day
- Greater earning potential and a more direct connection between effort and reward
- Tax benefits
- Variety offered by working on a number of different projects and the mobility of working anywhere

Disadvantages of Working for Yourself

- Capital usually needed to start a business
- Uncertain income makes it hard to plan financially
- Lack of paid-for benefits such as health insurance, sick leave, and a retirement plan
- Uncertain work hours
- Pressure of having sole responsibility for your livelihood
- Possibility of business failure and loss of capital
- Perceptions of family and friends who think negatively that you don't have a real job
- Having to chase clients to get paid

No doubt there will be trade-offs if you decide to leave corporate life. Again, the major issue for many people is money. The money issue works both ways, however. You may wind up making less money or more money. For people like Adrian Chong, a lower income is an acceptable sacrifice for the freedom and flexibility that comes with self-employment.

One study conducted by the University of Zurich on workers in twenty-three countries found that the self-employed are substantially more satisfied than people who labor for someone else, even if the self-employed work more and earn less. One response by a self-employed person given to a researcher was, "I used to do this work as a hobby. I'm making half what I used to make in my previous job, but I'm one hundred times happier."

> Each man has his own vocation; his talent is his call. There is one direction in which all space is open to him.
>
> — Ralph Waldo Emerson

You don't necessarily have to earn less money as a self-employed person, however. Contrary to what a lot of people believe, self-employment does not mean that you have to live in poverty. In fact, there is opportunity to end up being better off financially than 99 percent of corporate workers. According to an AARP Policy Institute report, the self-employed in the United States constitute 10.2 percent of workers — but 66 percent of the millionaires.

Providing a service or product in which you truly believe is the key to making it on your own. Studies have shown time and time again that individuals who go into business because they want to perform a service they love performing or selling a product they love selling make more money in the long term than individuals who go into business just to make money.

In his best-selling book *The Millionaire Mind* (Andrews McMeel Publishing, 2001), Thomas J. Stanley studied America's wealthiest individuals. He looked at characteristics such as IQ, college major, type of business, standing in college, and family history. Not one of these factors, surprisingly, seemed to matter all that much. What the millionaires had in common was they were working at something they loved. "If you love, absolutely love what you are doing," concluded Stanley, "chances are excellent that you will succeed."

The degree to which you love your field of endeavor will determine how motivated you are to bring creativity, innovation, and overall success into your field. Self-employment is for individuals willing to work to develop their personal creativity, willing to use their creativity, willing to try out innovative products and services, and willing to enjoy the results of their work.

Thanks to technology, today it is much easier than ever to jump into self-employment. Software programs, the Internet, and the availability of other forms of technology allow individuals to perform research, work from home, and handle other aspects of their business that they never could have done in the past. It is also easier for individual workers to get tax breaks from the government to fund their own businesses.

> Being in business is not about making money. It is a way to become who you are.
>
> — Paul Hawken

Regardless of how great self-employment sounds, however, be clear that it may not be for you. Surprisingly, even highly intelligent and abundantly skilled people have a difficult time making the transition from corporate life to something better, such as self-employment and the personal freedom that comes with it. Responsibilities associated with self-employment or running an unconventional business are fundamentally different from those associated with working for an organization or corporation. Thus, many individuals who have had someone else plan a major portion of their waking hours are at a loss when there is no one else there to do it for them.

As a member of the self-employed, you must be motivated enough to follow your dreams and change course if adversity strikes to put a dent in your plans. The most fortunate of corporate refugees are those who through good planning, experimentation, and risk-taking succeed in making self-employment the best time of their lives. Here are ten questions to help you decide whether you have got what it takes to make it on your own:

Test of Whether You Can Become Joyfully Self-Employed

1. Are you willing to make personal sacrifices today in exchange for undetermined rewards in the future?
2. Are you willing to trust your decisions when others aren't?
3. Are you willing to take risks?
4. Are you willing to accept rejection?
5. Are you willing to use your creativity and be more innovative than the average person?
6. Are you willing to experience a lot of failure, and learn from it, before experiencing a lot of success?
7. Are you willing to do a lot of research?
8. Are you willing to admire successful people, learn from them, and adopt their success principles?
9. Are you willing to get paid for the actual results you produce instead of for the time you spend at a job?
10. Are you willing to forego a regular paycheck and get paid sporadically, sometimes a little, sometimes a lot?

If you answered no to all the questions, then undoubtedly you are best suited for government work and the comfort and perks that it provides. If you get such a job, hang onto it dearly even

> All the things I love is what my business is all about.
> — Martha Stewart

though it will confine you to a cubicle every work day for the rest of your career life. Note that you will have to give up a lot in exchange for the comfort of a government job. As will be discussed in greater detail later in the book, living in physical comfort doesn't necessarily mean personal fulfillment, nor does it mean personal joy, nor does it mean experiencing a feeling of true success.

Obviously the more times that you answered yes to the above test, the more likely that you will succeed in working for yourself. If you had one to four negative responses, you don't have to disqualify yourself entirely. You do, however, have to work on whatever it takes to make a genuine commitment to achieving success in your own personal way.

The bottom line is self-evident: If you can tolerate risk and uncertainty, cope well with failure while you are learning the ropes, and work creatively and independently, then self-employment is for you. Re-creating yourself as a self-employed person working in an unreal job will be challenging, but through patience, productive thinking, and positive action, you can do it. The rewards will be more than worth it.

There's No Better Business than Your Own Unconventional Business

"What the hell do you want to work for somebody else for? Work for yourself," Irving Berlin once advised a young songwriter named George Gershwin. Clearly, I am giving you the same advice. But my advice comes with one more major qualification: If you are convinced about the benefits of working for yourself, stay away from running a business that is too big or too complicated.

> A business has to be involving, it has to be fun, and it has to exercise your creative instincts.
>
> — Richard Branson

No doubt if you want to be self-employed, you must own some sort of business, regardless of how small your operation. The key is to discover your passions and attempt to turn them into a successful business enterprise. You will have a much better chance of making it on your own if you create a small business out of your passions than if you try to make a business — such as a twenty-four-hour restaurant — fit you. Look into your soul, find out what makes you tick, then choose a business to match your passions.

It is true that you can create a life with more money, more free time, and more enjoyment by running your own business and being your own boss. The key is to give a lot of thought to the lifestyle you would like, the time you want to spend at work, what you want to achieve, as well as what precisely you want to do in a business.

Be clear that running most traditional businesses can be harder than working in most conventional jobs. Indeed, owning your own business can even be spiritually devastating to your soul. It is well-known that after a year or two many business owners become disillusioned and yearn for something else. If the business depends on you, the work grinds you down, and you have no freedom, what is the point of being there? You don't own a desirable business; you have nothing more than a lousy job.

Many new businesses fail due to fierce competition, a lack of capital, or changing trends. Just as many businesses fail because the owner is not able to deal with the many unpleasant tasks necessary for the successful operation of the business. Equally important, business owners often do not recognize necessary skills that should be learned at some point.

To increase your chances of success, you may want to avoid certain types of businesses. Buying a franchise such as McDonald's, for instance, can only lead to much harder work and more work than you will have to do in most corporate jobs. Besides having to put up several hundred thousands of dollars for start-up and franchise costs, you will end up working long hours seven days a week and having to deal with frustrating activities such as hiring and firing employees.

The good news is that there are many alternatives to running a franchise or starting any other business that requires a lot of capital and a lot of employees. A home-based business supplying professional services is an option for people with expertise in areas such as law, engineering, accounting, editing, translation, and human resources.

> Business is not financial science, it's about trading, buying, and selling. It's about creating a product or service so good that people will pay for it.
> — Anita Roddick

For example, people with human-resources experience have set up shop as executive recruiters and professional résumé writers. The great advantage is that most of these small businesses don't require a large initial capital investment, yet offer the opportunity to earn a decent living.

All things considered, there's no better business than an unconventional business that differs from most traditional businesses. Your chances for success are much greater when your unconventional business has these great things going for it:

Characteristics of the Ideal Business

- You have no employees.
- You can contract out work you don't want to do yourself through services such as www.elance.com.
- The capital required for start-up is minimal.
- Your overhead is low.
- You can start making money from the outset

instead of months or years down the road.

- ◆ You can work out of your home office; better still, you can do most of your work on a laptop in a coffee bar and watch members of the opposite sex at the same time.
- ◆ You don't have to commute or your short commute to your favorite coffee bar doesn't have to be made during the rush hour.
- ◆ Your income potential is unlimited.
- ◆ You have the opportunity to create intellectual property that will give you residual income for many years to come.
- ◆ You have to work a maximum of eight hours a day, which gives you plenty of free time to enjoy life.
- ◆ The business is adaptable to a wide variety of locations, including other countries.
- ◆ You can merge your personal goals with your business goals. You can make a business trip to Spain, for instance, which you have long wanted to visit.
- ◆ The business is adaptable to a broad range of health-and-wellness needs that you may experience as you get older.
- ◆ Even if you are seventy years old, you can continue working in the business for another ten to fifteen years.

No doubt many people will say that the ideal business with the above characteristics is a fantasy. I have to agree; it was a fantasy to me at one time. Yet today I operate such a fantasy business and so do millions of others in this world. Later in this chapter over one hundred unreal jobs are listed that lend themselves as the foundation for an unconventional business that you can operate with most of the above characteristics.

> It is awfully important to know what is and what is not your business.
>
> — Gertrude Stein

Conventional wisdom states that small businesses fail due to lack of capital and fierce competition. This may be true for conventional businesses, but what you want is an unconventional business, an unreal job that does not require a lot of capital and where competition is not that much of a problem. You want to move beyond the conventional to an unreal job where you can utilize your creativity doing something you enjoy and that enhances the lives of others.

Once you know what you want to do, you want to get it right the first time if you can. We have all read the statistics about new businesses — some 80 percent of them don't make it. So how do you give yourself the best chance? Don't fall for the first money-making scheme that someone tells you about. People who chase the dollar and the "get-rich-quick" schemes fail miserably more often than not.

Another key ingredient for business success is keeping your overhead low. Employees, for instance, can cost you a lot of money, not to mention time and energy. Instead of hiring someone full- or even part-time, hire a virtual assistant. By virtual assistant, I mean someone whom you hire on the Internet.

For example, I used the website Elance (www.elance.com) to hire a freelance professional to design my seventeen-page website. After putting out my project for bid, I received nineteen offers to design the website, with prices ranging from $240 to $650. I ended up paying $400 to a Web designer in Allentown, Pennsylvania, instead of the $1,000 to $2,000 that Web designers in my hometown wanted.

If you want to go into business for yourself, you may need a nest egg to get you started. In many cases, however, having a lot of money can be detrimental to achieving success. With a lot of capital you are liable to throw money at any problem instead of using your creativity to come up with innovative solutions that pulverize your competition.

Many businesses were started on kitchen tables with virtually no capital and went on to become hugely successful multimillion dollar businesses. On the other hand, many businesses supported with millions of dollars of venture capital have taken only a year or two to bite the dust.

Although many people have opted for unconventional work when they were broke or heavily in debt, it probably helps to have some financial resources. Of course, if you have substantial financial resources, the best investment is to start a business that is so much fun you don't care if it fails.

The main thing is, will you be doing something that you enjoy? If you don't answer yes to this question, then why the heck are you thinking of doing it? If you want to start your own business mainly

> Well, you know, I was a human being before I became a businessman.
>
> — George Soros

> I know of nothing more despicable and pathetic than a man who devotes all the hours of the waking day to the making of money for money's sake.
> — John D. Rockefeller

because you had a jerk for a boss in your last ten corporate jobs, it is highly likely that you will still have a jerk for a boss when you are self-employed.

Today, being an entrepreneur has become a goal for people because it is trendy. If you want to be an entrepreneur for the sole reasons that being an entrepreneur is trendy and you would make you a lot of money, surely you ain't a genuine entrepreneur. As a true entrepreneur, you should have some purpose such as making the world a better place to live for yourself and others.

If you want to succeed as an entrepreneur, you must pick a viable business, preferably one that is different and serves a market niche. But don't overlook the fact that your business must fit you as an individual. To be effective in running a business, you want to engage yourself in work that you enjoy immensely and not in tasks that you dislike, which should be delegated or contracted out to someone else. Your time and energy should be focused largely on work that benefits from your strengths, skills, and personal goals.

The joy and satisfaction you will receive from making a modest living selling a product that enhances the lives of other people will be tenfold greater than the satisfaction you will receive if you make lots of money from something that is not beneficial to the world, such as being involved in a pyramid scheme or selling contraband cigarettes.

If you enjoy what you're doing in a business, you will have a lot of fun and you will ultimately be more successful than someone who doesn't. Even if your venture fails for whatever reason, if you enjoyed doing something you are passionate about for three years, then it won't be such a great loss. Many people don't get to enjoy three years of work in a forty-five-year career.

To increase your chances for success, think about how you can use your skills to work creatively and independently. Also think about acquiring a few new skills to diversify your sources of income. You may have to do several things initially to make ends meet. The idea of doing a variety of things also gives you a variety of interesting work to pursue. Web designers, for example, can give speeches, do seminars, and publish newsletters.

Even if you are financially ready, you must still be mentally ready. You have to know yourself well to make the right decision.

Take your time. The key is to use a rational decision-making process that gives consideration to your health, your finances, your dreams, your family situation, and your present-day well-being. You may want to use the following process:

Decision-Making Model for Whether to Start an Unconventional Business

Step 1: Write down all the pros and cons of running your own business. Look for hidden disadvantages. It's all too easy to focus only on the advantages.

Step 2: Decide whether the pros outweigh the cons. What net benefits do you receive by leaving corporate life? What benefits do you lose that may turn out to be far more important than meets the eye?

Step 3: Find objective assistance from your spouse as well as friends and professionals. These people will be able to support you in your decision to go on your own; alternatively, they can ask insightful questions to ensure you aren't making the biggest mistake in your life.

Step 4: Make the decision. If the pros win out over the cons, it's time to go. As the Nike ad says, "Just do it." If things don't work out, it's not the end of the world. You can find another traditional job, possibly better than the one you have now.

This book won't go into much more depth about how to start your own business simply because this is not its intent. But there are hundreds of books that provide a lot of valuable information. Try one such as *Working Solo: The Real Guide to Freedom & Financial Success with Your Own Business* (Wiley, 1998) by Terri Lonier. Getting started in a new field may not be easy, but plenty of help is available to accomplish anything you want. Books alone provide a vast reserve of knowledge that can be exploited by practically anyone.

Every answer to any problem you can ever imagine is in publication somewhere; you just need to find it. When I first started in my business, for instance, I didn't have the faintest idea about how to write a book,

> Nearly every glamorous, wealthy, successful career woman you might envy now started out as some kind of schlep.
>
> — Helen Gurley Brown

get it published, or promote it. Many people are of the opinion that I still can't write, but the joke is on them because today I make a very good living from my writing. Everything I needed to know — the art of writing, how to self-publish, creative ways to promote books, even how to sell foreign rights — I was able to learn by reading books.

An incredible amount of information is available to you as well, regardless of what you want to accomplish. Besides using books, you can utilize other excellent resources such as consultants, seminars, radio talk shows, and the Internet. Other people have acquired a lot of knowledge and wisdom that they make available either for free or at relatively low cost. Not only is this information a bargain, your life will be a lot easier than if you had to go out and make the same mistakes that these people had to make.

No doubt if your decision is to start your own business, there will be a lot of people out there who will be all too happy to burst your bubble and try to convince you that what you are contemplating is unreasonable and unattainable. At the extreme, they may even try to convince you that it is your patriotic duty to work at a corporate job you hate, particularly if you have spent four to six years at a prestigious university acquiring an education relevant to the job.

> The woman who can create her own job is the woman who will win fame and fortune.
>
> — Amelia Earhart

Clearly, these people are terrified to do the thing you are contemplating. They may also be envious of your plans and even afraid that you will succeed while they remain miserable for years to come.

If you look at your bosses and more experienced colleagues and don't want to be like them in five or ten years, what more encouragement do you need? If you end up being a real success after leaving corporate life altogether, you will have these people to thank.

Being an entrepreneur is always risky, but not that much more uncertain than life in the corporate world, where constant pressure to cut costs and remain competitive results in even the most valued employees being put out on the street. Read the newspaper each day and you will learn about the latest round of layoffs in Fortune 500 corporations. You may also hear from friends or acquaintances who have been let go from the best of jobs.

The great thing is that once you get established as an entrepreneur you are in control of your future in more ways than one. Recent surveys by Dream Bean Morin Inc. show that corporate restructuring — arising from mergers, acquisitions, and reorganizations — remains the main reason for job loss among American workers. When you are an entrepreneur, the only person who can downsize you is you. But why would you want to? A career without a real job can be the most adventurous career that anyone can have.

The World's Coolest Unreal Jobs

To be sure, it's never easy to leave a career in which you have spent a good portion of your life. What makes it even harder is having reached a high level of traditional success where you have a large salary, great benefits, a generous expense account, and a good measure of prestige. But you must leave if you are unhappy and see no way to make yourself happy.

If you agree with even 80 percent of what I have said in this book so far, corporations need you more than you need corporations. A creative person like you wanting a corporate job is like a dolphin wanting a gun. Why bother? Indeed, if having to work at Starbucks would make you think that you have been denied your rightful place in the world's vocational order, the rest of this book will help, provided you commit yourself to the principles advocated herein.

The most successful creative people make the great escape from corporate life and don't work in real jobs; they choose self-employment or unconventional jobs such as those in the entertainment field. These people don't talk excessively about their dreams — they just make their dreams happen through their intention. They also don't listen to their negative friends and relatives who doubt that anyone can make a great living outside of a corporation. Indeed, millions of people in this world earn a decent living without a real job.

Take Miki in Toronto, Ontario, for instance, who is a clairvoyant. According to an interview she did with *Report on Business* magazine, in the average week Miki rolls through thirty to thirty-five people with about 75 percent being women. Her clients vary from people in the entertainment business, police officers, and stockbrokers, to bank presidents. She charges $120 for a one-hour reading. Run through the numbers and you can see that Miki makes a decent living. She says her job isn't always a

> Get happiness out of your work or you may never know what happiness is.
> — Elbert Hubbard

> Find a calling you love and you will never work a day in your life.
>
> — Confucius

bowl of cherries, but I bet she wouldn't trade it for a real job.

Many people like Miki march to the beat of a different career drum, particularly those who recoil with horror at the prospect of a conventional corporate job. They have created a cool, unreal job for themselves. A cool, unreal job is anything you joyfully do for a living instead of a conventional job. The unreal job becomes your real work. But if it's fun, it can't be real work. So we have to stick with the term unreal job.

Look for a job where the normal concerns don't apply. An unreal job is one in which we don't have to worry about achievement factors such as status, power, financial rewards, and advancement opportunities. Equally important, an unreal job is hard to differentiate from leisure; it's an opportunity to work at something for the personal satisfaction of doing it well and having loads of fun at the same time. At its best, a cool, unreal job is something that you would happily work at — or play at — for no pay.

Today there are more opportunities to work at unreal jobs than any time in history because of changing lifestyles and an incredible number of niche markets. Of the many other interesting ways to make an unconventional living, the following stand out:

100 of the World's Coolest Unreal Jobs

Auctioneer	Audio marketer
Advertising agent	Audio-visual consultant
Audio-visual technician	Book reviewer
Busker	Cabaret singer
Calendar creator	Cartoonist
Cat/dog boarding service	Choreographer
Clothes designer	College instructor
Color expert	Commissioned salesperson
Computer expert	Copywriter
Contract employee	Computer programmer
Corporate trainer	Crossword-puzzle maker
Daily money manager	Dance therapist
Desktop publisher	Dramatic coach
Entrepreneurial artist	Events producer
Executive chef	Exporter
Family therapist	Fiction writer
Floral designer	Freelance editor

Furniture designer
Ghostwriter
Home tutor
Illustrator
Importer
Information broker
Infomercial producer
Interior designer
Landlord/leasing specialist
Licenser of products
Lyricist
Makeup artist
Marriage counselor
Media expert
Model
Multimedia designer
Negotiator
Newsletter editor
Orchestrator
Photographer
Personal coach
Psychic reader
Publicist
Screenwriter
Self-publisher
Speech coach
Stunt performer
Telecommunicator
Travel writer
Video-game consultant
Website designer
Wedding planner
Writer

Game designer
Graphic artist
Humorist
Image consultant
Freelance product designer
Infomarketing coach
Instructional designer
Internet expert
Landscape expert
Literary agent
Mail order entrepreneur
Management consultant
Massage therapist
Mime artist
Movie critic
Multilevel marketer
Networking franchiser
Online content developer
Painter
Professional speaker
Printmaker
Public-relations consultant
Real estate broker
Sculptor
Seminar producer
Street performer
Syndicated columnist
TV-program producer
Tattoo artist
Web consultant
Web master
Wine expert
Yoga teacher

These unconventional jobs are just a few of many that lend themselves to making a living outside the corporation. Tomorrow, there will even be more new dream jobs that you didn't even know existed. A decade or so ago, who would have imagined a job as a Web designer?

Whether it's an unreal job or an unconventional business venture, don't

> Never be afraid to tread the path alone. Know which is your path and follow it wherever it may lead you; do not feel you have to follow in someone else's footsteps.
>
> — Eileen Caddy

rush into a new career without considering many alternatives. Today's large selection of cool careers gives you a great chance to select one that matches your skills, talents, and experience. Real success without a real job can be yours if you really want it.

Today's Most Exciting Unconventional Business That Allows You to Make Money While You Sleep

To some people the best way to make a living without a real job is being a landlord. Of course, being a landlord is not easy, particularly if you have no capital to invest in rental property. Sure, you may be able to acquire property without any capital using Robert Allen's book *Nothing Down for the 2000s* (Free Press, 2004). Even so, once you acquire property, being a landlord is not easy; I found this out during my short-lived stint as a landlord when I wound up with lousy tenants. What's more, there are high risks involved and you must know your market.

> My son is now an "entrepreneur." That's what you're called when you don't have a job.
> — Ted Turner

A much better career than owning real estate and being a landlord is an unconventional job associated with the information business. Some people call the information business "the real estate of the twenty-first century." For many decades, the best way to become wealthy was through real estate. Today it is information. The person who creates timely information, and markets it effectively, can prosper and generate more wealth than most people can with real estate.

What I like about the information business is that it is an exciting business, in fact, one of the most exciting in the world. It can also be a difficult business if you don't have a decent product or don't know what you are doing. If you develop a good service or product, and pay your dues to learn the ropes, however, this exciting business can be highly lucrative financially and very rewarding personally.

The information business has been experiencing unparalleled growth for several years and will continue to do so for decades. Why not get into this business? You can be the source of ideas, data, and entertainment that people and businesses want. Here are some of the benefits of being in the information business:

- Easy to create
- A large global market
- Easy to research, particularly on the Internet
- Inexpensive to produce
- Can sell information from practically anywhere in the world
- Fun to sell
- Prestigious career compared to most jobs

Since there is no lack of information in the world, the opportunity is not so much in coming up with new information as it is in packaging it properly. You want to make the information user-friendly. User-friendly means time-friendly — information that is easy to read and takes as little time as possible to read.

The great thing is that you don't have to come up with anything new. Better still, you can sell the same information that other people are selling and make a lot more money than they are. To do this your information should be simpler, cheaper, easier to understand, smaller, and/or more timely. It can also have more value because it has more features.

> Welfare is not a career opportunity.
>
> — Unknown wise person

Another great benefit to being in the information business is that you can develop multiple layers of products and programs by leveraging your information into residual streams of income. You don't want to specialize in too narrow of a field; the more specialized you become, the more dependent you are on that specialty. Broadening your opportunities allows you to make much more money in good times and still be able to do well when one of your information-making programs falls on bad times.

Ways to Sell Information

- Books
- E-books
- Audio books
- Audio programs
- Video training
- Multimedia programs
- Workbooks or manuals
- Coaching programs
- Consulting
- Keynote speaking

- Seminars
- E-zines
- Newsletters
- Branded retail products such as T-shirts
- Foreign rights
- Licensing for websites and cell-phone promotions
- Mentoring and apprenticeship
- Infomercials
- CD Rom/DVD Training
- Joint ventures

What makes the information business so delightful is its expansive nature. You can start with only one product or service but additional opportunities are sure to keep evolving over time. What's more, the inherent nature of the information business provides you with an ongoing education as you learn more and more about your subject or area of expertise.

The information business is all about ideas. Figure out what the market wants and deliver it in a way no one has before. A key to making it big in the information business is to create and market information that you are passionate about. Put another way, you have to be in love with your product, whether it's a book, video, or branded retail product. If you are crazy about the information you repackage, the marketing part becomes so much more enjoyable — even a breeze.

Note that the information business meets all the characteristics of the ideal business that are listed on pages 57 and 58. Possibly the most powerful aspect of the information business is that you have the opportunity to create intellectual property that will give you residual income for many years to come. New or repackaged information can become your intellectual property. Whether through games, training franchises, books, tapes, or videos, intellectual property can provide you with residual income that continues to come to you long after you have created the product.

Indeed, the staying power of intellectual property will earn you money while you sleep. Take, for example, *The Joy of Not Working.* This book was first published in 1991 and today it still earns me over $20,000 a year in royalties. To bug my friends working in real jobs, I say, "Why do you think I often sleep in until noon? I do this to earn an extra fifty bucks or so

> A #2 pencil and a dream can take you anywhere.
>
> — Joyce A. Myers

from my intellectual property. I also often take a nap late in the afternoon and make myself another twenty-five bucks."

> Make good use of bad rubbish.
>
> — Elizabeth Beresford

One of my favorite examples of the staying power of intellectual property is the album *Bat out of Hell* by Meat Loaf, the legendary rock-opera singer, born Marvin Lee Aday. Aday was given the nickname Meat Loaf by his abusive and alcoholic father. At the age of eighteen, after the death of his mother to cancer, Meat Loaf left his Dallas home to make it on his own, and in 1977 he released his first album *Bat out of Hell.* The amazing thing is that almost thirty years later the album still sells over 500,000 copies a year and has now sold thirty million copies. As you can well imagine, Aday and members of his band still get a handsome royalty check every year.

Of course, I don't expect you to become a singer to capitalize on the power of intellectual property — although you would probably have a better chance of doing this than I, given what a terrible singer I am. The point is that rock stars aren't the only individuals eligible for royalties. You can create an audiotape, syndicate a cartoon, invent a product, or sell an idea to a major corporation.

Keep in mind that not only am I a terrible singer, but I am also a lousy writer — according to some people, anyway. But I still make a decent living. You can also earn a decent living from intellectual property, particularly if you agree by now that I am a lousy writer and are sure that you can write better than I can. What more proof do you need?

Many obscure individuals are starting out today in the information business about whom you will be reading in two or three years. You can be one of these people. You don't have to be a genius and you don't have to own a big company. Best of all, you can do it from your kitchen table or home office. It's within your grasp. Get started today.

You may object that we are already bombarded with way too much information; so who needs more? A lot of people, in fact, want the information. Corporations want it also, simply because a lot of corporations, particularly large ones, are too sluggish to effectively generate useful and timely information. As a creative and ambitious individual working on your own, you can produce

> Syzygy, inexorable, pancreatic, phantasmagoria — anyone who can use those four words in one sentence will never have to do manual labor.
>
> — W. P. Kinsella

much more valuable information.

The key is to make your presentation of old information — whether through videos, training programs or documentaries — more timely and more user-friendly than what is already out there. Several readers have told me that although virtually all the principles in *The Joy of Not Working* were well-known to them, they loved reading the book because of the unique way I presented the information.

Real estate guru Robert Allen claims, "There's a lot more money in the information business than there ever will be in the real estate business." Old information reorganized, repackaged, and remarketed in new ways provides many people with an interesting livelihood and has made some of them millionaires. As already emphasized, the cool thing is that you don't need to create new information.

> The more I want to get something done, the less I call it work.
>
> — Richard Bach

Here is another personal example of how I repackaged existing information in creative and user-friendly ways: Two months before starting this book, I thought about how money and work were two of the most talked about subjects in Western society. That led to the idea that there should be a book of great quotations about each topic.

Immediately, I started working on the two books of quotations for about three hours each day. Remember that there are dozens of quotation websites and there have been hundreds of quotation books published. This would have deterred most people from pursuing the ideas further. This didn't stop me, however, because I knew that presenting the quotations in creative and user-friendly ways was key. Besides, if I couldn't sell the books to publishers, I had several ideas on how to use them as viral marketing tools to help sell my other books.

About a month after starting the projects, I had completed both in PDF format. I called them *The 777 Best Things Ever Said about Money* and *1001 Best Things Ever Said about Work (and the Workplace)*. I spent $350 for approximately 200 images from www.istockphoto.com to enhance the books and made sure that the quotations in each book weren't the stale, boring ones that are found in most quotation books.

My three hours of work each day for a month paid off. Within three hours of my sending the PDF file for *The 777 Best Things Ever Said about Money* to a Japanese literary agent (actually by mistake since I thought I was sending it to another agent), my contact there had an offer for me. It so happened that a Japanese publisher was coming to the agency an hour after I sent the agent the PDF file. The publisher ended up offering $8,000 as an advance, which I gladly accepted.

Clearly, the payoff from packaging and marketing information does not always come that quickly. Opportunities abound, however, to make a great deal of money from a modest amount of effort. With a few winning ideas on how to repackage existing information, and proper marketing, you can spend the rest of your lifetime experiencing real success without a real job.

Write Yourself out of Poverty into Satisfaction and Riches

Assume that you are placed in a prison cell against your will and your jailers tell you that you have to write a publishable book in order for you to gain your freedom. You are given access to the Internet as well as a writing coach and any book on writing and publishing that has ever been written. Do you think that you could write a decent book? Clearly, many people — likely you included — under these conditions would knock off a book within two or three months that is better than thousands of books that have been published by major publishers.

So why not write a book? Perhaps, like many people, you have always wanted to be a writer. Deep down, there has always been something about the Starbucks cappuccino-and-laptop crowd that appealed to you. If you have thought intuitively for a long time that you should have been a writer, you should give it some serious consideration. Indeed, if deep down you have always wanted to write a book, not writing one can be more difficult than actually writing it.

Apparently 81 percent of Americans think they should write a book, but only 2 percent have completed a manuscript. Alas, the large majority of people are not prepared to pay their dues. Most people don't start or finish their books because of a lack of commitment. How about you?

I have decided to devote a bit of space to what it takes to be a writer simply because there are so many people who want to write. Fact is, being a writer is one of the best ways to earn a living without a real job. There aren't a large

> Why do writers write? Because it isn't there.
>
> — Thomas Berger

number of unreal jobs that can give you as much personal freedom as the writing business.

> Writing is easy. All you do is stare at a blank sheet of paper until drops of blood form on your forehead.
>
> — Gene Fowler

But the writing business has to be run like — a business! That's why the vast majority of writers don't make a great living. They fail because they don't learn the business end. One of the most important aspects of any unconventional business is the marketing aspect, which will be covered in chapter 5.

For now, let's stick with what it takes to generate a publishable product. Many options and opportunities await you if you look for them. Whether it's writing a novel, a self-help book, or a newspaper column, you must choose what will give you the most interesting challenge and satisfaction.

To be sure, not everything about writing is easy. Richard Bach, author of best-selling *Jonathan Livingston Seagull*, admitted that it was tough for him to write his next bestseller, *Illusions*. Ernest Hemingway stated, "I read my own books sometimes to cheer me when it is hard to write and then I remember that it was always difficult and how nearly impossible it was sometimes." Joseph Heller, author of *Catch-22*, summed it up very well when he stated that all great writers have difficulty writing.

No doubt some people are born with more talent than others. This superior talent gives them greater potential to excel at certain things, including becoming an accomplished author. Writing is largely dependent upon commitment and perseverance, however.

A week doesn't pass by in which I don't meet someone much smarter and literarily more capable than I am, who desperately wants to write a book, but hasn't gotten around to it. I tell the person, "If I can write a book, so can you." Granted, no one has ever classified anything I have written — even one sentence — as literature. This is missing the point, however.

As much as possible, I won't allow my limitations to stop me from writing the books I am capable of writing. What I realized some time ago is that I can't write a book on the same level as William Shakespeare, but I can write a book by me. In fact, by the time I realized how bad of a writer I really was, surprisingly, I was too successful to quit. To deal with my bad writing, I decided to write more books and improve in the process.

Above all, my writing accomplishments are the result of my agreement with myself to write a minimum of three hours a day. I try to write four pages during this time. These pages don't have to be masterpieces. Sometimes, they contain some pretty pathetic writing, but at least I have four pages to work with. Even if I break my agreement to write three hours a day, and write for only fifteen minutes, I am still closer to completing a book than the lazy characters who talk for ten hours about writing one, but never spend a minute on it.

Most people cop out by saying that they can't write. Others say that they don't have enough time. Still others think that no one would be interested in what they have to say. These are excuses, far from being good reasons. If people are too lazy to write, at least they should admit it, and take responsibility for their own laziness.

Write a novel, write a poem, write a movie script, write a play, write a short story, write a newspaper article, or write an opera. Whatever you have wanted to write, start today. Even write an unauthorized autobiography, but make sure you write. All told, you can write yourself out of poverty into satisfaction and a livelihood simply because others have.

I know that we are ignorant and lack artistic talent but is this any reason to give up on our self-help book? That crackpot Ernie Zelinski has written several.

Frank Kaiser is an example of someone who wrote himself to satisfaction and a livelihood. In 2000 Kaiser entered retirement age with a $616 Social Security check and nothing else — no corporate pension and no savings. After having gone broke starting StreetSmarts Coalition, a non-profit organization whose mission was to help south Florida's homeless men and women attain self-sufficiency, Kaiser needed an income-producing venture so that he and his wife wouldn't lose their house.

Kaiser thought about how seniors are the most avid readers of newspapers and, yet, how dull most newspapers are. That's when he came up with the idea for a regular column where he could provide more interesting topics for these seniors. "In school, I was taught to write what I know," Kaiser remarked. "I decided to write the truth about what it's like to be a geezer."

The regular column was tagged "Suddenly Senior" and his first article was called "Have Sex the Way You Did 40 Years Ago." An editor at Florida's *Key Largo Independent* liked the first article so much that he decided to carry the writer's regular column. Soon

Kaiser's inspirational and funny writing caught the attention of more editors and eventually led to Kaiser's regular column being syndicated to several newspapers and magazines.

With his popularity growing, Kaiser then decided to promote his humor and philosophy on the Internet. He put his creativity to good use by including cartoons, humorous photographs, and funny stories on his website (www.SuddenlySenior.com). Within a relatively short time, the website was receiving 200,000 visits every month. In February 2002, individuals from seventy-two countries had logged onto his site. Here is a sample of what you will find on Kaiser's website today: "Remember: Every 8.4 seconds yet another baby boomer reaches age fifty and, to their horror, gets invited to join AARP!"

As is to be expected, writing the newspaper column and maintaining the website has been a big thrill for Kaiser. The column and website have also been a big thrill for his readers, who, in Kaiser's words, have "become senior before their time." The best news is that Kaiser is actually making a living from Suddenly Senior. "No one is more surprised than I," he admitted.

> I feel very rich when I have time to write and very poor when I get a regular paycheck and no time at my real work.
> — Natalie Goldberg

There is no question that being a writer offers one of the few opportunities to make a great deal of money in a short period of time. There are far greater payoffs, however — adventure, personal satisfaction, and acknowledgment from readers. Most accomplished writers profess that the biggest reward isn't financial. It's the thrill of sharing their views of the world with others, and having others tell them that they experienced pleasure — even spiritual fulfillment — from reading their poems, articles, blogs, or books.

You can also share in these benefits if you are prepared to do all the difficult things that are necessary to write, particularly a book that becomes a bestseller. If you can't find a publisher once you have written a book, publish it on your own if you believe in it. Many books that went on to be bestsellers were self-published. But don't equate success with producing a bestseller. If your book or any other work is enjoyed by one person other than yourself, it's a success — anything over and above this is a bonus.

You can take a writing course but it's not necessary for many people. Indeed, most famous writers never took a creative writing course. Again, as Nike advises, "Just Do It." You have to ask yourself: Would others benefit from my article, poem, newsletter, or book? If the answer is yes, then you have a responsibility, not only to yourself, but to the world to write.

> Writing is turning one's worst moments into money.
> — J. P. Donleavy

Writing, plain and simple, is putting your knowledge and ideas into words on paper and then trying to arrange them in publishable form, whether it's for a book, newspaper, magazine, or a website. Above all, writing is one of the best ways to express yourself to the world, and make some money at it at the same time.

Sit down at your computer and write 500 to 1,000 words today. To date *The Joy of Not Working* has made me about seven dollars per word since it was first published. If you can put together a book that goes on to be just as successful, writing 500 words (about one page) today will end up making you $3,500 over the next several years. Whenever I have a choice whether to watch TV or head down to a coffee bar and write a new book on my laptop, the coffee house and laptop win out every time. To the best of my knowledge, few success-seekers have become finders while watching TV.

Retire to a Job You Love Instead of One You Love to Hate

As indicated in my book *How to Retire Happy, Wild, and Free*, planning for retirement, if and when it is pursued, generally focuses on financial issues. Particularly if you are a baby boomer quickly approaching retirement, you may be concerned whether you are saving enough for retirement. The good news is that many people may be overestimating how much money they need once they leave the workforce. Several research studies show that people generally spend a lot less as they age.

If you have the money issue handled, you may be wondering whether there is life after retirement. There is good news here as well. With a retirement pension, you can retire early from your present boring job and find another job that is more interesting, even if it does not pay as much. This will make your retirement life more exciting and satisfying than your work life.

> Most people perform essentially meaningless work. When they retire that truth is borne upon them.
> — Brendan Francis

In fact, many soon-to-be retirees intend to find some sort of new job in order that they enjoy retirement life. A survey by Metropolitan Life Insurance

> Sixty-five is the age when one acquires sufficient experience to lose one's job.
>
> — Unknown wise person

Co. found that 57 percent of baby boomers between fifty and fifty-nine want a "feel-good job" in their retirement years. About 70 percent of women want a job that gives them purpose and 48 percent of men said it is important to have such work. Overall, almost 60 percent of men and women indicated that they would like "feel-good jobs" in the non-profit or public-service sectors.

A similar survey conducted by Merrill Lynch found that 76 percent of baby boomers plan to do some kind of work during their retirement. Many are planning active retirements that include a variety of jobs. One of the people surveyed stated, "I'd like to travel a lot when I retire, but I'd also like to work part-time — not at my current job — but something slower paced and more fun!"

Another baby boomer claimed, "I plan on spending my retirement giving back. I'd like to do volunteer work in the area of special education. I'll maybe do a little consulting to have extra money to help others but for the most part I will continue with the work I love but will be doing it without pay." Still another remarked, "Health permitting, I plan to work part-time at a book store (I'm in IT now) and do some traveling."

Clearly, for those stuck in a job rut, early retirement from their present career is a way to replace it with one filled with joy and meaning. For retirees who are financially stable, starting a business is another option. "Boredom is a key reason why retirees start a business," says George Krassner, a consultant and lecturer at Durham Technical and Wake Technical Community Colleges and in Duke Continuing Education small-business workshops. Some retirees try consulting. Others turn a hobby into a business. Still others will start franchises. All these can lead to real success without a real job.

If you are retired or soon-to-be retired, you may find Dorothy Cantor's *What Do You Want to Do When You Grow Up: Starting the Next Chapter of Your Life* (Little Brown & Company, 2001) helpful. This self-help tome is directed at retirees, wannabe retirees, and mid-life job swappers. Cantor outlines practical ways for readers to figure out strengths and interests so that they can set out a blueprint for the last third of their lives. The book is especially useful to people in middle age who have the sense that golf and bridge and visiting grandchildren can't be all that there is to retirement.

Leaving a traditional job for self-employment or an unreal job can offer a smooth financial and lifestyle transition into retirement or semi-retirement. For retirees who find their true calling, retirement actually becomes semi-retirement because they work part-time at an unreal job that allows them to work according to their own schedule. Semi-retirement is a time to work for the love of work rather than for the love of money. Going to work when one knows one doesn't have to work in itself can be satisfying. More important, working at a job one loves instead of a job that one loves to hate is highly rewarding.

Take, for example, Ron Sadownick of Nanaimo, B.C., who retired at the age of fifty-six. While he was a schoolteacher, Sadownick's passion was making fused-glass art. Taking early retirement allowed him to devote much more time to his creative pursuit. Because twenty-five galleries in B.C. sell his work, his hobby earns him $1,000 a month, a nice supplement to his $28,000-a-year pension.

As for Ron Sadownick, working for many baby boomers will be out of interest rather than necessity, with most of those who plan to work during retirement planning to move into a completely new career. If you are one of these baby boomers contemplating early retirement, it's easy to dream about how you'll spend your retirement days. It's entirely another matter to make those dreams come true, particularly if you don't have a major purpose. Several research studies show that retirees who have no real purpose to their lives are prone to feel unneeded and fit for nothing, even severely depressed.

> There's one thing I always wanted to do before I quit . . . retire!
> — Groucho Marx

One research study was conducted by Jungmeem Kim and Phyllis Moen of Cornell University on retired men and women based on the definition of "retired" as eligible for or receiving Social Security, an employee pension, or both. Kim and Moen concluded that regardless of their income, health, or age, retired males have high morale and little depression if they adopt second careers. Much higher levels of depression and lower morale are experienced by men who make retirement permanent. Retired women have the most difficulty with morale and depression if they are retired and their husbands aren't at home.

Many individuals are lucky enough to have had their career work and some passionate pursuit be one and the same. Thus, they can continue happily working part-time in their field well past retirement, without having to discover their true calling.

> Sooner or later I'm going to die, but I'm not going to retire.
>
> — Margaret Mead

Unfortunately, this is not true for many retirees and soon-to-be retirees. If they are not able to discover their mission in life, the prescription for these retirees and soon-to-be retirees is an enjoyable job.

By an enjoyable job, I am referring to what some semi-retired people call a "fun job." For example, Cliff and Babette Marten of Des Moines, Iowa, get their kicks in retirement by driving vehicles across Iowa, across the Midwest, and even clear across the United States. They get a chance to drive many types of automobiles — including Cadillacs and Lexuses — and they get paid for it. "About every drive is a different situation," Cliff Marten, seventy-seven at the time, told the *Des Moines Register*.

For a fee, the Martens drive new and used cars for Betts Cadillac, a Des Moines auto dealership. The couple is in a pool of fifteen to twenty drivers who drive cars to dealerships in other states or to private individuals who have purchased a car from Betts. The drivers are paid by the hour and reimbursed for expenses such as food, tolls, and lodging.

On out-of-state deliveries, Cliff Marten will drive the car to be delivered and Babette Marten will follow in another car that will later be used to bring them back home. The Martens have driven from Iowa to Florida, California, Michigan, and Connecticut, and passed through many states in between. They sometimes get the opportunity to visit family or friends along the way. "We get paid to have fun," declared Babette Marten, seventy-years old at the time.

Bob Laabs also got himself a fun job after he "retired." A former high-school principal, Laabs took a job as a historic interpreter in his hometown of Williamsburg, Virginia, a popular tourist center.

> It is not real work unless you would rather be doing something else.
>
> — J. M. Barrie

Now he gives tours of the buildings in Williamsburg and lectures tourists on the events of 1774—1776. "It's not so much a job, but a fun thing to do," stated Laabs, sixty at the time. "I like history, I like people, and this is a melding of both of these things."

Although the extra money Laabs makes allows him to live in more financial comfort than if he weren't working, this isn't his main point of working in retirement. "You've got to retire to something, not from something," Laabs advises people who are about to retire. "Don't just get away — do something that enhances your lifestyle."

All things considered, if you are going to work in retirement, the nature of the work should be much more important than the money you can make at it. Should it be the case that you need a reasonable income from your retirement career, careful thought and preparation will be needed to find part-time work that is both enjoyable and profitable. On the other hand, if you have a good retirement income without a job, even one that pays the minimum wage should be taken in the event that it provides you with satisfaction and enjoyment.

While pursuing a fun job, we should do the right thing for ourselves, regardless of what others may think of the job. It's okay to take a job that has less status than the one we had in our primary careers. A good example of a person who did just this is Dick Remy, a can-company supervisor before he retired at the age of fifty. For the first five years Remy worked part-time as a consultant. Regardless of the fact that being a consultant gave him a measure of status, Remy didn't find his retirement job much fun. Eventually he did something about it. "I decided to see what was out there," stated Remy.

As it turned out, Remy's fun job ended up being a truck driver, a job some retirees may have dreamed of doing as a kid, but never got around to pursuing due to the job's perceived lower status in society. This didn't stop Remy. He was first trained as a truck driver by Kreilkamp Trucking Inc. of Allenton,

> Retirement is waking up in the morning with nothing to do and by bedtime having done only half of it.
>
> — Unknown wise person

Wisconsin, before the company hired him. Now he spends up to forty hours a week behind the wheel of an eighteen-wheeler that he has nicknamed "Sweet Pea." Remy declares, "This is a great job for me because it keeps me moving — I'm happiest when I'm on the go."

Particularly if you have a nice retirement nest egg, you, too, can easily make the transition from "I have to work" to "I want to work for the fun of it." Getting the right fun job will allow you to work at something you like, at your own time, at your own pace. The beauty is that you don't have to get a job for the whole year and you can work as much, or as little, as you want. You can experiment with various short-term (a week or a month) or part-time positions (one or two days a week).

Following are several other fun jobs that will appeal to certain retirees and that you may want to consider for your retirement years:

- Spend a year in Mexico working alongside Franciscan nuns in a home for elderly women.
- Teach English in a Costa Rican village.
- Work on a golf course and learn more about the game from the experts.
- Work as a travel agent to learn more about other countries and get some deals on travel.
- Engage your musical abilities by joining a band that plays on a cruise ship.
- Get work as an extra with a studio doing a film or a TV documentary in your area.
- Use your carpentry skills to remodel old farm houses in the south of France
- Take off for the winter on a two-month-long trip to Las Vegas and work as a blackjack dealer in a casino.
- Get a summer job driving a tourist bus in Banff in the Canadian Rockies.
- Offer your public-speaking abilities to conventions in major cities in exchange for travel expenses, food, and lodging.
- Book a working vacation and help native Maoris in the Cook Islands improve their healthcare system.

Particularly if your career work was all labor and drudgery, a fun job may bring you a measure of enjoyment and satisfaction that you didn't think was possible. Indeed, getting a fun job after you retire from your primary career gives you the best of both worlds. Having enjoyable work while also having more leisure time is a great way to enjoy life. You can have a freer lifestyle because of the increased leisure time, and still enjoy the many positives of having a job.

> Don't simply retire from something; have something to retire to.
> — Harry Emerson Fosdick

Best of all, retirement is your opportunity to try out many different lines of work just for the adventure of it. If you find a job that really turns you on, you may want to stick with it for the longer term. The most fascinating aspect of a fun job is that it may actually end up being your true calling in life. As inspirational author Louise Hay said, "New careers can start at any age, especially when you do it for the fun of it."

3

Extraordinary Success Is Achieved by Ordinary Individuals

Real People Attain Unreal Success — So Can You!

As already emphasized, the best way to experience a funky work environment in which to hang out is to free yourself from the normal shackles of the corporate world and create a fun or dream job that really turns you on. No doubt this is much easier said than done. In many respects, however, you are probably limiting yourself in what you can accomplish in this world.

Perhaps you are like the majority of humans on this planet who believe that it takes extraordinary character traits for a person to successfully pursue a dream career and actually make a living without a real job. I like the way Mark Twain put it: "The trouble with most of us is that we know too much that ain't so."

Popular belief has it that the highly successful have achieved extraordinary accomplishments due to their extraordinary traits. This may be true to a large degree in sports, but most individuals who have escaped the dreadful enslavement of corporate life have not been born with exceptional talent.

What's more, being blessed with exceptional qualities does not guarantee real success without a real job. On the contrary, even traditional career success is not guaranteed by virtue of superior intelligence, a sky-high level of formal education, special skills, hard work,

> I don't have a lot of respect for talent. Talent is genetic. It's what you do with it that counts.
>
> — Martin Ritt

knowing the right people, or being in a high-status field such as law, medicine, or architecture. North America is full of well-educated, highly trained, and extraordinarily skilled people who have yet to experience any real success in their lives.

It's not that these people aren't smart — they are. Obviously they have proven their intelligence by getting a great education, which makes it all the more disappointing that they haven't gotten their acts together and done something extraordinary with their lives. What these individuals lack more than anything is the willingness to take creative action instead of opting for whatever comfort they presently enjoy.

Fact is, most extraordinary success is achieved by ordinary individuals. These people pull off remarkable achievements because they take action whereas others don't. Just as important, the difference between successful people and the rest of the pack is something American researcher Angela Duckworth calls "grit." She defines "grit" as "tenaciously pursuing something over the long term."

Duckworth, a psychologist who specializes in studying high achievers, has developed a "grit scale," to measure achievers' determination. The researcher believes people with this quality are more likely to succeed in work, school, politics, and other arenas than people with higher IQs and more talent.

Duckworth found grit was the key to the success of undergraduates, selected Internet users, West Point plebes, national spelling-bee contestants, and eighth graders. "Perseverance or grit does make a difference in the long run," she told *The Philadelphia Inquirer*. "It allows a person to learn through their mistakes. Also by trying to achieve something day in and day out, you get better, and sooner or later there is a breakthrough."

Interestingly, Duckworth, along with many other psychologists, believes that the most important act parents can perform to help kids succeed is to guide them in finding whatever it is they can love over the long haul. Now, doesn't this sound familiar? This is what many career consultants advocate for adults, and what I have been stressing in this book.

When you start living your purpose and pursuing your passions, you will have true grit, the incredible energy and drive to overcome the obstacles that appear. Eventually you will make a breakthrough and from then on your success will come more naturally.

> All acts performed in the world begin in the imagination.
> — Barbara Grizzuti Harrison

By now you know that the main purpose of this chapter is to convince you that you can be a lot more successful in your life than you think you can. Thus far, real success without a real job is likely sounding great, but nevertheless, too good to be true. Perhaps you need some good excuses — besides the ones you already have — to convince yourself that you can't make it outside the corporate world. Luckily for you, I can help. Here are a few that even David Letterman may like:

> Man is always more than he can know of himself; consequently, his accomplishments, time and again, will come as a surprise to him.
>
> — Golo Mann

Top Ten Excuses You Can Use to Convince Yourself to Stay in the Corporate World

1. I don't believe people can work at an unreal job and make a good living at it unless they are offspring of Edison or Einstein.
2. I once had a nosebleed and I am afraid of getting more if I don't work at a real job.
3. George W. Bush would think I was unpatriotic if I were not part of corporate America.
4. Finding an unreal job that I like may be too relaxing — I think I feel more comfortable tense.
5. I am three-times divorced and I estimate that I have at least twelve kids.
6. I prefer to live in the past because most of my life has been spent there.
7. I have arthritis, and although I know people with much more serious disabilities have been extraordinarily successful, I don't think they know what it is like to have arthritis.
8. Although my present job is really boring, I kind of like it — I may actually be addicted to boredom.
9. My dog died and I need to get another one real fast.
10. I am much too afraid of becoming a member of a better class of people.

All right, this is more than enough. You may find some of the above excuses useful for explaining some of your other shortcomings in life, particularly when you don't want to take

My philosophy is that any success worth pursuing is too hard. I may not end up rich and famous, but I get to spend a lot of time at the beach where I drink beer and complain a lot about life to people like you.

responsibility for having created these shortcomings. My point is best made by the Jewish proverb: "If you don't want to do something, one excuse is as good as another."

Let's be honest. All of us are good at justifying why we haven't been more successful in following our dreams. I have likely done it a few thousand times myself. Alas, excuses don't bring results; we only hurt ourselves with excuses. Fact is, virtually all excuse-makers progress at the same speed just like all procrastinators wait at the same speed. Moreover, there is no time like the present to use a good excuse to postpone what is important, but appears somewhat difficult to do.

Excuses are convenient, but as always, there is a downside to anything convenient. Individuals who are not able to get rid of excuses find it virtually impossible to succeed in the long term. On the other hand, once people get rid of excuses, they can succeed at a lot more things than they think they can.

Oprah Winfrey said that one of the most important things that helped her become successful was that she read two books a week. If you are like most people, you will immediately discount reading two books a week as either too much work or something that may benefit Oprah, but not you. Yet if you were to read two books a week for the next five years, you would have read 520 books and have acquired an incredible amount of knowledge. This knowledge would give you a tremendous advantage over people with more natural intelligence or talent than you, and also put you in a position to achieve more than you think you can.

In the same vein, have you ever thought about someone you know who has succeeded in something quite remarkable? This could be starting a highly successful business, writing a blockbuster-selling book, designing an award-winning house, or dating a stunning member of the opposite sex. You were wondering how someone like this could pull it off. The individual didn't appear to have as much talent as

> One is not born a genius, one becomes a genius.
> — Simone de Beauvoir

you, be as smart as you, or be as attractive as you. You may have even asked yourself, "If this person can do it, why can't I?"

To the extent you have abilities that at least come close to those of the average person in society, you are likely right about the accomplished individual not having had something over you. This shouldn't come as a big surprise because many successful people admit they don't have an advantage, particularly genetic, over the mass of humanity. David Ogilvy, the advertising genius of Ogilvy & Mather, claimed in his book, *Blood, Brains and Beer* (Atheneum Publishers, 1978), that he had an IQ of ninety-six, which in his opinion is "the norm for ditchdiggers."

Whether you have an IQ that is the norm for ditchdiggers, or one that is the norm for brain surgeons, the basic equation for escaping corporate life is plain and simple: What are you willing to give up now in order that you can live the life you want to live later? The success of your get-out-of-corporate-life venture depends on a personal list of trade-offs. If you want to exchange a high-pressure job for life without a real job, your unwillingness to make sacrifices can wreck your dream.

Perhaps you are envious of successful artists, actors, and entrepreneurs because they appear to truly enjoy what they do. You are well aware that the majority of workers in society are not so "fortunate" or "lucky" to love their work.

> The best augury of a man's success in his profession is that he thinks it the finest in the world.
>
> — George Eliot

What you must keep in mind, however, is that not all artists, actors, and entrepreneurs are successful enough to earn a great income. In fact, some don't even earn a modest living; all the same, they are happy because they are astute enough to know that money is not everything. The ones who make a lower-than-average living adjust financially and do whatever they must in order that they can continue working at something they love.

One thing is certain: You always have to give up something you want for something you want more, particularly something that will make you happier in the long term. The biggest thing you may have to give up is your belief that you don't have what it takes to get something that you dearly want.

Granted, there are some valid concerns about pursuing dream careers. If you are American, for instance, the biggest reason you may give for not leaving corporate life is that you don't want to give up your healthcare plan provided by your employer. In fact, two or three reviewers of *The Joy of Not Working* on Amazon.com trashed the book because I did not provide them with a sure-fire way to pay for their healthcare insurance (even though the purpose of the book was not even remotely related).

There is no doubt that paying your own healthcare premiums will cost you plenty. Have you considered, however, how much working in a corporation may cost you? Either you are in a system that works for you or you are in one that doesn't. If you are still a regular employee, don't forget the role that the corporate world plays in your future health and overall life plan.

Some time ago Michael Ventura wrote in *LA Weekly*, "My employer uses twenty-five years of my life for every year I get to keep. And what do I get in return for the enormous thing I am giving? What do I get in return for my life?"

> You have to know exactly what you want out of your career. If you want to be a star, you don't bother with other things.
>
> — Marilyn Horne

Indeed, what will you get in return — including the state of your health — for dedicating yourself to corporate life for thirty or forty years? Following is some food for thought:

Why the Corporate World Isn't All That It's Cracked Up to Be

- One in three employees is chronically overworked according to a survey by the Families and Work Institute.
- Unprofessional, obnoxious co-workers — morons, in other words — are driving American employees bananas according to a survey by CareerBuilder.com. Fifty-three percent of workers said they feel like they work with a bunch of monkeys and one in five said they think their boss is a monkey.
- According to a recent article in *The Washington Post*, the dread of having to go to work on Monday morning, the onset of which is experienced early Sunday evening, even afflicts corporate workers who like their work.
- Being exposed to stress in the workplace is a major factor in the development of heart disease and diabetes, according to a 2006 research study reported in the *British Medical Journal*.

- ◆ According to the United Nations, work injuries and illnesses kill more people in the world than alcohol and drugs together.

The above studies seem to indicate that corporate life, at the extreme, can be dangerous to your health. It follows that remaining in the regular workforce and having a healthcare plan may be more detrimental to your health than leaving corporate life and not having a healthcare plan. You may be surprised to know that many creative individuals who escape corporate life are not willing to trade their great health that comes with an unreal job for a traditional corporate job that has a great healthcare plan.

Of course, a fact of life is that many American corporations don't even have an employee healthcare plan for their employees. Just as serious, employees who work for corporations with a healthcare plan often have a difficult time collecting compensation when they become ill.

> A lot of us are working harder than we want, at things we don't like to do. Why? It figures! In order to afford the sort of existence we don't care to live.
>
> — Bradford Angier

The old adage that prevention is much better than the cure applies here. I truly believe that had I not left corporate life, I would either be dead today, or suffering from some serious stress-induced illness. It may appear far-fetched for me to say this, but many workers actually wind up with serious illnesses due to the stress that comes with corporate life. Even worse, some people wind up dead long before their time.

No one agrees with this more than Ingrid Bacci. A graduate of Harvard, Bacci became a college philosophy professor at twenty-seven, married a successful and wealthy man, and seemed to have it all. Bacci was a success in the traditional sense of the word until an unknown disease emerged and left her bedridden and in constant pain for almost three years. Although she consulted many doctors, there was no answer forthcoming from the medical community about the nature of her illness. It wasn't until Bacci gave up her marriage and academic career for good that she started healing herself.

In her book *The Art of Effortless Living* (Perigee Trade, 2002), Bacci states, "My illness was an inevitable and natural product of the cultural values I grew up with. I followed the rules to the letter and they made me sick. All around me I see other people who, like me, are seriously sick as a result of living lives enslaved to the cultural norms. Others who are not sick are nonetheless suffering. They are saddled with dissatisfying relationships, or with demanding but unrewarding professions, or with a loss of creativity."

Bacci realized that the secret to health, happiness, and success was to let go of trying so hard and face the fear that had ruled her life. Incidentally, this woman totally healed herself using alternative health methods, which are usually not covered by healthcare insurance. By getting away from the traditional values embraced in corporations, she was able, not only to heal herself, but also to adopt a healthy lifestyle that reduces her chances of requiring traditional healthcare.

> You are never given a wish without also being given the power to make it true. You may have to work for it, however.
>
> — Richard Bach

Today, Bacci works at her dream job as a healthcare practitioner who helps her clients develop techniques of effortless living so that they can achieve optimum health and creativity in their lives. She says, "What happened to me through those long years of my disability was just a very dramatic result of living by unconscious rules and patterns that others also live by."

Given what happened to Ingrid Bacci, there is the danger that your staying in a dissatisfying job can lead to a serious illness that immobilizes you for a year or more. Even if healthcare insurance pays you a limited wage while you recover, this is not a great way to live and be rewarded for your work. Wouldn't it be better to create a job that you enjoy immensely and at the same time minimize your chances of contracting some stress-induced illness? Besides, if you start earning decent money at what you enjoy doing, you can purchase healthcare insurance.

The alternative is to create an unreal job or operate an unconventional business in another country where you can purchase healthcare for a third of what it costs in the United States. Even if you don't move abroad, there are some alternatives to using expensive American healthcare facilities. Robin Sparks, a San Francisco native who works at her unreal job as a global travel writer, recently wrote an informative online article (available on www.robinsparks.com) about how Americans and Britons travel to countries such as Thailand to receive inexpensive, but quality healthcare.

Again, I agree that healthcare insurance for Americans wishing to work outside the corporate world is a valid concern. As a Canadian, I have better government healthcare insurance than most Americans, but some people say that disability insurance is just as important as healthcare insurance for self-employed people. Even so, to this day I have never purchased any. Fact is, there would be a hundred times more chance of my dying in a car accident while commuting to a corporate job as my requiring disability insurance to give me an income because I couldn't make a living without a real job anymore.

The overriding point is, if every creative American wishing to accomplish something extraordinary used the lack of adequate healthcare and/or disability insurance as a reason not to pursue an unreal job or start an unconventional

> It may be that those who do most, dream most.
>
> — Stephen Leacock

business, no one would leave corporate America for a better life. Yet millions do. Many of these individuals, such as Buckminster Fuller and Steven Jobs, are the ones who have made major contributions to humanity and whom you read about in books, magazines, and newspapers.

If you want to achieve real success without a real job, take a cool, appraising look at what truly successful people are up to, not what your typical wage earner is doing. Successful people are usually not engaged in traditional jobs because they want to accomplish something different and significant. They also do what has to be done, including not having a healthcare plan for a few months or even years, during which time they establish themselves financially so that they can afford healthcare insurance.

If earning a good income and having healthcare insurance are important to you, it is worth repeating the importance of finding an unreal job or creating an unconventional business that is your passion. By creating a sense of meaning and purpose in your work, by linking your dreams and your motivation, you increase your chances dramatically of earning a lot of money. The higher income can be used to purchase healthcare and disability insurance along with anything else that you deem important.

Unfortunately, taking responsibility for our potential and following our passions in search of a dream career means standing alone. As is to be expected, this is terrifying to most of us. It's much easier to do something similar to what the masses are doing, which is relying on the corporate world to provide them with a decent wage, healthcare insurance, and a rewarding lifestyle.

> First say to yourself what you would be, and then do what you have to do.
>
> — Epictetus

Alas, employees in today's corporate America — ditto corporate Australia and corporate United Kingdom — do not have that much to brag about: little or no savings, excessive debt, no residual income from intellectual property, no passive income from investments, and very little saved for retirement. For good measure, throw in the dreadful enslavement that revolves around corporate employment and the majority does not look like a group to which you should aspire.

The most important question in this chapter is: How much are you limiting yourself by thinking the only place that you can make a good living is in the corporate world? As you ponder this question, keep in mind that millions make a great living without a real job. These people believed in themselves and were willing to take the necessary risks so that they could eventually earn a decent living — even a remarkable one — without a real job.

> All glory comes from daring to begin.
>
> — Eugene F. Ware

One eye-popping example of an ordinary person who achieved extraordinary financial success without a real job is Rosalind Gardner, who lives in British Columbia, Canada. In the late 1990s, Gardner worked as an air-traffic controller. "The crazy, inhumane shift schedule was literally making me sick," claims Gardner, "so I had to find some way to replace my income. Fortunately, right around the time I fell ill, I got connected to the 'Net. I'm no genius, but it didn't take long to see the potential for a fun and lucrative home-based business using the 'Net. Boy, was I was ever right!"

Because she saw greater possibility for her life, not only obstacles and limitations like most people see, Gardner earned enough income from her home business in her first year to match what she was making as an air-traffic controller. She was able to quit her job just one year later. This gets much better, however. In 2002, Gardner earned — get this — $657,801 from the home business and, in 2003 and 2004, she earned much more!

Did Gardner have any advantage over other people who continue to toil away as air-traffic controllers, or any other jobs for that matter? "When I started, I had zero business experience," emphasizes Gardner. "As a matter of fact, I barely knew how to surf the Web! What I had was a strong desire to become my own boss, and huge motivation to make some good money to make up for the retirement plan I was being forced to give up."

What you should commit to memory more than anything else about Gardner is the role that desire and motivation played in her success. Indeed, one does not end up achieving real success without a real job by accident. This is not all that difficult; it's just that people don't want to escape corporate life badly enough. If they did, they would do whatever it takes to attain it.

For the record, what Gardner does to make a great living outside the corporate world is promote other people's products on her websites. This is known as affiliate marketing, which is an arrangement between an online merchant and the affiliate marketer whereby the affiliate marketer earns a fee or commission for generating sales or sales leads for the merchant's website.

> One of your most powerful inner resources is your own creativity. Be willing to try out something new and play the game full-out.
>
> — Marcia Wieder

Of course, when you are successful in one line of work, other areas open up, adding to your multiple streams of income. Due to her success, Gardner wrote the *Super Affiliate Handbook* (Webvista Inc., 2005), a book that is sold both on Amazon.com and through one of her websites (www.superaffiliatehandbook.com). She also writes a column for *Revenue* magazine. Still more, because Gardner has taken up public speaking, she is invited to talk about affiliate marketing at conferences all over North America.

I realize that I make this sound all too easy. No doubt Gardner had her share of obstacles and frustrations in setting up her business and making it work. To be sure, all corporate refugees who eventually become successful in their own right do. Obstacles and frustration are good, however. You won't discover your capabilities by undertaking something easy.

Incidentally, as I was revising this chapter, I decided to e-mail Rosalind Gardner to ask her about any obstacles she had to face. She was about to leave for a month-long winter vacation in Mexico, when she sent me the following reply:

> Obstacles . . . Hmm . . . it's a learning process, but I've never had a problem with that. I love a challenge. And lots of people laughed at how I was every spare moment at the computer when I was first starting out, but I've always been very good at ignoring the snoring masses, and doing my own thing.
>
> My motto from a very early age has been "dare to be different." Those who laughed, by the way, are all still working at the same place — and guess who's laughing her way to a month in Mexico?

So which direction would you like your life to go? Do you want to be a member of "the snoring masses," as Rosalind Gardner calls them, or would you like to eventually have the financial and emotional freedom to head to Mexico any time you want? Gardner wouldn't be in the financial position she is today, and have a lifestyle that is the envy of over 90 percent of the corporate world, if she hadn't believed in herself. She also had to be receptive to the opportunity in this world.

Common wisdom has it that there are two certainties in the game of life — death and taxes. Here is another one: Keep thinking the way you have always been thinking and the degree of your future success will pretty much match your past success. If you want to eventually join the real-success-without-a-real-job clan, start with the premise that you have the talent, skills, and potential to achieve much more than you have so far in your life.

> There isn't a person anywhere who isn't capable of doing more than he thinks he can.
>
> — Henry Ford

One fascinating aspect of humanity is that some ordinary people achieve great results in their lifetimes while others with much greater talent, intelligence, and education merely eke out an existence. The core of the matter is that you don't have to be a saint or a genius to make an impact or big difference in this world. Fantasies and dreams don't have to be a waste of time. Real people attain unreal success — so can you! Particularly if you have always wanted to achieve in some career field, you are selling yourself short by sitting back and talking about it.

Practically every spectacular achievement was once thought impossible. What is impossible today to most people may be tomorrow's breakthrough success for some ordinary, but motivated individual. In many cases, one highly talented — but negative — person is saying, "I don't have what it takes and it can't be done," while another ordinary — but empowered — person is responding to the same situation with "This looks like a great opportunity to create something new and interesting." Guess which one will eventually experience real success without a real job?

Ultimately, getting much more of what we want in life is not all that difficult. It's not so much a matter of being exceptional compared to others; it's a matter of how effectively and efficiently we utilize what we have. This means putting our talents, skills, and available resources to the best possible use.

Commit Yourself to Being Successful and You Won't Have to Be a Victim — Ever Again!

A great mystery to any ordinary individual who attains extraordinary success is why so many people choose to be victims, instead of empowering themselves to do something positive with their lives. In this day and age, in fact, being a victim is even trendy. Weird, but true. Reporters with the various media are always looking for victims to feature in their stories. In any society that promotes the victim mentality as acceptable and, in some cases, desirable, it takes a strong personality to resist the temptation to be a sufferer.

Sadly, it's all too easy and irresistible for most humans to play the victim game. They attribute their dissatisfaction with their lives to society, their parents, their country's economic state, or the world in general. They see themselves as victims when, on the contrary, they aren't. The thing that is impressive about self-proclaimed victims is how tenacious they are in directing their energy into shunning responsibility and complicating their lives.

I hope that you won't fall into the trap of experiencing victimhood too often given that people who do are seldom successful. Being a victim is the ultimate expression of selfishness because you are basically saying that "everything is about me." If you play the victim game, you should get yourself one of those T-shirts that says, "Yes, it is all about me."

> God gives every bird his worm, but He does not throw it into the nest.
>
> — P. D. James

The truth is, it's not all about you. It never has been and never will be. With one trivial exception, this world is made of 6.5 billion other human beings, a good portion of them with minds thinking in one form or another, "It's all about me." If it's all about you, then do something — everything possible — for yourself. Don't expect any of the 6.5 billion others to do something for you. You will be waiting a long, long time.

Victims are known for their incredible ability to complain, which is probably the worst possible thing you can do if you want to succeed at anything, including being a real success without a real job. Complaining about your job keeps you a sufferer and does nothing to liberate you. When you are constantly a victim, you

> There are no hopeless situations; there are only people who have grown hopeless about them.
>
> — Clare Boothe Luce

remain in a rut — and the only major difference between a rut and a grave is the dimensions!

If you want to get out of the rut, you must stop being the victim. The best way to begin is to see how long you can go without complaining. Pay close attention to how much you complain, not only in speech but in thought as well. This applies to everything you complain about, not only the job you are presently in, but also what other people do or say, how they drive, and the state of the economy. The goal is to filter out all the negative thoughts that can keep you from being successful.

First, try going one day without complaining about anything. It may take several weeks of sustained effort before you can go a whole day. If you can eventually go a whole week without complaining, you will be well on your way to making a significant difference in your life. Brain experts say that our brains can rewire themselves to virtually avoid all complaining if we put our efforts into this for thirty straight days. Soon your efforts will reward you. If you can stop complaining altogether, miracles will start happening in your life.

Clearly, if you have been passing blame for your shortcomings, particularly in your career, now is the time to stop — not tomorrow, but today. Stop blaming the education system. Stop blaming your employer. Stop blaming the economy. Stop blaming career consultants. Stop blaming President George W. Bush or whoever else is president at the time you read this book.

So the mystery deepens. Who or what else is there left to blame? Yourself, of course. Who else? Who is responsible for your life situation? Rainer Maria Rilke put blame in its proper place: "If your daily life seems poor, do not blame it; blame yourself. Tell yourself that you are not poet enough to call forth its riches."

Indeed, blaming yourself in a positive way is the best way to respond to your shortcomings and setbacks. After you have signed an agreement or contract of sorts, for instance, it's pointless to blame anyone else when you discover the terms aren't as generous to you as you had initially thought. Having failed to read the small print is your fault and no one else's. You have no option but to fulfill your part of the contract. You may not have gotten as much as you had anticipated, but you did

> I attribute my success to this: I never gave or took an excuse.
>
> — Florence Nightingale

get an important extra you hadn't anticipated. The extra is the lesson that from now on you should read the small print carefully.

The day you start blaming yourself in a positive way is the day you are well on your way to a life that works. Winners blame themselves; losers blame others. Are you overextended financially like most people in Western society today? If you want to be in a better financial position than the masses, blame yourself; you are a victim of your own scheming. It's time to take control of your life and find ways to either reduce your spending or earn more money.

I was irritated to find out that Mary is working much less and making twice as much money since she quit her job here and started her own Internet business.

Me too! I guess few things are harder to put up with than someone with less talent, but who has attained much more success than you.

The choice is yours. You can be a victim or you can be a real success without a real job — you can't be both, however. With the negative attitude that invariably accompanies a victim mentality, you are three-quarters of the way to defeat without even having started. Blaming others will keep you on the road to perpetual failure. Still don't believe me? I have yet to go to an awards celebration where the person with the most blame of others and personal excuses for not accomplishing anything significant was featured as the main attraction.

Fortunately, getting what we want out of life is not about circumstances. It's about taking responsibility and overcoming, or changing, our circumstances. If we are willing to suspend our beliefs about our limitations, all of us can be more successful.

Keep in mind that J. K. Rowling was on welfare when she decided to write her first *Harry Potter* book. She is now a billionaire. Needless to say, Rowling did not get to where she is today by thinking the thoughts that negative people think, and proclaiming herself a victim. She also did not get to where she is today by thinking that getting a real job was the way to free herself from her dependence on welfare.

Lest you fear that things won't work out if you pursue something different, allow me to add that, as for most people, your limitations are in your mind. Sadly, your false doubts about yourself often become real. Negative expectations bring about negative results. To put it succinctly, keep saying that you are not capable of accomplishing something worthwhile and you will be a prophet with a damn good track record.

It is in your best long-term interest not to be the person telling everyone something can't be accomplished. Instead, join the successful people already doing it. To succeed, you must know how to look for opportunities and try to capitalize on these when you find them. You must also have ambition, determination, and the ability to learn from your mistakes if everything doesn't work out.

Above all else, overcoming the victim mentality requires commitment. You can have great goals and the best of plans on how to attain these goals, but without commitment these goals will never be attained. The problem with self-proclaimed victims is they don't even know what commitment means. It is just another word that sounds nice. Commitment is a major disconnect that always loses out to excuses. In contrast, commitment to successful people means doing whatever has to be done to get anywhere worth going — regardless of the nature of the obstacles that they face.

> When a man blames others for his failures, it's a good idea to credit others with his successes.
> — Howard W. Newton

Prior to becoming an actor, Chuck Norris was a martial arts expert. Some of his students included Priscilla Presley and the Osmonds. Norris founded thirty-two martial arts schools and taught karate to actor Steve McQueen. Although Norris was highly successful as both a competitor and a teacher in the martial arts, he dearly wanted to become an actor.

When Steve McQueen learned of Norris's acting aspirations, he urged Norris to pursue his dream. "Remember that philosophy of yours," McQueen reminded Norris, "that you always stressed to students: Set goals, visualize the results of those goals, and then be determined to succeed by overcoming any obstacles in the way. You've been preaching this to me for two years, and now you're saying there's something you can't do?" McQueen's words were enough to motivate Norris to pursue his dream career in the same diligent manner that he pursued his martial arts career.

Obviously, Chuck Norris attained his huge dream of becoming an actor because he was committed to this dream. Some of us who want to succeed don't necessarily lack commitment. The problem is that we are committed to small goals and not large ones. The difficult thing for us to accept is that the biggest thing we are committed to is the life we are leading right now. That is why we are getting what we are getting.

You won't achieve anything big by playing small. Working for a corporation, particularly if you hate your job, is playing small. You should be able to tell how big you are playing by the results you have been getting in your life. Playing big brings big results. Once you truly commit yourself to something bigger and better — as Chuck Norris did — you will be on the right path to achieving something bigger and better.

> Ninety-nine percent of failures come from people who have a habit of making excuses.
>
> — George Washington Carver

Another reason why people lack commitment to their dreams is that they allow themselves to be easily distracted. To be more committed, you have to make your internal dialogue about what you want to accomplish clearer, louder, and stronger. Tune out the other voices in your world, including those of your colleagues, friends, and family. Make the strongest voice in your life your own. This way you will be less influenced by the psychological obstacles that invariably appear when you listen to others.

You don't necessarily have to know how you are going to achieve your dream or your goal. Commitment and perseverance — not watching TV and complaining about the world — will create the magic of how you get to where you want to go. When you decide to do something, the "how you get there" will materialize once you take bold action to get there.

I can make this point much better if once again you will allow me to use myself as an example. When I decided to self-publish my first book, I knew nothing about desk-top publishing, typesetting, cover design, printing, and editing, not to mention the all-important art of marketing. As naive as I was at the time, I rightfully suspected that a good way to get these things done was to plunge into them headfirst and see how far I could get. I did not have to know in advance all the things that I eventually learned to make things work.

> One of the strongest characteristics of genius is the power of lighting its own fire.
>
> — John Foster

In short, commit yourself to being successful in your own personal way and you won't have to be a victim — ever again! The "how you get there" will materialize soon after your genuine commitment to succeed materializes. In time, other people will be wondering how you could have succeeded in something quite remarkable, even though you aren't as talented, intelligent, attractive, or hard-working as they are.

Receiving a Lot of Criticism Is a Good Sign That You Are Well on Your Way to Success

Having escaped the corporate world for such a long time, I must warn you about the occupational hazards of being a success without a real job. These include having to deal with freedom, responsibility, and joy in your life. You must also deal with envy and criticism from the complainers, critics, and misfits of the world, all of whom you must avoid if you want to become successful yourself.

Let me give you an example of one type of critic you may encounter. Not so long ago my computer indicated that it was receiving an e-mail with an attached virus. After I had quarantined the attachment, I looked in the body of the e-mail. The message simply said, "You are a bad writer." Over the next two weeks I received about ten more similar messages, all with viruses attached.

I suspect that the messages with the viral attachments were sent by someone who resented my success as a writer and thought that he could get even by trying to belittle me and mess up my computer at the same time. A person operating in this state of mind does not realize how much he is contributing to his own lack of success and misery in life. Truth be known, criticizing the works of others does not contribute to success. Even worse, trying to keep others from being successful is at best a self-destructive act.

In regards to my writing, I will be the first one to admit that I am not a great writer. As I have indicated previously, by the time I realized how bad of a writer I was, I was too successful to quit. In spite of my bad writing, it still has made me almost one million pretax dollars. This means that as bad as my writing is, it has already been worth almost a million dollars to me. What's more, I know that it has been worth at least the same amount to others, given the hundreds of positive letters and phone calls I have received from readers.

> He was a self-made man who owed his lack of success to nobody.
>
> — Joseph Heller

What I would like to say to the person who sent me the viral e-mails and other critics like him is: "Whether your own writing is good, bad, or ugly, how much money and how many compliments has it earned for you? From the nature and tone of your e-mail, I would suspect the financial and personal results of your writing would be pretty much on the ugly side. I can assure you that the results of your writing or other creative efforts — if you have ever come up with even one creative idea in your whole life — will pretty much remain on the ugly side as long as you put your energy into criticizing others and trying to sabotage their efforts."

It's interesting and somewhat dismaying how the pathological critics of this world will look up to anyone who wins a multimillion-dollar lottery, but will attempt to belittle anyone who has worked either hard or smart to attain prosperity and real success. Jules Renard put this in proper perspective, however: "Failure is not the only punishment for laziness: there is also the success of others."

> Any fool can criticize, condemn and complain . . . and most fools do.
>
> — Dale Carnegie

It has been my experience that with any type of pathological critic nothing is so small or insignificant that they can't blow it out of incredible proportion with sustained criticism. They will deride practically anything and anyone. Of course, if all you have going for you is a hammer, everything looks like a nail. The biggest problem with critics is they spend so much energy and time trying to ridicule the extraordinary accomplishments of others that they never accomplish anything significant themselves.

The lesson here is not only to avoid becoming a pathological critic yourself, but also to refrain from casually belittling anyone or anything successful. American composer Irving Berlin, who led the evolution of the popular song from the early ragtime and jazz eras through the golden age of musicals, wrote more than 800 pop songs. One day Berlin gave a young composer named Cole Porter counseling on how to become more successful in the music business. "Listen kid, take my advice," Berlin told Porter. "Never hate a song that has sold half-a-million copies."

No doubt Cole Porter took Irving Berlin's advice seriously, given the huge success that Porter himself achieved as a composer. Berlin's advice to Porter, in fact, is great advice for all of us. Instead of hating and criticizing something that has been successful — whether it's a song, a painting, or the latest computer model — we should be admiring and blessing it. Moreover, we should be learning why it is so successful so that we can adapt its positive features into whatever product or

> Deceive the rich and powerful if you will, but don't insult them.
>
> — Japanese proverb

service we are ourselves trying to sell to the world.

Fact is, anything that is successful in the marketplace can teach us a lot. So can people who develop these products. If you resent and criticize successful people, chances are you will never become successful yourself. How could you? You would have to become someone whom you resent. Thus, you will always set yourself up, consciously or unconsciously, so that you don't succeed. What's more, you will have a lot of great excuses — but no good reasons — for why you are not a real success in life.

> It is observed that successful people get ahead in the time that other people waste.
>
> — Henry Ford

The thing that is quite striking is how so many people spend most of their time and energy complaining and trying to belittle successful people. The universe, however, has ingenious ways of keeping pathological critics in their rightful place. It makes them incredibly miserable inside.

Moreover, the universe ensures that real success eludes these faultfinders for their entire lives. Oh sure, they become successful critics, but that's about all. The last time I checked, there was no Nobel Prize awarded for criticism and I have yet to see a statue made in honor of a critic.

Instead of getting you on the road to Success City, trying to belittle successful people will get you headed full tilt in the opposite direction toward where the misfits of this world hang out. It's called Loserville. So where would you like to hang out? Loserville or Success City? It's your choice. Personally, I prefer Success City.

If you choose Success City as the place you want to be, entertain no notions about avoiding criticism directed your way. Those who are motivated out of a higher level of consciousness do; those who are too lazy or too ignorant to do become critics. The thing to remember is that the more successful you become, the more criticism you will receive.

Avoiding criticism is an unattainable task — even to the most renowned individuals of this world — because the most degenerate of misfits can easily belittle the greatest of accomplishments. There

> For things to change, you must change. For things to get better, you must get better.
>
> — Jim Rohn

is no reason to despair, however. Receiving a lot of criticism from the misfits of this world is a good sign that you are well on your way to success — or that you have already arrived.

Clearly, some people are nothing more than opposition looking for something to oppose. This is where they are coming from; it is their essence and their reason for being. Criticizing others and telling them they can't accomplish something gives the world's critics some feeling of importance, as perverse as it is. Perhaps criticizing anything they can is their way of achieving success as they define it. If you want a feeling of true enlightenment and satisfaction, however, don't become like them.

As much as possible, disregard the comments made about you by the negative people of this world. A critic's most cherished beliefs are often in inverse proportion to their actual worth and relation to reality. Truly successful people get bashed a lot, mainly by the lazy, jealous, and broke, who apparently have nothing better to do with their time, aside from watching a lot of bad TV. Successful people, however, are used to — and spiritually above — the misconceptions, criticism, and untrue statements that negative people utter about anybody and everybody who is successful.

> The law of floatation was not discovered by contemplating the sinking of things.
>
> — Thomas Troward

Today when critics tell me that what I am attempting is unreasonable or won't work, I sarcastically thank them for their valuable advice. I also ask them how I ever could repay them for showing me how much I got carried away with my dreams of being a successful writer. Then I go about my business and do the unreasonable. Sure, to do something difficult and different is outrageous — but this is probably why it will eventually succeed and prove the naysayers wrong.

Critics can be a good thing, as it turns out. I can be motivated after reading or listening to the negative remarks thrown my way by the faultfinders of this world. I tend to be more inspired to attain even greater success with more books so that I can give the critics even more great things to belittle. After all, my success — along with living well — is the best revenge. I have this strong suspicion that most people who deride my books and accomplishments would gladly trade places with me financially and occupationally.

> If you can't be a good example, then you'll just have to be a horrible warning.
>
> — Catherine Aird

Putting things in the best possible way, these negative, faultfinding people are just ignorant and don't know any better. What's more, they are not complete failures — we get to use them as great examples of the type of people we don't want to become ourselves.

Action Has Magic, Power, and Grace in It

Let's say that you have explored your dreams and selected the field in which you would like to succeed. You may want to own a fancy restaurant. You may want to make a big difference in the environmental movement. You may want to make a name for yourself in the field of public speaking. Whatever area you have chosen, however, you can't turn ideas into reality overnight.

> You have to have a dream so you can get up in the morning.
> — Billy Wilder

We each have our own strengths, weaknesses, and particular challenges in life. This is one of the great things about being alive. We get a particular hand dealt to us, and it's one of the great joys in life to figure out how to best play it.

Keep in mind that trying to attain real success without a real job is like trying to climb a great mountain. They both involve great risk, a chance for major disappointment, and a sense of adventure. On your journey to success you will encounter many new problems — but you will encounter many new opportunities and wonderful experiences as well. Let me warn you, however, that attaining your goals will likely take a lot longer than you may think.

Not only does the mountain always look closer than it is, the mountain gets steeper as you get closer. One reason is that Murphy's Law has a habit of throwing a wrench into the best of plans. In case you haven't been introduced to Murphy's Law, allow me to do so. Murphy's Law says, "Nothing is as easy as it looks. Everything takes longer than you expect. And if anything can go wrong — it will at the worst possible moment."

Over the years several astute individuals have added hundreds of bylaws to Murphy's Law that are variations of the main law. Here are some of them:

Bylaws Associated with Murphy's Law

- Nothing is ever as simple as it first seems.
- Even if something cannot go wrong, it will.
- Things go right so that they can go wrong.
- Given a bad start, trouble will increase at an increasing rate.
- A shortcut often turns out to be the longest distance between two points.
- Things always take longer than you think they will — even when you compensate for this fact.

- The most expensive component is the one that breaks, and which is not in stock at the parts store.
- There is no job so simple that it can't be done wrong.
- A surprise source of revenue will be accompanied by an unexpected expense of a larger amount.
- Beware the rest of the day in which you yet haven't had something to complain about.
- Regardless of what you are trying to achieve, likelihoods are 90 percent against you.
- Nothing ever comes out as planned.
- Just when you think that victory is yours, something goes wrong.
- All great discoveries are made by mistake.
- Brilliant opportunities are cleverly disguised as insurmountable obstacles — the reverse is also true.

> There are no shortcuts to any place worth going.
> — Beverly Sills

The above bylaws are just a few variations of Murphy's Law in action in the real world. Perhaps you feel that I am being negative when, in fact, the opposite is true. Some people who have become successful in their own ways go so far as to say Murphy was an optimist. The bad news is that there are many factors that are beyond your control. The good news, however, is that you have the ability to overcome these factors.

The point is, without exception, there is no such thing as success without failure. Moreover, whatever you attempt, you aren't going to do it perfectly, even if you do succeed to a large extent. Strangely enough, planning for lots of obstacles and failure can add to your chances of success.

Ultimately, however, those perplexing roadblocks to real success can be overcome only with action. Getting off the couch can magically start making things work out to your advantage, and with time, turn your dream career into reality. The moral is to be found in what could be the most elegant and powerful words Johann Wolfgang von Goethe ever spoke: "Whatever you think you can do or believe you can do, begin it. Action has magic, grace, and power in it."

> Even a thief takes ten years to learn his trade.
> — Japanese proverb

> The greatest pleasure in life is doing what people say you cannot do.
> — Walter Bagehot

In this regard, extraordinary things are accomplished by ordinary people who have extraordinary dreams and take sustained action toward achieving them. In the short term, the results of sustained action may not appear that spectacular; in the long run, they are.

As you pursue your vocational dreams, you will find out — as I did — that creating a life worth living can be difficult at times. Sorry, there are no seven easy steps to paradise. Indeed, getting the most out of this book will take a lot of dedication, commitment, and keeping your word. This means that the demands of this book will be far too much for most readers; it will work only for the committed and very determined.

Alas, when the going gets tough, most people disappear. Don't be one of them. You must pay your dues to have a meaningful, fulfilling, and well-paid unreal job. This means you have to be totally dedicated to the purpose you have chosen. With anything short of this, you will probably bail out at the first sign of trouble.

At the risk of boring you and also embarrassing myself, allow me to share my most memorable experience of how I had to pay my dues to get where I am today — experiencing real success without a real job. For the record, I first shared a portion of this personal adventure in my book *The Lazy Person's Guide to Success*.

As is invariably the case when any individual achieves a measure of success, I now have to endure critics who imply in one form or another that I had to be lucky, or have had some huge advantage over others to be able to escape corporate life for over twenty-five years. In my view, a "lucky" person is someone who takes the wrong turn on the path to nowhere and winds up with a big windfall. Based on this measure, I have been anything but lucky.

What's more, I had no advantage over anyone who can think clearly, can write at a grade-nine level, and is willing to commit to a project. In fact, when I first started out in this business, I received less respect than the late comedian Rodney Dangerfield — and remember that Rodney didn't get any!

Let's go back in time to when I wrote my first book. Even though I had a literary agent to represent me, no publisher was willing to take a risk on the book. Based on the comments that the agent forwarded to me, it appeared that most publishers thought that the manuscript was written by a ditchdigger whose last three years of education were spent trying to get through grade nine.

Nonetheless, like a lot of first-time writers I have met, I thought that I had the next blockbuster that would put both *War and Peace* and *Moby-Dick* to shame. In retrospect, I was suffering from a case of megalomaniac delusion. Given that I wanted to prove that all the publishers who looked at the manuscript were a bunch of morons who should be in another line of business, I did not have too difficult of a time convincing myself to self-publish the book.

The initial 2,000 copies of the book cost me $7,500 to have printed. Because I was having one of those weird out-of-money experiences, as I had been for many years, I had to borrow half of the money from my mother. At some point she thought I would lose my shirt and not be able to pay her back. Regardless of my mother's lack of confidence in my entrepreneurial abilities, I figured that I was in a privileged position because I had the opportunity to prove her wrong and, even more importantly, the moronic publishers.

> Empty pockets never held anyone back. Only empty heads and empty hearts can do that.
>
> — Norman Vincent Peale

With one book to my name on how to be more creative, I speculated that I was destined for greatness in the exciting field of professional speaking. In no time, I could be like Tom Peters or Antony Robins, making $20,000 or more per speech. The place to head to was Vancouver, B.C. (B.C. stands for bring cash), which had more progressive and innovative organizations than Edmonton, Alberta — or so I thought. I had no doubt that corporations would be lining up for my blockbuster speeches and mind-blowing seminars on how to be more creative.

My move to Vancouver in September of that year turned out to be the best of times and the worst of times. Finally, I could experience a winter away from the frozen, barren tundra known as Edmonton — my hometown. Upon my arrival in Vancouver, however, my financial position was so precarious that I couldn't even afford a nervous breakdown. My apartment was only half-furnished, with stuff the Salvation Army wouldn't accept. My car was a ten-year-old beater — it doubled in value every time I filled it up with gas. A cheap umbrella to deal with the Vancouver rain was my only status symbol.

> I don't measure a man's success by how high he climbs but by how high he bounces when he hits bottom.
>
> — George Patton

With a meager income of about $500 a month for teaching a course at Simon Fraser University, $1,000 in savings, $30,000 in

> There are days when it takes all you've got just to keep up with the losers.
>
> — Robert Orben

student loans, and no seminars coming up in the future, buying a Rolls-Royce and hiring a butler were definitely out of the question — at least for a year or two. Plain and simple, things were getting so desperate that I thought about asking the buskers and panhandlers on Granville Street for a handout, before they could ask me for one.

Nonetheless, I tried to keep things in proper and positive perspective. There was a heroic side to my predicament. Sometime in the future, someone would write a book — or even make a movie — to try to account for the drama that happened to me after I left corporate life. Some of my life would appear that weird and that twisted, but at the same time, would make a great plot leading to my eventual accomplishments that only the elite of humanity ever attain. Today's severe predicament would be one of tomorrow's most inspirational stories cited in *People*, *Fortune*, *Entrepreneur*, and *Business Week* magazines.

Despite my remarkable lack of understanding of what it would take for me to be a successful speaker and seminar presenter, the eight months that I spent in Vancouver had their good moments. I experienced adventure and fulfillment from spending time in a different city. To this day, I call Vancouver my second home. Although I didn't have much money, I made it a point to go out to dinner at a good restaurant at least once a week. I was able to ride my bicycle in relative comfort most days, something I couldn't normally do in Edmonton because of the cold and snow.

Now for the not-so-good news: After eight months, my finances were even more strained. Not one speaking engagement came my way. To boot, I had given away more copies of my book than I had sold. My move to Vancouver was a brilliant idea that had gone bad. I escaped an extremely cold Edmonton winter to encounter a very damp, and sometimes almost as cold, Vancouver winter. In early spring, things really started to heat up when I couldn't pay my bills anymore. I headed back to my hometown, admitting to others and myself that I was a failure as a professional speaker and creativity consultant — a despicable situation that my ego was trying its hardest to ignore!

> Quit now; you'll never make it. If you disregard this advice, you'll be halfway there.
>
> — David Zucker

Believe it or not, it gets worse from here. Upon my return to Edmonton in mid-April, I was seriously contemplating — of all things — getting a regular job. I was hoping that if

I was "lucky" to get one, it would be on a temporary basis. Needless to say, having to work in the corporate world until I was sixty-five would have ended up making a mockery of my life.

Put in metaphorical terms, my life at that point was a sea of troubles. I had one seminar booked for May; that was it. My car was on its last legs. Beans and rice were gourmet to me. I was riding my bicycle, hoping that it wouldn't break down, because I couldn't afford to fix it. Even worse, I was putting up with two obnoxious housemates to help pay the costs for the half-duplex I was renting. One housemate was a pathological critic coming from the far left. The other was a pathological critic coming from the far right. Each one thought the other was crazy — all things considered, both were right.

One particular day, after listening to the two housemates complain about everything imaginable, I wasn't sure whether I should kill myself or go play some tennis instead. Because I had no money to buy a gun, I headed to the tennis courts, where I lost the match. I attributed the loss to a broken string in my racquet, which I couldn't afford to have repaired until I got a job or won a lottery. Winning a lottery was out of the question, however, since I didn't have any spare cash to buy a ticket.

But again, I tried to keep things in proper and positive perspective. I was busted, cleaned out, flat broke, stony broke, bankrupt, insolvent, and without a bean. I was not reduced to poverty, however, nor was I on skid row, nor was I impoverished, nor was I pauperized, nor was I broken, nor was I beggared, nor was I with nothing to hope for, nor was I without prospects. Remarkably, I was still working at what I most wanted to do — write books and present seminars.

> Nothing is troublesome that we do willingly.
>
> — Thomas Jefferson

Soon after, something magical happened. Call it Divine Intervention, blind luck, synchronicity, or God on your side; sometimes when you need things to go your way, they do. This is particularly true when you indulge in sustained action and refuse to give up. By May, I had managed to get $15,000 worth of seminar bookings for September and October.

By September, I also managed to sell enough copies of my first book to pay my mother back and justify another print run. Was I happy? Happy does not cover it; I was elated. There were no seminar bookings after that until January of the following year — then another $4,500 worth. Things really improved from then on. In the fall of 1991, almost two years after venturing to Vancouver,

I self-published *The Joy of Not Working*. Happily, I did not have to borrow any money to have the book printed. What's more, I did not even consider submitting the manuscript to publishers because I had gained enough confidence from having self-published the first one.

> The greatest discovery of my generation is that man can alter his life simply by altering his attitude of mind.
> — William James

By following the success principles advocated in this book, I have gradually increased my income over the years to where it is in the top 20 percent, the odd year even the top 10 percent, of wage earners, on which I live comfortably and from which I have accumulated a net worth in the low six figures. To be sure, this still isn't a lot of money to the overly ambitious of this world. The important thing is that I enjoy what I do; better still, I work only four to five hours a day and experience more freedom and true prosperity than most millionaires do in their vocations.

All told, had I not taken sustained action toward my dream of being a successful writer, and done what most people figured I couldn't do, I wouldn't be writing this book today. When I started writing it, I had eighty-four book deals with publishers in twenty-four different countries for thirteen of my previous books. I have no doubt that sooner or later I will reach my goals to have at least one hundred book deals and be published in at least thirty different countries. I cannot get there without more action, however.

I do not know exactly how I will reach these goals, or several others that I have. You must take the same approach. The planning is more important than the actual plans. The sooner you take action, the better. Action brings momentum. As a matter of course, by being adventurous, you will make things happen. You may not wind up exactly where you had intended, but where you end up may be just as good, if not better.

> Take care to get what you like or you will be forced to like what you don't like.
> — George Bernard Shaw

If you want to improve your lifestyle, if you want to have an opportunity for your creativity to make a difference in this world, you have to make changes in your career. The only motivation you need is the knowledge that millions of people with questionable intelligence and talent — myself included — succeed at this game. If they can do it, so can you!

4

Get Creative — You Will Surprise Yourself and Change the World!

Creativity Is Your Biggest Asset — Bar None!

In my view, Mark Twain expressed a great deal of wisdom with these words: "Thousands of geniuses live and die undiscovered — either by themselves or by others." The fact that so many people haven't discovered they are geniuses is a major reason why they toil away at jobs they hate. As is to be expected, most corporations aren't about to help their employees realize they are geniuses for fear of losing them.

By geniuses, I refer to individuals with the potential to make a difference in this world if they ever get around to developing and using their creativity. Unfortunately, most people have allowed organizations, educational institutions, and society to suppress their creativity for so long that they don't realize how creative they can be. Truth be told, most people can be more creative and, in turn, more successful.

In this regard, there are two principles for creative success — one general and one definitive. The general principle is that virtually everyone has the ability to be more creative and accomplish extraordinary things in this world. The definitive principle is that almost everyone has volunteered to be exempt

> The guy who invented the first wheel was an idiot. The guy who invented the other three, he was a genius.
>
> — Sid Caesar

> Creativity comes by breaking the rules, by saying you're in love with the anarchist.
>
> — Anita Roddick

from the general principle. Put another way, few people spend time, effort, or thought cultivating their creative ability, which is an essential element for achieving real success without a real job.

The majority of adults don't get halfway to reaching their full creative potential due to their self-imposed limitations. Sadly, many people have suppressed both their desire and their ability to be creative for so long that they think they are naturally uncreative. You may be one of them.

How many times have you said to yourself or others, "If I only had the creative ability to pull that off" or "If I could invent something like that, my life would change forever"? All told, each one of us has greater inventiveness than we exhibit in ordinary life, but most of us are unaware of it, or refrain from using it. Again, there is no heavier burden than great potential that we are squandering. To deny our creativity is to lie to the world and, worse, to lie to ourselves.

Creative thinking, if diligently practiced, allows each and every one of us to accomplish feats that appear to be unattainable miracles to those who don't practice it. Creativity combined with action is a simple, easy, and sure-fire way to achieve health, wealth, and happiness in our lives; it is also an invaluable tool to help us experience harmony in this fast-moving and constantly changing world in which we live.

If you are serious about attaining real success without a real job, start with the premise that from both a financial and a personal point of view, your most valuable asset is not your job, your house, or your bank account. Plain and simple, it's your creative ability. Your creative mind has great value because it can solve problems. All employers have problems that they pay employees to solve. In the same vein, individuals have various problems, such as needing something to entertain them, that they pay others to solve.

The value you place on your creative mind should be at least one million dollars because you can use it to generate many times this amount over your lifetime. This makes creativity the poor person's wealth. Indeed, when you list the monetary value of your personal assets, the total should make you a millionaire simply by including the value of your creative ability.

> Creativity is the sudden cessation of stupidity.
>
> — Dr. E. Land

I know that my creative mind is my most valuable asset. What's more, I know it is worth over a million dollars because it has already made me at least that amount in pretax earnings and will make me much more in the future. Interestingly, if I worked for a corporation, I would not be listed as an asset anywhere on their balance sheets. Strictly from an accounting point of view, the company would have the wages already paid to me listed as an expense on its income statement. Moreover, any unpaid wages and vacation time would be listed as a liability on its balance sheet.

Go figure: My creativity is worth over a million dollars. Yet my name would appear only in the expense and liability columns if I worked for a corporation. Just on general principles alone, this is a good reason for me to be self-employed. Another reason that I choose to be self-employed is that I get rewarded fully for my imaginative projects. In contrast, as a regular employee, I would likely wind up as the finalist in the wishful-thinker-of-the-year award if I expected to get properly rewarded for any valuable idea that I generated or any product that I invented.

Perhaps you have heard about how the NBC TV network spent $750,000 to have a graphic design firm develop a brilliant new logo, which it unveiled on New Year's Day in 1976. The trouble, however, was that the Nebraska Educational Network, a small TV station in Lincoln, Nebraska, had been using an almost identical logo for quite some time, and was not about to give up its right to it without a legal battle.

> Real wealth equals ideas plus energy.
> — Buckminster Fuller

At this point, NBC paid the small Nebraska station an out-of-court settlement of $55,000 in cash and $500,000 in used television equipment for the right to use the "new" logo. The most interesting aspect of this case is the Nebraska TV station actually paid only about $100 in wages to one of its employees to develop its logo.

The $64,000 question is: What monetary reward was given to the Nebraska station's employee who designed the original version of the logo, which ended up netting the station a total of $550,000 in assets? My educated guess is not that much, if anything, besides his wages. Keep in mind that the graphic design firm that NBC used to develop virtually the same logo pocketed $750,000.

Clearly, rare is the highly creative corporate employee who actually gets rewarded fairly for his or her own brilliant ideas that make the company piles of money. In most cases the whole company, or a group within the company under the guise of teamwork, will take credit for an invention or an individual member's brain wave. But it's one creative character who comes up with an innovative idea and who should be rewarded handsomely for it, but usually isn't.

John Steinbeck in his famous novel *East of Eden* makes the important point about the relationship between creativity and the individual. "Nothing was ever created by two men. There are no good collaborators, whether in music, in art, in poetry, in mathematics, in philosophy. Once the miracle of creation has taken place, the group will build and extend it, but the group never invents anything. The preciousness lies in the lonely mind of man."

Notwithstanding the miracle of an individual employee's imaginative project and how much money it can end up making for a company, the company's upper management often claims full credit for it. The employee is left with nothing more than the experience of being mesmerized by the audacity of the company's elite.

It follows that being creative while operating your own unconventional business is a much better way to experience joy and to get ahead financially than being creative while working in a large organization. It has been my experience that there is nothing quite as exhilarating as coming up with a brilliant idea, putting it to good use, and eventually being rewarded handsomely for my efforts by the marketplace.

So get creative — you will surprise yourself and change the world! Perhaps you will still insist, "I know that I am not creative regardless of what anyone else says." These thirteen words are not likely to help you move mountains or attain real success without a real job. It is important that you don't let your lack of creative achievement in the past blind you to what opportunity there is for you to be a creative success in the future.

You are a living, thinking human being with a mind and imagination of your own. Why do you want to be grouped in with all the corporate lemmings following whatever they are following blindly with their herd mentality? To be a free and independent thinker, you must first recognize the genius within, and then put it to good use.

> The best ideas come as jokes. Make your thinking as funny as possible.
>
> — David Ogilvy

Psychologists and creativity specialists claim that, on average, we use only 15 to 20 percent of the cerebral cortex, that portion of the brain where the most important thoughts occur. Such being the case, most of us have incredible potential to create a product or service that will change the world in some measure. We don't want to own up to our latent genius within, however. After all, it's easier to settle for mediocrity in our lives than to take responsibility for all of that potential.

But you must take responsibility for your creative potential if you want to escape corporate life. In many regards, creative thinking is unorthodox thinking. To be a real success without a real job you will have to think outside the "nine-to-five box." Clearly, it is a box — prison is probably a better word — if you hate being there.

Luckily, there are many resources on how to utilize strategies and techniques to discover our latent genius within and to become more creative in our business and personal lives. Michael Michalko's two books, *Thinkertoys* (Ten Speed Press, 1991) and *Cracking Creativity* (Ten Speed Press, 2001), are highly recommended. *Thinkertoys*, particularly, is an invaluable resource that presents creative thinking techniques with breadth, depth, coherence, humor, and originality. If you are serious about learning how to be more creative and haven't read this book, you will be glad when you do.

Another one of my favorites is Julia Cameron's *The Artist's Way* (Tarcher, 2002). If you are an engineer, an accountant, or even a ditchdigger, don't be misled by this book's title. This classic is not just for painters and sculptors. The book will benefit you even if you don't want to pursue an occupation involving the arts. Perhaps you are doubtful that any book can actually help you develop creative spirit. Here is one Amazon.com reviewer's testimonial for *The Artist's Way*:

If we come up with one great original idea, we could wind up being rich and famous instead of obscure ex-government workers.

An original idea? That shouldn't be too difficult to find. The public library must be full of them!

> This book has completely changed my perspective about my creative ability. At first my practical side felt very silly doing some of the exercises. But after a while I began to realize how much better I felt about myself and my ability to be creative . . . not do everything by the book. I began oil painting, which I've even entered into contests. I went to Professional Culinary School, in

spite of everyone telling me I was crazy. Now those same people are envious of my ability and attitude to discover something that makes me happy and actually pursue it. So many people dream, but never act on those dreams. As practical as I am and probably always will be, thanks to this book, I'm happy that I'm taking these steps toward self fulfillment, and I've established a balance in my life I have never previously experienced.

> Even the woodpecker owes his success to the fact that he used his head.
>
> — Unknown wise person

You too can be more creative if you set your mind to it. Don't stop after reading one or two books on creativity. The more books you read, the more your inventiveness will become your key resource for attaining real success without a real job. In fact, years ago I used to read everything I could on creativity and I just realized that I myself should tune up my creative ability by rereading the books I already have and reading any new ones that I can find.

The thing that is quite striking about creativity is that it can be developed at any age. Indeed, many people get involved in creative projects for the first time when they are fifty, sixty, seventy, or even eighty years old. Often this happens after they leave the corporate world. What's more, they generate an income from their imaginative projects to add to their experience of creative success.

Take Charlotte Tell, for instance, who at the age of fifty-seven retired from her long-time career as an accountant. Today she is an avid photographer and strongly recommends that people "find a more creative side to themselves." This is exactly what she did and wound up with a truly enjoyable way to experience joy and freedom in her retirement years. "When you can do exactly what you want to do every single day," says Tell of Asheville, North Carolina, "what could be better than that?"

Although she enjoyed taking photographs when she was still in the corporate world, Tell didn't get serious about photography until after she retired. A year before she left her accounting job, she and her husband, Barrie, took a trip to Key West, Florida, to indulge in some "practice retiring." Here she took a number of photographs of the Gulf of Mexico and the sunsets in the background.

Back home again, Tell had the photographs developed. Surprisingly to her, these turned out to be masterpieces. Inspired by her husband's compliments, she continued to take many more pictures after she retired, which brought her tons of additional compliments from friends and neighbors. To polish her talents, she did a lot of research, such as studying impressionist painters and their use of light.

Eventually Tell started selling her photographs and named her photography business Apple Pics. Although Apple Pics is a profitable business, Tell doesn't give this much significance. "It's not about the money; it's about enjoying what I'm doing."

Surprisingly, at one time Tell was actually reluctant to hang her photos in her own living room. This has changed due to the self-confidence that she gained from her success. Not so long after, the Asheville hospital commissioned a set of her photos for a new wing. Today, her work is sold in about twenty-five galleries. The fascinating aspect of this example is that because Tell was willing to develop her creative side, a fun and profitable vocation was born. "I would have to say," she concludes, "that right now is the best time of my life."

Charlotte Tell should be an inspiration to those of us who want more creative fulfillment in our lives. You, too, can joyfully earn a living without a real job if you develop your creative side and in doing so provide an imaginative product or service that people want. In fact, it's

> He is very rich and he is very poor. Money cannot buy him creative fulfillment.
>
> — Julia Cameron

harder to suppress your creativity than to use it. The core of the matter is that everyone has the deep-seated desire to produce something innovative. In everyone there is a creative person wanting to break out and make a difference in this world.

To be more creative, you don't necessarily have to take unique photographs, write a novel, or create a painting. You can be innovative in your own way, in your own chosen field. This could involve developing a new service or advertising a product in a new way for your unconventional business. You could also use your genius to develop new ways of presenting and marketing information in books and DVDs on how people can minimize their energy costs, for instance.

All things considered, if and when you choose to leave corporate life, your creativity becomes your biggest asset — bar none! Trust me on this one: You must recognize the latent genius within and stay in the habit of being innovative if you want to attain real success without a real job. To maximize the use of your creative mind is to maximize the career and financial aspects of your life.

Bold, Creative Effort Will Dispel Your Fears and Bring You Good Fortune

What is somewhat strange to virtually any individual who has attained real success without a real job is the number of talented people who pursue jobs and careers that do not bring them creative fulfillment or job satisfaction. The obvious reason why so many people do this is that, due to societal influences, most people place traditional success and money ahead of enjoyment, fulfillment, and satisfaction. Just as telling, however, is the all-too-common issue of fear.

Fear, above all else, prevents most of us from living our dreams. Unfortunately, there is a lot of support in our society for fearful thinking. When you have a promising idea for a new product, new service, or unconventional business, you won't have any trouble at all in finding people who are critical of your idea, find fault with it, or focus on its negative aspects. The more attention you pay to these people, the more fear you will experience.

The only way to conquer any fear is to confront it head-on. Clearly, our main fear is that we will fail. It may come as a surprise to fearful people who never attempt anything daring that most individuals who have had a great measure of success in their lives still experience the fear of failure. Take, for example, Bruce McCall, who, above all, considers himself a humorist.

> There is often less danger in the things we fear than in the things we desire.
>
> — John Churton Collins

McCall, also an illustrator and author, has attained a good measure of real success without a real job, given that he has had over 200 pieces published in *The New Yorker*. Even so, McCall still submits all his work on spec and admitted to a reporter with *The Globe and Mail* that he is surprised when a project is accepted. McCall, it would seem, is one of those able individuals, like millions of us, who underestimates his own creative ability. The point is, we all have our doubts and our fears about our projects and career aspirations, even if we already have had great success in our field of endeavor.

The most successful of us don't use these fears and doubts to stop us, however. Instead, we keep on going in spite of our doubts and fears. If you would like to be as successful in your personal way as Bruce McCall has been in his personal way, your willingness to confront fear is crucial. If you want to move to another level in your life, you have to learn how to be terribly uncomfortable while you experience your fear. The only way to conquer fear is to experience it while actually doing whatever you fear.

> Fear keeps your life small. On the other side of fear is fortune.
>
> — Robin Sharma

Lest you think that you can totally eliminate the fear of failure forever by being a major success in your field, perish the thought. You will always experience some fear when there is risk involved. Even though I have spent many years reprogramming myself and learning as much as I can about what it takes to be successful in my own way, I know this old programming based on fear still exists. No doubt it doesn't affect my behavior as much as it used to, but it still does, and can become intense at times.

A recent experience comes to mind. Shortly after I completed my book *How to Retire Happy, Wild, and Free*, I sent the manuscript to twenty-five American publishers and ten British publishers. I thought that I would have no problem getting a publisher, but the opposite happened. Here are excerpts from four of the rejection letters that I received from American publishers:

1. From St. Martin's Press: "After reading your proposal, I am impressed with your obvious zest for life. Unfortunately, the retirement shelf is tough at the moment and I just don't think there is room for another title."

2. From Warner Books: "Even though I'm well aware of your successful track record as an author, there was a strong sense from my editorial colleagues here that most people really wouldn't have much of a problem in trying to plot out their retirement years."

3. From Harmony Books: "Especially in light of the current economy, my sense is that there's not a large audience at present for retirement books."

4. From Broadway Books: "Thank you for the opportunity to consider *How to Retire Happy, Wild, and Free*. This is a quirky, informative, and often motivational look at retirement. We discussed this at our editorial meeting this week, but I'm afraid our consensus was that a book-length work on the subject just wouldn't have enough widespread potential for us to publish it."

Much to my surprise, all twenty-five American and ten British publishers that received my manuscript felt there was no market for retirement books, or if there was, the market was too saturated with too many similar books. I estimated at the time that there were anywhere from one to two hundred retirement books published in English, with the likelihood of many more to come.

At this point it is worth asking: What would you have done if you were in my situation? I believe that most people would have been too fearful to take matters into their own hands as I did. Notwithstanding the major publishers' negativism about the potential market for retirement books, I decided to self-publish after Ten Speed Press agreed to distribute the book for me in the United States. I felt that I had likely written the best book in the world on the personal aspects of retirement and that it should eventually prove itself in the marketplace.

> No pessimist ever discovered the secrets of the stars, or sailed to an uncharted land, or opened a new heaven to the human spirit.
>
> — Helen Keller

Even so, after I had arranged for the editing, cover design, page layout, and printing, I was still fearful that the project would fail and that I would end up losing money. I started doubting myself largely due to the fact that so many major American publishers — the so-called experts in the field — didn't think there was a market for the book.

It even got to a point where I was trying to figure out some way to convince Ten Speed Press to take over the project and assume the financial risk. I finally talked myself into pressing forward when I concluded that even if I lost $10,000 on the venture, it wouldn't be the end of the world. Because I had made hundreds of thousands of dollars from my books over the years, I could certainly take a hit of ten grand for once. Besides, as they say, "it's only money."

It's a good thing, as things turned out, that I confronted my fear head-on. Taking the financial risk paid off big time. *How to Retire Happy, Wild, and Free* has now sold over 40,000 copies and has seven foreign publishers. Today when I typed "retirement book" into the major search engine Google, the top listing overall was a link to Amazon.com's webpage for *How to Retire Happy, Wild and Free* — out of over 50 million webpages! It won't be long before I have realized a tidy pretax profit of at least $200,000 on the book. Just as important, given that I am Canadian, I have experienced an incredible amount of satisfaction from seeing the book do so well in the United States market when so many major American publishers felt it had no potential.

Clearly, had I not confronted my fear of self-publishing *How to Retire Happy, Wild, and Free*, I would be poorer both financially and psychologically. Fear of failure and fear of losing money are things that we all have to face and conquer if we want to work outside the corporate world. But it is not fear that is the problem. It's how we handle fear. We must get over the fear and realize that even if we fail, we can handle failure. This is what makes all the difference.

There is another moral associated with my aforementioned experience — so much for listening to the experts! Since most "experts" don't even come remotely close to knowing whether something innovative will work in their line of business, why not take some chances and disregard what they have to say? In fact, it is wise not to listen to the experts even if they have been in the business for thirty-five years and you are a recent newcomer. Find out for yourself what you can accomplish.

> Always listen to experts. They'll tell you what can't be done and why. Then do it.
>
> — Robert Heinlein

The core of the matter is that individuals who achieve creative success are willing to confront their fears and take risks that others — even the experts — won't. How many times have you read about a person who took a chance with an idea, encountered some real obstacles, and made it to the top? How many times have you thought: "Wow, look at what she accomplished! I wish I had the courage and commitment to have done that, given that I have come up with many promising ideas."

No doubt you have generated at least a few creative ideas that had great potential in the marketplace. I believe it was Will Durant who stated that in every work of genius we recognize our own discarded ideas. No matter how gifted you are, you will have to experiment with different ideas if you want one to click. Most important, you will have to confront your fear of failure, and test the ideas. Bold, creative effort will dispel your fears and eventually bring you good fortune.

A Bit of Craziness Is Good for Business

This may be a little difficult for some readers to believe: While I was writing my first book, there were many times when I thought that I was at least a little crazy. "Who am I to write a book?" gripped my mind more than once. To add to my feeling of insanity, several of my friends and acquaintances told me that I must be a lunatic to think that I could actually write a book and get it published. A big part of the reason may have been their knowledge of my having failed English three times in a row when I was in university studying for my engineering degree.

Here are the results of my craziness: Before starting this one, I had completed thirteen books. Each has had at least one major publisher somewhere in the world. Every year my books sell in the thousands in American, Canadian, and European bookstores. Given that I now have over eighty-five book deals with various publishers around the world, my success at selling foreign rights far surpasses that of major American publishers.

My point here is that whatever new field you decide to enter in pursuit of real success without a real job, chances are someone is going to think that you are nuts. Relatives, acquaintances, friends, life coaches — even you — may doubt that you have what it takes to make it. The good news is that if others and you yourself think that you are at least a little bit crazy, this is a good sign that you can attain creative success.

Perhaps you are, in fact, a bit crazy. Not to worry — this is even a better sign! In his book, *The Hypomanic Edge* (Simon & Schuster, 2005), John Gartner establishes a link between craziness and success in America. Gartner, a psychologist at Johns Hopkins University, claims many of today's successful entrepreneurs and business people exhibit hypomania, an energetic and ebullient state, which is a milder form of the mania associated with bipolar illness. Moreover, he contends that leading figures in American history, including Andrew Carnegie and Henry Ford, had the condition as well.

All things considered, a bit of craziness is good for business. While many successful entrepreneurs are not entirely crazy, they are not entirely normal, which leads others to believe they are crazy. Talk to America's successful entrepreneurs and you will find that most of them had at least one friend or acquaintance, even a spouse, who thought that they were crazy to attempt what they did. Yet it was their willingness to be a little bit crazy that allowed these entrepreneurs to achieve creative success.

> Do not fear to be eccentric in opinion, for every opinion now accepted was once eccentric.
>
> — Bertrand Russell

Along with a little bit of craziness, eccentricity is the companion of creative success. Eccentricity is the quality of being different and deviating from the normal, established, or expected.

"Eccentricity has always abounded when and where strength of character has abounded," observed John Stuart Mill, "and the amount of eccentricity in a society has generally been proportional to the amount of genius, mental vigour, and moral courage which it contained."

Unfortunately, most people are trying to fit in with colleagues at work, or be the same as practically everyone else in society, instead of being different and deviating from the normal, established, or expected. Yet anything of major consequence in this world was initiated by characters who were different than the rest of society. In fact,

> A man with a new idea is a crank until the idea succeeds.
>
> — Mark Twain

they were out of step with society in large measure. Think Nelson Mandela! Think Oprah Winfrey! Think Steven Jobs! Think Anita Roddick! Plain and simple: These individuals all made a big difference in this world because they were willing to be different.

Investigate characters such as Virgin Group founder Richard Branson and you will discover that being a creative achiever and making a major difference in this world require being different and feeling good about it. After he attained a good measure of success with a mail-order company selling music records, even Branson's own associates doubted that he could succeed in a new venture. "Almost all my colleagues at Virgin said I was completely mad to go into the airline business," revealed Branson. "The newspapers said calling an airline Virgin was mad. The company is now worth over one billion pounds." Notwithstanding Branson's incredible success, to this day there are members of the British business establishment who claim that he is "a flake."

The important lesson here is that you should be prepared to be different than the masses if you want to be successful in your own right. Some people may be uncomfortable with you and others may dislike you for it. No doubt you will be criticized a lot. The more success you have at being different, the more you may be disliked, including by people in your own industry. But people will respect you for it, particularly when you start making that big difference. You will also have your own respect.

The degree to which you learn how to be different and feel good about it will determine how many "crazy" ideas you generate. Spending time generating unorthodox ideas is important because

> People will accept your idea much more readily if you tell them that Benjamin Franklin said it first.
>
> — David H. Comins

these ideas often have the most potential. Indeed, these ideas can be worth a million times more than ones you generate thinking "sanely" like the masses. Richard Branson has proven this more than once.

Be clear, however, that when you generate a great money-making idea, not everyone — maybe no one — is going to look at you and exclaim, "Wow, what a great brain wave! Why didn't I think of that?" On the contrary, most people will likely make fun of you and predict that your money-making venture is going to land you in the poorhouse.

> Trust that still, small voice that says, "This might work and I'll try it."
>
> — Diane Mariechild

As a truly creative individual, you must trust your intuition, which tells you that an idea has great potential even when all the naysayers — including the experts — tell you otherwise. You must proceed in the direction in which you ought to be going even if the masses think that whoever found your marbles should give them back to you. When David Bach, an investment advisor with Morgan Stanley Dean Witter at the time, decided to give seminars specifically directed at women on how to manage their money, all his colleagues thought that it was a dumb idea. "Everyone laughed at me," claims Bach. "I was a joke."

Guess who had the last laugh? Today when people are interviewed for possible employment at Morgan Stanley Dean Witter, David Bach's ex-colleagues proudly point out that one of the offices used to be occupied by him. The reason is that Bach's seminar, *Smart Women Finish Rich*, proved to be highly popular and led to his first book of the same name. Since then, he has written many books and has even had six of them on the *Business Week* bestseller list all at one time. Ironically, the man who was a joke to his colleagues became one of the most well-known and richest financial gurus in the world.

As the Richard Branson and David Bach examples indicate, your chances for a financially rewarding and psychologically satisfying career life will increase in direct proportion to how much you are willing to be out of step with the rest of the pack in your industry. Indeed, the more unconventional you are, the better. It has been my experience that individuals who are different — even a little crazy — change the world; those who are ordinary keep it that way.

> It takes a strong fish to swim against the current. Even a dead one can float with it.
>
> — John Crowe

Just One Great Idea Can Change Your Life Dramatically — It's There Somewhere!

As already emphasized, creativity is your best resource for generating a great product or service to offer to the world. Even if you don't want to be a millionaire, but just want to earn a decent living without a real job, you must spot and capitalize on the many opportunities that the world has to offer. Paying attention to the world around you — looking at commonplace things and seeing the miraculous — will lead you to opportunities that others don't see.

Keep in mind that you don't have to go halfway around the world and spend a ton of money to spot an opportunity and take advantage of it. Opportunities for creating new sources of income are all around us, including our backyards. Robert G. Allen and Mark Victor Hansen, co-authors of *The One Minute Millionaire* (Harmony, 2002), claim that they will be able to spot at least fifteen money-making opportunities in your living room alone.

Clearly, there are always opportunities in human needs around which we can build a new business. Things that fulfill our needs and that we take for granted were once just creative thoughts. Everything you encounter during the day — the Internet, your computer, this book, your car, and your TV — began as an idea in someone's mind. Sadly, many people have had a great idea and discounted it, later to find that some ambitious character became successful, rich, and famous with the same idea.

> The only place opportunity cannot be found is in a closed-minded person.
>
> — Bo Bennett

To take advantage of opportunities you must develop the habit of recording all your ideas, regardless of how crazy they may seem when you generate them. "A man would do well to carry a pencil in his pocket, and write down the thoughts of the moment," advised Francis Bacon. "Those that come unsought for are commonly the most valuable, and should be secured, because they seldom return."

Carry a small notebook or a small computer at all times to record all your creative revenue-generating ideas. Keep notebooks and writing implements in your coat, bicycle saddle bag, automobile, briefcase, purse, and even near computers and phones. Research indicates that most ideas are forgotten forever if not written down.

Ensure that you review and update your revenue-generating database on a regular basis. In chapter 5 (on pages 143 to 146) I cite a marketing idea that ended up making me a substantial amount of extra revenue. This idea would have likely earned me nothing, however, if I had not recorded it, and later retrieved it from my list of revenue-generating opportunities.

While reading The Joy of Not Working, *I came up with a brilliant idea to start a worldwide leisure movement called Why Can't Everyone Be Lazy Just Like Ernie Zelinski? It's already the craze in Nepal and should hit Bhutan any time soon.*

Try to give your mind a creative workout every day. For example, set a personal quota for revenue-generating opportunities. Come up with at least five new ideas every day for a whole month. The first few will be the most difficult. You will find yourself hitchhiking on the initial ideas, however, and creating many new ones. The more ideas you have, the more confident you will be that you can make a decent living. What's more, the more ideas you generate, the more likely that you will wind up with a winner.

By a winner, I can give no better example than the one that New Jersey resident Paul Hartunian generated in the 1980s. One morning while he was watching the television news, Hartunian saw a construction crew foreman being interviewed about the renovations being done to the Brooklyn Bridge. Of course, virtually everyone has heard and continues to hear references to this landmark such as "If you pay money to attend Ernie Zelinski's self-help seminar, you will find it the biggest rip-off since the last time you bought the Brooklyn Bridge."

The construction crew foreman was standing on a pile of the original, old, and rotten wood used on the pedestrian walkway of the bridge, which was being replaced with new wood. Hartunian experienced a brain wave and quickly jotted down the phone number that was on the door of the truck parked next to the foreman. Within half an hour Hartunian was able to get the supervisor on the telephone.

Hartunian asked the foreman what he was going to do with the old wood. "I'm going to toss it out," answered the foreman. "It's junk." Hartunian offered the foreman $500 to deliver the wood to

Hartunian's home, which the foreman gladly agreed to do. Hartunian then paid someone else to cut the wood into small pieces.

> Make visible what, without you, might perhaps never have been seen.
>
> — Robert Bresson

That same day Hartunian used fifteen minutes of his time to prepare a press release with the headline "New Jersey Man Sells Brooklyn Bridge . . . for $14.95!" He also drafted a certificate on which he placed a little history and current information about the Brooklyn landmark. On the certificate he added "Attached to this certificate is a genuine piece of the original wooden pedestrian walkway of the world famous Brooklyn Bridge. You now own the Brooklyn Bridge."

After he had made arrangements to print copies of the certificate, Hartunian sent the press release to about one hundred key media people. Mailing the press release cost him about $100. Within two or three days Hartunian's phone was ringing off the hook with media people from across the United States wanting to interview him. The publicity went on for well over six months and eventually even famous TV talk-show host Johnny Carson did a ten-minute spiel on Hartunian's sale of the Brooklyn Bridge.

With all the publicity he received, Paul Hartunian ended up making a nice fortune selling his certificates with a small piece of wood attached to each one. Several thousand other people were likely watching the TV morning news the day Hartunian saw great opportunity in some rotten wood. Everyone else watching the TV show could have just as easily tried to capitalize on this opportunity. No one else did, however, simply because they failed to spot the opportunity, or if they did, they didn't do anything about it.

> I will take beers with dreamers over cocktails with the realists any day.
>
> — Unknown wise person

This "crazy" idea led to others and today Hartunian is rich and famous. The biggest thing that he attained was the freedom that comes from real success without a real job. Hartunian claims that the Brooklyn Bridge idea changed his life dramatically and his life has never been the same. He has used publicity in the media ever since to promote a number of other products and has now been interviewed on over 1,000 radio and TV stations in the United States and several other countries.

Of course, as Paul Hartunian demonstrated, it is not a simple case of coming up with a winning idea and then watching the big bucks roll in. What you need just as much as a great idea is that

> Ideas are a dime a dozen and they aren't worth a plugged nickel if you don't do anything with them.
>
> — Unknown wise person

miracle trait that we discussed earlier. It is called action. In other words, you must do something with the idea.

If you fail to take action — preferably courageous and substantial action — you may as well have come up with the world's worst idea ever. Unless you commit yourself to doing everything you can to get your idea to work, it's destined to remain forever in the file called The Universe's Wastebasket of Great Ideas. Based on my extensive research, at last count this file held approximately 1,453 trillion ideas that various people have let slip through their minds.

My idea that led to my best-selling book could just as easily have been part of "The Universe's Wastebasket of Great Ideas". A few months after I got fired from my engineering job over twenty-five years ago, I realized that many people have difficulty handling leisure time and I should write a book to help them deal with it.

It took me over a decade to start writing *The Joy of Not Working*, however. But at least I eventually took advantage of the opportunity that was staring me in the face for such a long time. Occasionally someone claims, "I could have written that book." My reply is, "So, why didn't you? I gave you lots of time. I played with the idea for over ten years before I actually did anything with it."

Although my writing *The Joy of Not Working* was not anywhere near as heroic an accomplishment as Paul Hartunian's selling of the Brooklyn Bridge, it did change my life remarkably. My success with that book proved that my creativity will do more for my financial and personal well-being than anything else in this world. Your creativity can do the same for you. Just one great idea can change your life dramatically! Look for it. It's there somewhere! Combine the idea with that magic called action and real success will find you in remarkable ways.

Hard Work and Real Success — Oil and Water!

Although I have stressed the importance of imagination, perseverance, dedication, commitment, and action so far, it may come as a surprise — to a few people at least — that I am not a proponent of hard work. By hard work I mean working strenuously, for long hours, and on as many tasks and projects as possible.

Here is a Zen story to make my point:

> A student, most eager for enlightenment, went to the Master and expressed his desire to be his student and become enlightened. The Master welcomed his enthusiasm and told him he would be honored to help him. "How long will it take?" asked the student.
>
> "Usually about two to three years," the Master responded, "but it depends on how hard you work at it."
>
> "Oh," the student declared, "I will work extremely hard — I will try to work at it both day and night."
>
> "Well, in that case," the Master advised, "it will take you at least seven years."

Plain and simple, the moral of this story is: hard work and real success — oil and water! Put another way, hard work and real success don't mix all that well. Real success, in fact, is about working smart and not hard.

Personally, the only time I am a big fan of hard work is when someone else is doing it and I am paying for it. This is not to say that I won't work hard at times, particularly on projects that excite me immensely, or ones that I must complete within a certain time frame. But for all intents and purposes, I find most hard work detrimental to my well-being.

Why do I work so hard? The best reason I can give you is that millions who collect welfare depend on me.

Contrary to popular belief, the work ethic is a terrible mistake, a cute term gone haywire. It is promoted most vehemently either by employers who want to exploit pathetic workaholics or by pathetic workaholics themselves who are trying to justify why they work so many hours and have no real life.

As is to be expected, everything has a price attached to it. There is a price for not working hard enough; there can be an even larger price for working too hard. Not so long ago I received a letter from Jeffrey Carson (his name has been changed due to the personal nature of the letter) from the eastern United States. Incidentally, the letterhead indicated that Carson's occupation was Attorney at Law.

Dear Ernie,

It's Monday and I've taken the day off. I've just finished reading *The Joy of Not Working*, which I found at the bookstore last Saturday. It's always exciting when a bit of revelation occurs in one's life. After two heart attacks and a near-death cardiac arrest last winter, you'd have thought I'd have gotten the message, but this work ethic doesn't go down easy.

So, after six months of near-suicidal depression about work and how much I hated it, I found your book. I can only say, from the bottom of my heart, thank you.

Best regards and sincerely,

Jeffrey Carson

> If you burn the candle at both ends, you are not as bright as you think.
> — Unknown wise person

The really good news for me was that this attorney had no intention of suing me on behalf of a client or himself. The good news for Carson was that he had realized how the work ethic could end his life if he didn't stop believing in it so fiercely.

Of course, corporations would like you to believe that "hard work is good for you and it never harmed anyone." There are reasons to believe otherwise, however.

Evidence That Hard Work Can Kill You

- According to a 2002 study in the *British Medical Journal*, employees with stressful jobs are twice as likely to die from heart disease as those who have jobs with little or no stress.
- Employees who work over forty-eight hours per week double their risk of heart disease, according to a 1996 UK government report.
- According to a 2003 American study, long-term job strain is worse for your heart than gaining forty pounds in weight or aging thirty years.
- Approximately two million workers die annually due to occupational injuries and illnesses, according to one United Nations

report. This means that work kills more people than war (650,000 deaths per year).

The core of the matter is that hard work can kill you. Another dark side of the work ethic is how many rainbow-chasers end up working hard all their lives, expecting success, but with nothing to show for it. The key to success, in fact, is to work on the few things that are truly important and make a difference in this world, and to disregard the rest.

> Don't overdo things that shouldn't be done in the first place.
> — Unknown wise person

In this regard, Peter Drucker advised, "Do the right things instead of trying to do everything right." To ensure that you don't spend time on projects that don't produce meaningful results, and instead have time for creative thinking and leisure activities, get in the habit of asking yourself the following questions:

- What is the best use of my time right now?
- What is the best book I could read right now to learn more about running my unconventional business?
- What is the best way to market my product or service right now?
- Is what I am doing today going to enhance my life today and in the future?
- What project will make me the most money with the least risk?
- Who are the best people to spend time with so that I can learn more about my career or business?

Clearly, if you are channeling your hard work into areas that offer little chance for big payoffs, your hard work will likely be in vain. On the other hand, if you work only four or five hours a day at creative endeavors that offer the likelihood of immense payoffs, four or five hours a day may be all that you need to hit it big so that you can live a comfortable life. Even two or three hours a day can do the trick in Britain, Canada, the United States, and Australia, given the opportunity that exists in these countries.

In the same vein, perhaps you have been told by the career experts to gain broad experience. In my view, it is better to focus one's energy in one key area, certainly not more than two or three. Too many projects will divide your focus at the expense of all your important ones. The ideal is to specialize in a very small niche, a

> Things that matter most must never be at the mercy of things that matter least.
>
> — Johann Wolfgang von Goethe

niche that you enjoy, where you can excel and become a master.

Some people may want to pursue more than one source of income, as advocated by Robert Allen in his book *Multiple Streams of Income: How to Generate a Lifetime of Unlimited Wealth* (Wiley, 2004). His advice on cultivating more than one source of income is sound. A person in an unreal job or unconventional business can only devote his or her attention to so many projects, however.

If you want to keep your business a simple operation and a one-person show, as I do, the number of sources of income should probably be limited to three or four. Although in the past I have handled being a writer, self-publisher, professional speaker, and part-time college instructor all at once, I wouldn't attempt to undertake more sources of income. No doubt if I had attempted to add being a landlord and multi-level marketing to the other four streams of income, I would have experienced a serious drain of mental and financial resources to the point that my writing and self-publishing would have had to be abandoned.

The key is not to overdo things. Pablo Picasso was one of the most prolific and influential artists of the twentieth century. No doubt you will agree that Picasso, who excelled in painting, sculpture, etching, stage design, and ceramics, attained an impressive measure of real success without a real job. Yet Picasso, like me, did not believe in being an achiever at all costs.

"You must always work not just within but below your means," claimed Picasso. "If you can handle three elements, handle only two. If you can handle ten, then handle only five. In that way the ones you do handle, you handle with more ease, more mastery, and you create a feeling of strength in reserve."

There is much more to say about why overwork can ruin you, but the topic in itself deserves another book. Come to think of it, I have already written two that cover the topic quite well. But, instead, let me recommend Richard Koch's *The 80/20 Principle* (Doubleday, 1998), which will teach you the secrets to achieving much more impressive results with much less effort.

Suffice it to say that, regardless of your field of endeavor, creativity ultimately produces the biggest payoffs. Although both creative effort and hard work require action, the former is at the heart of real success without a real job. The latter has been known to lead to nervous twitching, heart attacks, and dubious results.

5

It's Not Just an Unreal Job — It's a Real Business!

It's Not Creative Unless It Sells!

Over the last few years I have been approached by many individuals who want to learn how to write a book and get it published. Because providing free advice was taking up way too much of my time, I prepared a two-page letter to send to aspiring authors. Here are two of the most important paragraphs from the letter:

> Once you have written a book and had it published, you are about 5 percent of the way to making it a success. Whether the book is self-published or published by a major publisher, you must promote it. The best promotion for a book is not done by publishers, publicists, distributors, or bookstores; the best promotion is done by the author. In the academic world, it's publish or perish. In the real world, it's PROMOTE or perish.

> Writing a good book takes creativity; effective promotion takes ten times as much creativity. Five years after I wrote *The Joy of Not Working*, I was still promoting the book with the same intensity as when the book was first released. Without this sustained promotion, it would never have eventually become an international bestseller.

Next to doing the right thing, the most important thing is to let people know you are doing the right thing.

— John D. Rockefeller

I made particular mention of promotion in my letter because

promotion is a critical factor for whether a book succeeds. Promotion, of course, is one aspect of marketing, and marketing is an essential ingredient for any business, regardless of its size. Marketing is also important for an unreal job that requires selling services to customers.

You can have the best idea or product in the world, but if you can't market it, you may as well have the worst idea or product in the world. Product here refers to you as a contract employee, any service you may be offering to society, or any innovative item you have developed with the potential to change people's lives.

If you don't want to become a marketing expert, then you have to hire one. Fact is, however, marketing experts don't come cheap. Therefore, you may have to do what I had to do for the first few years: Learn how to become a marketing expert yourself and enjoy it. If you don't like certain forms of marketing, then avoid them. Concentrate on the areas that work best for your product and your own nature.

> A market is never saturated with a good product, but it is very quickly saturated with a bad one.
>
> — Henry Ford

Regardless of your initial inspiration to undertake your unreal job, you must recognize that it's not just an unreal job — it's a real business. Unlike a traditional job, you are getting paid for results produced instead of time put in at the office. Whether you like it or not — and a lot of people don't — marketing brings more results than virtually all other work activities. This means that if you are an artist, for example, you must strike an adequate balance between how much time you spend painting and how much time you spend marketing.

A good balance often requires more time spent in marketing than in creation of the product. Some of the most successful people in the information business invest 90 percent of their time in selling, self-promotion, getting publicity, and hustling new business. Only 10 percent of their time is spent developing new products or services. If artists were willing to spend at least a third of their time marketing their art, a lot more of them would not have to experience the starving-artist syndrome so common in their community.

Marketing is the art of turning your ideas and dream projects into profits. You have to be clear, however, that just the fact that you think people should be buying your product or service doesn't mean there will be a market for it. Many people who decide to provide a service or product fall into the trap of believing that every human being is a potential buyer. Your opinion of what is important, or what ought to be important, to other people is totally irrelevant. People themselves will decide what product or service will benefit them and whether to buy it. This is the way it should be — it's their money that they are spending and not yours!

Strictly from a business point of view, your product or service is not creative unless it sells! It must satisfy some human need or want. The basic human needs and wants are sex, shelter, security, health, happiness, money, love, relationships, self-esteem, status, and prestige. With the right innovative product or creative service, you can tap into most humans' greed for all these needs and wants and become so successful and wealthy that you can satisfy all of your own greed for all these needs and wants.

> Everyone lives by selling something, whatever be his right to it.
>
> — Robert Louis Stevenson

One aspect of marketing is the nature of the product itself. The first step of marketing is to make your service or your product unique. Then keep changing it so that it remains unique. You won't have to focus so much on pulverizing your rivals, as many people must do in the marketplace, because your competition will be yourself.

So what are you going to sell to people? The most important principle here is to select a product or service for which there is a large market. You have to first ask yourself: "Who is going to want to buy my product or service?" Then you better have a damn good answer!

The key is to think big. You aren't thinking big if your intention is to write and sell poetry. Plain and simple, most of the world is not interested in poetry. Whatever your product or service, your market for it should meet the following criteria:

- Your market for your product or service can be easily identified.
- A large segment of people is interested in your product or service.
- The market for your product is growing.
- People who are interested in your product or service can afford it.
- People who are interested in your product or service are willing to spend money on it.

Once you have identified your product and your target market, you have just started your marketing task. Like everyone else with an unreal job or unconventional business, you must master the

> I wanted to be an editor or a journalist. I wasn't really interested in being an entrepreneur, but I soon found I had to become an entrepreneur in order to keep my magazine going.
>
> — Richard Branson

arts of distribution, sales, promotion, and publicity in order that you can show the world how your product or service will uplift and enhance humanity.

Most people who attain phenomenal success without a real job aren't super-human. In fact, often their products or services aren't even the best ones in their category. Why then are they so successful while their competitors with superior products struggle to make a living? The reason is simply that the most successful people in any field think and act differently than most everyone else in the respective field. They have a marketing mind-set that is very different from that of their major competitors. The difference between a best-selling product or service and a bomb is marketing strategy.

Truth be known, you can sell junk with the right creative marketing campaign. "There is hardly anything in the world that some man cannot make a little worse," claimed John Ruskin, "and sell a little cheaper." Junk, however, has no staying power in the marketplace. Moreover, junk will not be subject to word-of-mouth marketing, which is the best marketing you can get for your service or product.

Although junk can be sold with exceptional marketing, exceptional products are doomed to be stuck in no-man's-land without adequate marketing effort. Plan to market your product for a year or two before word-of-mouth advertising kicks in.

The impact of initial sustained action is hard to overstate. Even though I knew I had a great book, I spent over five years promoting *The Joy of Not Working* after it was released. I spend very little time on it now, however. The book continues to sell about 7,500 copies a year because of word of mouth. Talk to bookstore owners and they will verify that a book does not last in bookstores for fifteen years unless it has word of mouth generated by satisfied readers.

College marketing courses stress the so-called four Ps of marketing — price, placement, promotion, and product. Marketing, in all its weird and varied forms, entails such things as identifying the target market for your product, getting people in the target market to buy your product, finding out whether customers or clients are happy with their purchases, and persuading customers and clients to purchase more of your product or service.

Whether you are selling a product or providing a service such as coaching, speaking, or free-lance writing, you must develop innovative titles, tag-lines, and techniques that help your product or service stand out in the marketplace. Not only must your product or service be one of a kind instead of one of many, you must show your target market how your product or service is, in fact, different from any other in the marketplace.

Anyone who creates a one-of-a-kind product or service can charge a much higher price. People with wealth love to pay a lot for what they buy; this gives the service or item more value. At the time I write this book I can give no better example than Donald Trump and his 2006 scheduled speaking tour, from which he will earn $1.5 million for each one-hour talk. With ten speeches planned, Trump will earn a total of $15 million, plus expenses. Another similar example: Several Fortune 500 executives pay Tony Robbins one million dollars a year as a retainer for his services as an inspirational coach.

No doubt both Donald Trump and Tony Robbins are master salespeople. Selling, one aspect of marketing and an essential business skill, is difficult for some of us mainly because we must deal with rejection. But learning how to deal with rejection is good for us; our self-esteem increases and we end up liking ourselves more. We also end up more successful after we learn to brush off rejection as something perpetuated by idiots, morons, and misfits who all don't know a good product or service when they see it.

Even artists can learn how to deal with rejection and sell their work. They must learn what most art schools don't teach them — business know-how. If you are an artist, you don't have to sell your soul to be a marketing expert. Your marketing expertise, in fact, enhances your soul and allows you much greater opportunity to introduce your art into the world. All successful artists today are successful at marketing and at managing their careers. Either that, or they have delegated these two tasks to someone else.

A business-savvy painter once talked me into buying a piece of his modern art to place over a hole in my living room wall. I later decided that the hole in the wall looks much better.

Marketing art is not all that difficult; indeed, it can be much easier than creating art. One great resource is the book *Art Marketing 101* (ArtNetwork Press, 2004) by Constance Smith, which helps artists take care of their business, with tips on everything from making winning portfolios to cultivating clients

> Being good in business is the most fascinating kind of art . . . Making money is art and working is art and good business is the best art.
>
> — Andy Warhol

and selling at shows. It also teaches artists how to tap into the publishing, greeting-card, and licensing industries.

Unfortunately, there is not enough room in this book to cover even the most basic important information about marketing, whether for artists or Web designers. For this reason you should read anything and everything by marketing guru Jay Levinson that you can get your hands on. If you can afford it, go to a $6,000 marketing boot camp run by marketing masters such as Levinson.

Do not discount the value of books insofar as how much they can help you attain your unconventional career goals. One Amazon reviewer of *Making A Living Without a Job* (Bantam, 1993) by Barbara J. Winter had this to say about how much Winter's book helped him become more successful as an artist:

> I had art work and writings published; had an art show in NYC and several other cities; taught Marketing for Artists at a gallery; spoke publicly at art league meetings as the guest speaker; painted artsy furniture for the homeless people; became an Amazon seller and numerous other non-job profit centers! Besides all that, I learned html; created my own and several others' websites; learned yoga, tai chi, feng shui; and was able to travel and study with a famous TV artist for a month!

Besides books, other important resources that artists can use to promote and sell their art include marketing classes, seminars, workshops, and coaching. Use your creativity in your art, but use your creativity just as much in marketing your art. Whether you are an artist or pure businessperson, creativity is your biggest asset. You have to use it in all aspects of your business, not only in coming up with an innovative product or service.

In 1998 first-time author Charlene Costanzo self-published *The Twelve Gifts of Birth.* Excluding the introduction, the book had only 461 words and was published in hard-cover. (Yes, 461 words — I counted them and was astonished.) Much to the surprise of the publishing industry, eighteen months later the book had sold over 300,000 copies. Eventually a major publisher paid Costanzo a substantial advance to take over publication of *The Twelve Gifts of Birth* (Collins, 2001).

How did Costanzo — without any publishing or marketing experience — manage to sell so many copies on her own? This is a valuable case study of how an ordinary person accomplished extraordinary things. We can learn a lot from Costanzo regardless of what product or service we are trying to market. Here are the reasons for Costanzo's success with *The Twelve Gifts of Birth*:

- ◆ The book was well-packaged and well-priced.
- ◆ The book was spiritual without being religious.
- ◆ Costanzo spared no expense to take the book to the New Age Expo in Denver and to the Chicago Gift Show.
- ◆ Costanzo convinced Books Are Fun, a direct-marketing company, to carry the book, and the company ended up selling thousands of copies.
- ◆ Despite being a one-book and one-person show, Costanzo was able to convince wholesalers and catalogs to carry her book.

Costanzo was successful in marketing her product because she introduced it to those who would appreciate it most. As word of mouth about *The Twelve Gifts of Birth* spread among churches, schools, hospitals, and other organizations, individuals such as teachers, counselors, and therapists used the book in values training and character classes. According to *Publishers Weekly*, it was, above all, "Costanzo's unusual, often quirky and always expansive approach to marketing that helped immensely."

Costanzo's extraordinary success was a result of her creative marketing of a creative product. A creative service or product without creative marketing behind it is not all that creative. There isn't a marketplace out there that isn't more crowded than it was a decade ago. People won't be aware of your product or service unless you take unique steps to let them know about it.

All things considered, you must think like a businessperson, not like a writer or an artist or a musician or a Web developer. You are essentially an entrepreneur with a product or service to sell, and it's critical that you start thinking that way. Instead of always developing new art or any other new products, you must invest substantial time, energy, and money in marketing activities.

> Every child should be placed on a doorstep to sell something. It's the best possible training for life.
>
> — Robert Morley

Fifteen Minutes of Notoriety Beats the Best Advertising Money Can Buy

As already emphasized, one of the most important principles for unconventional business success is to create awareness of your product or service. If you're an artist, a life coach, a public speaker, or a business owner, you must get the word out about your product or service. The problem is that keeping your name in front of the public can be more expensive than ever.

Another major problem is that we live in a world where consumers actively resist most marketing, particularly advertising. When humans are foolish enough to read an idiotic advertisement, they realize that they have wasted their time and haven't gained anything useful. Eventually, most individuals don't look at most advertisements. I, for one, can spend a whole hour reading the newspaper and not read one advertisement.

Hiring a celebrity spokesperson to promote your product might help, but I bet that you can't afford this. Even if you can afford a beautifully executed commercial on the Super Bowl broadcast, it's still an extremely risky bet. You will be lucky to gain enough sales of your product or service to pay 10 percent of the cost of the celebrity and producing and running the commercial.

> Ninety-nine percent of advertising doesn't sell much of anything.
>
> — David Ogilvy

This means that you have to look for cost-effective alternatives. The best one is publicity. Publicity is information that concerns a person, a group, an event, or a product and that is disseminated through various media including newspapers, magazines, radio, TV, and the Internet. Notoriety is often achieved by the spreading of such information. An especially compelling advantage to this approach is that publicity requires little or no money; all it has to cost you is your time and effort.

You can hire your own public-relations person if you have to. But why would you want to? A professional P.R. firm can end up costing you anywhere from $2,000 to $10,000 just for a basic publicity campaign. If you use your creativity, you can get extraordinary results, better than most P.R. firms will get you. Let's say that you spend twenty hours and save yourself $5,000 that a P.R. firm would charge. You will end up making $250 an hour by doing it yourself. How often do you make this amount of money? What's more, it has been my experience that generating one's own publicity can be a lot of fun.

The biggest advantage that publicity has over advertising is that people see publicity as much more credible than advertising. Indeed, fifteen minutes of notoriety beats the best advertising money can buy nine times out of ten. Now is this cool, or what? Something that you can get for free can be ten to a hundred times as effective as something for which you have to pay thousands of dollars. In fact, even millions of dollars can't buy the same results that the best free publicity can give you.

Above all, publicity sets you aside from the competition much better than advertising ever can. One key to getting publicity is controversy, so this entails ruffling some feathers and even getting a good portion of the population downright upset at you. Using this approach means that perhaps a quarter to a third of the public will love you, with the remainder either hating you or being indifferent to your message.

> The secret to success is to offend the greatest number of people.
>
> — George Bernard Shaw

The problem with most publicity seekers is that they are trying to be too nice; they are not willing to take a stand or be the least bit controversial. I was successful in getting a ton of publicity because of the controversial title and content of *The Joy of Not Working*. Talk-show hosts particularly liked my boldness in saying things with which over half of their listeners and viewers disagreed.

For instance, within the first few months after I self-published *The Joy of Not Working*, I received a phone call from a producer for Peter Warren's radio show on CJOB in Winnipeg. I had never heard of Peter Warren, but I gladly accepted an opportunity to do a telephone interview for an hour. I expected this interview to be similar to those I had already done either on the telephone or in the studio with several talk-show hosts. With me as their guest, most of the talk-show hosts used a theme for their show such as "Are We Working Too Hard?"

Boy, was I in for a cool surprise! Peter Warren started his show by saying something like, "We have never had as many of our listeners wanting to get at a guest on our show as we do people wanting to get at Ernie Zelinski. Zelinski is the author of the recently published book *The Joy of Not Working*. Zelinski has not held a job for years and believes that anyone who works hard for a living is stupid." This left me perplexed, not quite sure whether I should be infuriated, and very much amused all at the same time. I came to the brilliant conclusion that I could have a problem

> If you don't feel well, tell your doctor, but not the marketplace.
>
> — Jim Rohn

benefiting from this interview if I didn't handle it properly.

As you can well imagine, all the phone lines at the radio station lit up immediately. For the first half hour, with the exception of one caller, everyone attacked me. One of the first callers said something like, "I am sure glad that you live in Edmonton and not Winnipeg. People like you contribute nothing to society."

With amusement, I responded, "First, because I live in a much better city, I am also glad that I don't live in Winnipeg. Insofar as my not contributing to society, I can say that *The Joy of Not Working* is already a Canadian bestseller. This means that many people are benefiting from the book and telling others about it. This year I am making more money working four hours a day than a lot of people are working eight hours a day. This makes me at least twice as productive as they are. So don't tell me that I don't contribute anything to society. Chances are I contribute a heck of a lot more than you do."

With verbal dexterity that I didn't know I was capable of, I managed to handle all the attackers in the first half-hour. The second half of the interview was less controversial, with most of the callers much more receptive to my message. I had a chance to clarify that *The Joy of Not Working* wasn't a book for people who want to live off the system, but a book for the retired, unemployed, and overworked to help them enjoy their leisure time and make the best of their lives.

All in all, this heated and controversial radio interview ended up being one of most beneficial I ever did. At the time, *The Joy of Not Working* was not readily available in Coles bookstores in Winnipeg or the rest of Canada. The interview generated so much demand for my book in the Winnipeg Coles bookstores that the national buyer for Coles ordered copies for all of their 150 stores throughout Canada.

My willingness to be controversial over the years has generated feature articles (most with a photo of me) about my books and my life in major newspapers including *The Washington Post, The Vancouver Sun, The Oakland Tribune, Toronto Star, and USA TODAY*. I have been interviewed by over one hundred radio stations and have appeared on CNN TV's *Financial News*, CBC TV's *Venture*, and CTV's *Canada AM*. If I had to purchase the equivalent advertising space or time, the cost would have been between $100,000 and $200,000, and not anywhere as effective.

Given my success with controversy, I would suggest that you not be afraid to offend someone. Not offending anyone might be a smart thing to do when you work for the government or when you go to your best friend's birthday party, but not when you are trying to get publicity to develop a market for your product or service.

Never let the urge to be nice interfere with your being different. The urge to be nice to everyone comes from wanting to be liked by everyone. "The disease of niceness cripples more lives than alcoholism," remarked British actor Robin Chandler. "Nice people are simply afraid to say no, are constantly worrying about what others think of them, constantly adapting their behavior to please — never getting to do what they want to do."

Just getting your fifteen minutes of fame, as promised by Andy Warhol, will be extremely difficult if you are a carbon copy of all the nice people out there. The news media aren't in the business of gratuitously writing about just anyone — the news media are in the business of providing interesting stories for their readers. It has been my experience that the chances of the media writing about me are increased dramatically if I follow these principles:

- Be first.
- Be different.
- Be daring.

> No one can be profoundly original who does not avoid eccentricity.
>
> — André Maurois

Being first is important. If someone were to ask you which team was second to climb Mount Everest, no doubt you would reply: "Who cares?" (If you are one of those weird trivia buffs who really cares, the answer is Jurg Marmet and Ernest Schmidt.) The point is, generally speaking, people won't remember who was second in accomplishing something extraordinary.

Being different and daring are just as important. "Good P.R.," advises Richard Branson, "is really about having something different to say in the first place." To be different, you must strive to be what no else but you can be. If you want to lead an anonymous life, then go ahead and be like everyone else — fit in and be part of the pack. Conforming to society, and thinking like the rest of the herd, will bring you the nebulous result of fitting in and being liked a little bit by everyone, but not being liked a whole lot by anyone. You will certainly never attain great recognition or any fame by following the herd.

Only by being different and daring can you be controversial. Clearly, the media loves controversy — take advantage of this. If you are sold on the power of publicity, which you should be, never forget the following:

Three Truths about Publicity

1. Media people are not there to help you promote your product, website, business venture, etc. and really don't care if you succeed at what you do.
2. Media people are bombarded every day of the year with thousands of press releases from public-relations firms and 99 percent of these press releases are either not read or ignored.
3. The only time that reporters will care about your product, service, or life story is when you provide them with an extraordinary pitch that their readers will enjoy.

You stand a much greater chance of getting publicity for your product or service if you make the media person's job easier by providing her with a controversial story that she doesn't have to dig up on her own. When sending out a press release, you have to ask yourself, "What can I do that will make this story more useful to a journalist?" This applies whether you are a sports psychologist or a writer or an artist.

> The shortest and best way to make your fortune is to let people see clearly that it is in their interests to promote yours.
>
> — Jean de La Bruyére

Ensure that you present your story from a reporter's perspective and not from your own perspective. If you are an artist, for instance, don't offer some self-absorbed account of your paintings that would bore even the best of your artist friends. Instead, give the reporter a story on how you have taken your biggest non-selling piece of art, cut it in four, framed the four resulting pieces, and placed each for sale on E-bay. You have now increased your chances a millionfold that a reporter will write about you. Heck, you may even end up selling every one of your four new "pieces" of art for more than any of your other pieces have ever sold for. (If you are an artist and use my "stupid" idea, you owe me half of your profits!)

There is something that every publicity seeker should remember, however, but most people don't: If more than two people are doing something, no matter what it is, it's no longer news. Too many people read about something unique that someone else has done and then try to copy it, expecting to get the same amount of publicity. Reporters end up thinking, "This person probably never

had an original idea in their whole life."
The reporters are probably right.

> Passion persuades and, by God, I was passionate about what I was selling.
>
> — Anita Roddick

If you want to get publicity for your product or business, you have to do something truly new to stand out. Tell the media something they don't know. Surprise them with something totally different. Find something bizarre to tell the world. Give the interviewer an astonishing new statistic or report a new survey that contradicts popular belief. What you need is a story with spice and vigor to it.

Try Something So Stupid That It May Pay Off Big Time

When it comes to marketing your product or yourself, it's important that you don't lose touch with the craziness in yourself and not be afraid to go public with it. The more attention you pay to what the masses are doing, the more you will realize that the everybody-else-is-doing-it approach isn't the way to put your mark on this world. While it's tempting to join the masses, always remember that you have meaningful career dreams and extraordinary things to pursue.

As I have said before, you should be excited, even crazy about what you are doing. Anything worth doing is worth having fun while doing it. Marketing your product or service is a great way to enjoy yourself. What sort of quirky marketing can you come up with? I suggest that you try something so stupid that it may pay off big time.

Here is an example of how I used an original promotional idea to differentiate myself from my competition and make a few extra bucks. The idea was used to market my first book and seminars on creativity. After self-publishing *The Art of Seeing Double or Better in Business*, I wound up with about twenty-five defective copies, which were either cut crooked or had missing pages. I took these back to the printer, expecting a refund. The printer, however, told me that he had given me eighty extra copies over and above those I had paid for. Because I didn't want to throw the defective copies away, I decided to hang on to them for a while.

> If an idea does not appear bizarre, there is no hope for it.
>
> — Niels Bohr

Not long after, I ran into Lance, a former

colleague of mine. We decided to have coffee together since Lance wanted to talk about how I had published the book. I mentioned the defective books that I was trying to put to good use. Lance jokingly said something silly like "Send them to people you don't like." With my competitive nature, when someone says something silly or foolish, I have an urge to do better. Without missing a beat, I said, "I can do better than that; I can cut these books in half and mail either a top half or bottom half to people."

Later I went home and retired for the night. But I couldn't sleep because I hadn't followed one of my important principles of creativity — write down all ideas, regardless of how stupid they sound! I forced myself out of bed and in my little black idea book wrote, "Cut books in half and send to people." Then I had no problem sleeping.

> Nothing sells by itself.
> — Ellen Chodosh

A week later I was trying to figure out how to get corporations more interested in my book and seminars. I didn't want to send any more free promotional copies of the book to more human-resource workers since the response had not been all that good. Luckily, I happened to look in my black idea book and saw "cut books in half and send to people." This is exactly what I did. First, I went down to my printer and had the books cut in half. Then, I drafted this letter:

Dear Mr./Ms. Vice-President of Human Resources:

You have just received half of my book, *The Art of Seeing Double or Better in Business.*

Why did I send you half a book? I had two problems: One, I had a few defective books that I wanted to use for something more purposeful than fill in my garbage can. Two, I needed some way to get you interested in my book and seminars.

So I decided to be creative. I believe that by cutting the books in half, I have solved both problems. First, I found a use for the defective books. Second, with all the material you receive, no doubt half a book has attracted your attention more than conventional forms of marketing.

Incidentally, creativity is the foundation for *The Art of Seeing Double or Better in Business*, which was written to help people and organizations be more innovative. To increase productivity many organizations are giving the book to their employees. Several radio stations, credit unions, school boards, professional associations, and universities have already purchased the book in bulk.

The Art of Seeing Double or Better in Business is available only directly from me through my seminars or if you purchase 10 or more copies (20 after July 1). A price list and an order form are enclosed. Information about my seminars is also enclosed.

Sincerely,

Ernie J. Zelinski

My reasonable mind jumped in at this point and tried to convince me this was a "dumb idea," which wouldn't work and wouldn't do much for my reputation. Luckily, my instinctive mind told me to be unreasonable and do it anyway. Truth be told, a bad reputation is better than no reputation at all — if you have a bad reputation, at least some people know that you exist!

> Nothing is ever accomplished by a reasonable man.
>
> — American proverb

I was sure that some people to whom I was about to mail the half-books would think I was unprofessional, or even crazy. But I also figured a lot of people would remember me. What's more, my curiosity was getting the best of me; I was wondering how human-resource professionals in corporations would respond to receiving either a top or bottom half of my book. To be sure, I felt a little silly while stuffing half-books along with a copy of the letter in envelopes.

I am happy to report that this idea was so stupid that it paid off big time! Sending the half-books with the above letter resulted in several orders for ten books, which further led to sales of several hundred books as well as several seminar presentations for one client. At this point, the extra revenues from this crazy idea had totalled somewhere between $10,000 and $15,000.

This gets much, much better, however! After I let the media know about my success using this stupid idea, I received a lot of valuable publicity via two feature newspaper articles, which led to other seminars and book sales. In fact, given the profits this crazy idea generated, I calculated that I could cut perfectly good books in half and still have this promotion be highly profitable. The cool thing is that two years later I was in Vancouver about to make a speech when I was introduced to a gentleman in the human-

> Deals are my art form. Other people paint beautifully on canvas or write wonderful poetry. I like making deals, preferably big deals. That's how I get my kicks.
> — Donald Trump

resource industry. He exclaimed, "Hey, I know who you are! You sent me half of a book some time ago. To this day I still show it to people who come in my office!"

One final note about this "stupid" idea: I set it aside for well over a decade, but I recently revitalized it and now utilize an electronic version. I offer the top half of my recent book *How to Retire Happy, Wild, and Free* on my website. (If you would like a copy, you can download it in PDF format at www.thejoyofnotworking.com — again, this e-book is free just like the other great things in life!) No doubt giving away the top half of *How to Retire Happy, Wild, and Free* has contributed to the book's respectable sales and overall success.

All things considered, if you want to be a successful marketer, you must realize that the best marketing techniques often go against common sense. There is no telling where a stupid idea might lead if you are willing to try it out. Be bold and be shameless. Try anything that is legal to get your product or service noticed. With the right stupid idea, applied to the right intelligent product or service, you will get extraordinary results.

Claim Your Way to Fame

One of the best ways to get publicity for your product or service is to make your own claim to fame. What you need is a title. Needless to say, I am not talking about a title such as "Your Highness" or "the Right Honorable" although you may well deserve both. For marketing purposes, your title should tell the world that you are one of the leading authorities in the field that you work in. It also helps if the title is a bit controversial.

I can give no better example than Frank Ogden of Vancouver, B.C., who calls himself Dr. Tomorrow. Ogden is a master marketer, and over the years his title has helped him establish himself as a prominent futurist, even though some people question his credentials and his expertise. The *Financial Post* newspaper described Ogden as a "20th Century visionary" and called his ideas and deeds "outrageous," an ideal combination of qualities for a life of profitable nonconformity. Ogden even went so far as to trademark "Dr. Tomorrow" in several countries, including Canada. This title helped Ogden become a highly successful speaker on the conference and convention circuit.

With a title, you can use publicity to build your business and personal brand by positioning yourself as a qualified and credible expert, particularly in the media. Again, media people are willing to help you if you give them what they want. Thus, you must find a way to make your expertise known to the media so that they can contact you whenever they need someone to comment on a particular product, service, or story.

> It's not enough to be the best at what you do. You must be perceived as the only one who does what you do.
>
> — Jerry Garcia

After Paul Hartunian — yes, the same guy who sold the Brooklyn Bridge — wrote a book called *How to Be Outrageously Successful with the Opposite Sex* (Ultimate Secrets, 1991), he claimed in his press releases to be "the nation's leading authority on dating and relationships." No one else gave Hartunian this label — it was his own claim to fame. Hartunian even challenged anyone who thought he or she was America's leading authority on dating and relationships to call any of the over 1,000 radio talk shows he was on. No one ever did. Hartunian says, "To this day, I remain the undisputed, unchallenged nation's leading authority on dating and relationships."

Giving yourself a title is a form of branding. The better the title and the more visibility you have, the easier it is to get media coverage — and keep getting more. A greater share of the marketplace for your product or service can belong to you if you can get the word out about it using a unique title. If you are an Afro-American artist, for instance, why not call yourself "The Afro-American Renaissance Man" or "The Artist with an Attitude" or "The Enlightened Artist" or "The Paint by Wonder Artist"? Once you have claimed a title, there are many avenues that you can pursue to further establish yourself as a renowned expert in your field:

Fifteen Ways to Claim Your Fame

1. Get yourself featured in publications.
2. Get interviewed on a radio talk show.
3. Appear on the television news.
4. Write a regular column about your field of expertise for print media and/or websites.
5. Publish a monthly newsletter that you send to subscribers and to all your media contacts.
6. Speak at conferences and seminars.
7. Volunteer yourself as an "expert source" for

media people who may need someone on short notice for breaking news related to your field.

8. Connect your product or service to a charity or cause.

9. Conduct a survey related to one of your products or services and then announce the results to the media with a press release.

10. Sponsor a contest to promote your service or product and announce it in the media.

11. Put on some stunt related to your product, service, or expertise and announce it to the media.

12. Write a letter to the editor and list your title (claim to fame) with your name.

13. Distribute your press release about your product or service via a publicity service that distributes news releases electronically to news rooms around the world.

14. Publish your press releases on your website.

15. Provide the producers of *Oprah* with a show idea or theme with suggestions for other experts besides yourself being on the show.

Use your title as much as possible. Start small if you have to. Of course, every person marketing a product or service would jump at the chance for a guest spot on Oprah. There is great value to a show that reaches millions, no doubt, but don't ignore the smaller shows — those that reach only a few thousand people. Astute marketing people will do the smallest of shows because they never know who is listening. One small thing often leads to another small thing and a number of small things can lead to a big thing — such as a feature on *Oprah* or *60 Minutes*.

I need to claim a title to promote myself. Should I use King George, George the Great, or George the First?

Stick to Able George. Members of royalty seldom become freelance ditchdiggers.

You must be able to demonstrate a passion for your subject. A great title and a great topic together aren't enough. A producer with NBC's *Today Show*, Andrea Smith, claimed she wants to book guests who are "passionate, dynamic, and care about what they're saying." What producers look for (which, of course, may vary from show to show) are topics that are fun, entertaining, fresh, topical, and presented by well-spoken guests. Don't be afraid to blow your own horn. Talk about your product or service, but do talk from your heart and not like a poorly trained used-car salesman.

The power of being featured as an expert even in a small newspaper or on the smallest of radio or TV stations is not to be underestimated. What happens when we hear a financial consultant on a radio talk show? He immediately commands credibility. We all think, "If he is on the radio, he must be good." Moreover, if he mentions that he has written a book, he must be even better. Yet this financial advisor may in fact have one of the worst track records while some obscure financial advisor is making his small group of clients filthy rich.

> If you aren't an authority on the product or service you're offering, get out of the business!
>
> — Paul Hartunian

The key is to keep your name, title, and even your face continually in front of the media. Sometimes we forget how many opportunities there are for us to get publicity about our products and ourselves. Each day there are thousands of broadcast shows alone that are hungry for good guests. In fact, every day more than 4,000 American radio and TV shows book more than 10,000 guests. You can be one to them.

Give Yourself Away to the Influencers of This World

All things considered, word of mouth is still the most important means of marketing a product or service. Word of mouth is created by getting your product or service in the hands of people who will appreciate it and will talk to friends and associates about it. The best way to get people talking is to give your service or product to key individuals — talk-show hosts, columnists, celebrities, and chat-line addicts — who are going to mention it to many people, who will mention it to even more people.

With the right product or service, the more you give away, the more you end up selling. I have now spent approximately $40,000 giving away over 12,000 copies of my books. But let me not dwell on my own case because I have one that is much better. A few years ago, Marlo Morgan self-published a book called *Mutant Message Down Under*. Three years later, Morgan had sold 270,000

> Do it big or stay in bed.
>
> — Larry Kelly

copies. This is a remarkable figure for any self-published book, but the most extraordinary fact was Morgan had given away over 90,000 copies of her book in three years. She donated the copies to prisons, women's shelters, and other institutions.

Giving away almost one hundred copies each day for three years straight is not something even major publishers would consider, but it paid off for Morgan. Her impressive sales were a result of the word-of-mouth advertising generated from the copies she gave away. Better still, when the book finally came to the attention of HarperCollins, the publisher paid Morgan a $1.7 million advance to take over publication of *Mutant Message Down Under* (HarperPerennial, 1995).

Giving away your product or service for free may seem like a silly way to try to make a living. There is no better way to create word of mouth, however, as Marlo Morgan proved. Many people end up buying your product or service after hearing about it from someone. The key is to give your service or product to the influencers of this world. By influencers, I mean the "big mouths" of this world who know a lot of other influential people and will recommend your product or service to everyone they talk to.

In the same vein, you can get publicity by giving free talks and consultations. You will establish yourself as an expert and publicize your product or service at the same time. Again, if you can create yourself as being controversial, you increase your chances of making appearances on talk shows, where you can offer free samples of your products. If you can't get publicity after sustained effort, your product or service is likely not distinctive enough. Do whatever it takes to make it more distinctive.

A product is a service is a product is a service. The marketing principles in this chapter apply whether you are promoting a speech or a painting or a book or a pizza or a website. Remember how Paul Hartunian used publicity to market rotten wood and make a fortune at it. Don't you think that your product or service has more value than rotten wood? If it does, you should be ashamed of yourself if you can't market it to the world.

I can't give enough ink to the fact that marketing is the mother — father, grandmother, aunt, and uncle too — of extraordinary success attained with any product or service. Again, strictly from a business point of view, it's not creative unless it sells! A creative product or service gets you to first base only; creative marketing gets you all the way to home plate.

6

Prosperity Comes When You Do the Right Things with Your Life

More Money Won't Bring You More Happiness — It Works the Other Way Around!

As I start writing this chapter at one of my favorite coffee bars, the time is 3:30 P.M. Today is November 23, a day when it is common to have two feet of snow on the ground in Edmonton and a temperature high of 21°F. The lowest temperature recorded for this time of the year is -29°F (yes, that's a minus). Because today's temperature reached an abnormal high of 61°F, and there was absolutely no snow on the ground, I went for a most enjoyable bike ride for an hour and a half in the early afternoon — and just for the record, I didn't get up until the crack of noon.

Yesterday, also a bright sunny day, was even better when the temperature reached a record high of 68°F. I went running for an hour wearing just a T-shirt and shorts, something I could normally not do on November 22 unless I flew to Las Vegas, at least 1,500 miles south of my hometown. Both yesterday and today I saw only a handful of people taking advantage of this great weather to run, cycle, golf, or walk. Not only did I feel prosperous, I felt truly blessed to be able to do what I wanted to do, when I wanted to do it.

Sadly, most people in conventional jobs, even if they earn $500,000 a year

> Money will buy you a bed but not a good night's sleep, a house but not a home, a companion but not a friend.
>
> — Zig Ziglar

or more, could not take advantage of these two great days as I was able to do. Some motivational speakers say that although money can't buy happiness, it can buy freedom. I agree that money can help buy a good measure of freedom, but the financial pursuit can also imprison people — in more ways than one. No doubt many Edmontonians, both yesterday and today, felt imprisoned by their jobs — the source of their money — when they couldn't take advantage of the great weather. In an indirect way, they were not able to do this because of their pursuit of the almighty dollar.

The purpose of the first part of this chapter is to put money in its proper place so that you have realistic expectations about what a great amount of cash can do for you — and what it can't do for you! If you need less money in your life, you won't have to work as much and as hard for it. Just as telling, you will find it much easier to give up a well-paid job to pursue a dream career or unconventional business and be able to enjoy the freedom I enjoy.

Contrary to public belief, earning or having more money can be a trap that leads to a diminished quality of life. More cash often leads to more spending on items that require a lot of one's time and more money for maintenance of the items. Of course, if the items have been purchased on credit, there is the pain of having to make even more money to make the payments in order to avoid personal bankruptcy.

> To be clever enough to get a great deal of money, one must be stupid enough to want it.
> — George Bernard Shaw

More money should bring more freedom and more security instead of more slavery and more worry. Yet research studies indicate that financial prominence can bring its own form of hassles and worries. More money leads to alienation from previous peer groups, the pain of having to lose a lot more of one's assets in divorce, and more acute feelings of fear of someone stealing one's property and money.

Weirdly, there is a certain luxury in not having a large portfolio. I discovered that having financial assets can be somewhat of a burden. Managing my nest egg is frustrating and time consuming. Where do I put it? Don't ask me for my cash and other financial resources, however. It's not as troublesome looking after my nest egg as it would be for me to give it to you.

Following is a letter that shows another way how we can get trapped by the almighty dollar. Thomas Allen (his name has been changed) from the city of New York wrote to me five months before I started this book. Up until then I had received several hundred letters about *The Joy of Not Working*, but none of this nature:

Dear Mr. Zelinski,

Recently, I went on strike, furious with my client, feeling that I was always abused. By striking, I put them in a very compromised position that they'd have no way out of except by meeting my demands, which was a six-figure-dollar amount. They prepared to fight, but it was a lost cause. All I had to do was hold out for a couple of months and they'd eventually give up and I'd be rich! So why couldn't I sleep at night?

One day my sister-in-law let me borrow your book, *The Joy of Not Working*. Three chapters in and I immediately realized what a terrible mistake I was making. My problems weren't with my client at all. I was the problem. I had lost my passion for the work months earlier, and as a result I began to find other ways to combat the emptiness in my life: guitar, taekwondo, learning foreign languages, dieting. I wanted to add more, but I couldn't; work blocked the way.

It seems so obvious now, but at the time I was quick to blame the people at work rather than the idea of work itself. Once I put these two parts of my life together, the solution became crystal clear. I called my client at once, explained my position, and we agreed to part on good terms.

Am I nuts? Did I really just pass up a small fortune because I couldn't put up with a little fight? I don't think so. I think I'm richer now because of it. A day lived to its fullest is worth far more than any money you could hope to earn by sacrificing it.

Thanks for helping me see what was always there.

Sincerely,

Thomas Allen

> There is a gigantic difference between earning a great deal of money and being rich.
>
> — Marlene Dietrich

To be honest, I am not exactly sure how the information in *The Joy of Not Working* put Thomas Allen's problem in proper perspective and convinced him to

> The only point in making money is, you can tell some big shot where to go.
>
> — Humphrey Bogart

forego over $100,000 from his client. Nonetheless, we should all pay at least some attention to Allen's observation: "A day lived to its fullest is worth far more than any money you could hope to earn by sacrificing it."

Clearly, we all need money but the pursuit of wealth can cost us precious time and, more important, our independence. One reason people pursue the almighty dollar zealously is they make an absurd assumption about money. Although many wise people over the ages have warned us that money can't buy happiness, most of us ignore this wisdom. We strive for happiness that is supposed to accompany increased wealth regardless of the required sacrifices. The belief system that more money can bring more happiness needs some severe auditing. Somewhat against my better judgment, I am going to take a stab at it.

> No amount of money can make others speak well of you behind your back.
>
> — Chinese proverb

Money, generally speaking, can't buy what your heart truly desires nor can it buy what you can't see. Yet what your heart truly desires and many things you can't see are fundamental to being happy. In this group you can list peace of mind, love, job satisfaction, and spiritual fulfillment. Many rich people don't have these elements of happiness and, regardless of their financial prominence, they can't buy these things.

Even health can't be bought. No doubt financial might can provide better quality healthcare, particularly in the United States, where public healthcare is not universal as it is in Canada. Once you destroy great health, however, you can't buy it back. Right living including having enjoyable work — and not the almighty dollar — is key to great health.

If you were to think about it for a while, you would realize that there are many more personal attributes contributing to happiness that are beyond the realm of money. Following is a list of thirty-three elements of happiness that I challenge you to purchase on the open market:

Elements of Happiness That Money Can't Buy

Purpose	Reputation	Physical fitness
Health	Longevity	Self-reliance
Personal creativity	Real friends	Achievement
Job satisfaction	Loving family	Respect of others
Integrity	Charm	Peace of mind
Good character	Sense of humor	Generosity

Street smarts	Patience	Gratitude
Compassion	Empathy	Emotional stability
Greatness	Warmth	Courage
Self-esteem	Time	Spiritual fulfillment
Wisdom	True love	A good night's sleep

If these are all elements of happiness, and they can't be bought, then it follows that happiness can't be bought with cash. When you finally accept this, it is much easier to break the relationship between work and money. This in turn gives you the opportunity to pursue your true work that may be totally unrelated to what you are presently working at to earn a living.

> Average sex is better than being a billionaire.
>
> — Ted Turner

Of course, if we are extremely poor (starving or homeless), more money can bring a much better life. But beyond a certain level — not as high as you may think — more financial resources don't translate into more happiness. The evidence is overwhelming, as indicated by numerous studies. Here are four:

1. A recent study compared average life satisfaction with the purchasing power of tens of thousands of people in twenty-nine different countries. In poor countries, not surprisingly, purchasing power and life satisfaction were clearly related. Surprisingly, however, in countries half as rich as the United States there is absolutely no relationship between money and happiness.

2. Another study confirmed that people in rich countries are not any happier than those in poorer ones. "During the 1980s, the West Germans had double the incomes of the poor Irish, who year after year reported more satisfaction with their lives," claims David Myers, a sociologist at Hope College in Michigan and author of *The Pursuit of Happiness* (Harper Paperbacks, 1993).

3. The Alfred P. Sloan foundation found an inverse relationship between self-reported child happiness and parental income in the United States. Blue-collar and middle-class kids identified themselves as happier than wealthy ones.

4. Two Canadian studies found that the unhappiest

Canadians live in cities where income is the highest whereas the happiest live in Atlantic Canada, the poorest of regions.

I could present a lot more scholarly evidence that more money doesn't translate into more happiness, including extensive research by renowned psychologist Ed Diener of the University of Illinois, but this could be in vain. Regardless of how good of a job I do, there will still be many readers who won't believe that money can't buy happiness. This coincides with the Law of the Lie: No matter how often a lie is shown to be false, there will remain a significant percentage of people who believe it to be true. I hope that you aren't one of these people.

It may be that you are almost convinced, but not quite, that the pursuit of more money at all costs is not the best way to spend the rest of your life. Then allow me to make one more attempt to convince you totally. Unless you were born into wealth, likely you have been truly broke at some time in your life. I am not talking about a time when you sold one of your three luxury cars or the cottage at the lake to help you through a recession as you continued to bask in relative comfort. I am referring to a situation when you were so broke that you couldn't think of a word or phrase to describe your true financial position. "Short of funds" or "having an out-of-money experience" wouldn't come close.

If you have been this broke, or have experienced something similar to my adventure that I shared on pages 104 to 108, undoubtedly you imagined that you would be truly happy when you could enjoy a much better financial position. Yet you are likely in that well-off position today. Your happiness today, however, is probably far from what you imagined it would be. Your happiness may have not increased a bit, despite your wealth having increased considerably. This should be evidence enough that more money won't bring you more happiness. You may even be unhappier and more miserable now that you have greater wealth.

Indeed, several callers to radio talk shows on which I have been a guest admitted that despite their making incomes in the top 10 percent of wage earners, they weren't happy. Some were miserable. The host of one talk show asked a man making over $100,000 a year how he would rate his happiness on a scale of one to ten. The man replied, "I would be pushing it if I said four or five." Another caller revealed that she and her husband were much happier years ago when they

> Money is a dream — in fact, it can be a fantasy as deceptive as the Pied Piper.
>
> — Michael Phillips

were making $30,000 a year, and had to be creative to make ends meet, than they are now making over three times as much money.

When you fall into the trap of feeling unhappy and thinking that more money will make you happier, you should ask yourself, "How many more material possessions and how much more money do I need to be happy?" Take at least five minutes to think about this. Be careful. Your devious mind may play tricks on you. If your answer is that you want it all, you better ask yourself, "You want what? And how much money?"

To be fair, perhaps you want fewer possessions and less money than I do. The point is that the less you need in material and physical comforts, the freer you become. These comforts have their place but they should not be the highest on your list. When you need fewer material and physical comforts, you are much better prepared to pursue an unreal job or unconventional business for the initial period when you may not make much money.

I agree that giving me a big raise will not make me any happier at work — or even when I am away from work. But at least I will be able to afford to be unhappy and miserable in pretentious style in luxurious places.

Perhaps by now you are thinking that I'm trying to convince you to forget about earning more money than you earn today. Not at all! That is not my intention. As much as anyone else, I enjoy earning money and spending it on things that enhance my life and the lives of others.

Although the rumor that money doesn't buy happiness is, in fact, true, earning more money is not a total waste of time. Having financial peace of mind can be liberating. There are enough other problems in life without having financial problems to add to them. I just want to point out that the less money you need to be happy, the freer you become.

There, incidentally, is another important relationship between money and happiness, one that I hadn't noticed before I started writing this chapter. In three of my other books I claimed that more money won't bring more happiness. But I hadn't noticed that, in fact, it works the other way around — more happiness will bring more money! Put another way, first learn how to be happy with little or no money and money will come much more easily in your life.

> If you want to feel rich, just count all the things you have that money can't buy.
>
> — Unknown wise person

Ludicrous, no? Let's go back to the thirty-three elements of happiness listed on page 154. I assure you that if you take time to develop all these elements you will be one happy camper. What's more, virtually every one of these elements of happiness will help you earn more money. Clearly, if you are already in possession of all thirty-three, you are well qualified — better than the vast majority — to earn a lot of money. Better still, you are also well suited to work at an unreal job or at an unconventional business and create a lot more freedom in your life.

Financial Freedom Does Not Have to Be Just a Dream

Clearly, the biggest benefit from working at an unreal job or operating an unconventional business is about much more than making a lot of money. It's about having the freedom to live your life as you choose. You can imagine how prosperous self-employed people feel to be able to spend a lot of time with family and friends, take vacations when they want to, live wherever they want, and have no boss.

Money is still important to the extent that it is a means of survival, a foundation for comfort, and a tool to accomplish some of your life's goals. It can't guarantee happiness or health or love, however. Just as important, regardless of how much money you have set aside, it can't buy job satisfaction. Heck, money can't even buy "a dinosaur," as Homer Simpson pointed out.

> What good is freedom if you've not got the money for it?
>
> — Lillian Hellman

The most desirable thing that money can help you purchase is a good measure of freedom. I am not naive enough to believe that it can buy total freedom, however. There is no such thing as absolute freedom. The point is, generally speaking, you can enjoy more freedom with money than without it. Combine financial freedom with the personal freedom that comes with having an unreal job, and you will come as close to absolute freedom as is possible.

Financial freedom is having more options for doing the things you would like to do. "What financial success does is provide you with the ability to concentrate on other things that really matter," indicated Oprah Winfrey. "And that is being able to make a difference, not only in your own life, but in other people's lives."

You must be clear, however, about what it takes to attain financial freedom. Luckily, there is no secret to attaining financial freedom. Contrary to popular belief, financial freedom is not having a million or two in the bank. Financial freedom is simply having more money come in than goes out. If you are a master at handling money, financial freedom is much easier to attain than most people realize.

Derek Foster is a great example. Foster was featured in an article in *The Globe and Mail* about the time I was preparing to write this book. Surprisingly to most people, but not to me, Foster managed to retire shortly before he turned thirty-five without having had a high-paying job and without inheriting any money. Foster, a former telemarketer and Radio Shack salesman, has recently spent some of his surplus leisure time writing a book called *Stop Working, Here's How You Can!* (Check out the book on Foster's website at www.stopworking.ca.)

Foster challenges the popular belief that financial freedom is attainable only after decades of working hard at a high-paying traditional job. "What are you going to do with two-million dollars when you're eighty years old?" asks Foster.

> Always remember: Money has no power of its own.
>
> — Suze Orman

Perhaps you are married and have already assumed that Foster is single and has no kids. Wrong again, Sparky! Foster, in fact, is married and he and his wife have two children.

Although Foster has never had a high-paying job, he started setting aside $200 a month in an investment account when he was an early-twenties university student. Any unexpected cash, such as a tax rebate or a Christmas bonus, was also saved. Foster kept up the $200 a month contributions even when he backpacked Europe and spent time working and scuba-diving in Australia. This allowed him to acquire a modest investment portfolio along with a house worth $179,000 in Wasaga Beach, Ontario, by the time he was thirty-four.

Today the Fosters' family of four lives happily and freely on about $30,000 a year. Although his wife has a part-time job at a local ski hill, Derek Foster himself does not work. According to Foster, the key to being financially independent is to build a nice nest egg. Also, make lifestyle choices that reduce your overhead such as living in a small town where real estate is inexpensive. Then if you can structure your finances to minimize taxes and maximize government assistance available for families with children, you will have it made.

You don't have to lead a Spartan existence on $30,000 a year, adds Foster. "There will be no financial reason for me to ever get a job again," he told the reporter from *The Globe and Mail*. Because he had no desire to work, Foster was busy participating in — and adding to — his list of "things to do before I die," such as learning to play a musical instrument, doing a night of stand-up comedy, and possibly buying a recreational vehicle to take his family on a leisurely trip across Canada.

Derek Foster has a lifestyle that defies the ordinary simply because he has learned how to handle money, which has allowed him to attain financial freedom. Of course, handling money while you work for yourself or operate an unconventional business is critical since you don't have a regular paycheck to rely on. Paradoxically, having a lot of money can't buy the ability to handle money, given that many people who at one time had millions to their name are now broke. Thus, you can add the ability to handle money properly to the thirty-three elements of happiness that money can't buy.

Master, I have come all this way to ask you: What is the best financial advice you have ever given?

Don't buy expensive socks if you can never find them.

As I initially stated in *The Joy of Not Working*, money is actually quite easy to handle. Indeed, there are only two secrets. The first secret is: Spend less than you make. If this doesn't work for you, then the second secret is definitely for you: Make more than you spend. That's all there is to money.

If you earn good money and still have financial problems, you have to get your act together and do whatever it takes to spend less money. You certainly aren't going to get a call from the guys on Madison Avenue in New York who devise the glitzy ads that say, "Buy this expensive car and be cool, happy, and successful." They don't want to tell you that the ads are really false and that no amount of material possessions can make you happy and help you achieve personal freedom and financial independence. You have to discover these things for yourself and then keep your wants in check.

Perhaps you have financial problems because you earn way too little and can't cut expenses. In this case, if you want to upgrade from a dump you're living in today to something closer to the Taj Mahal in the next few years, you have to make some changes in your life. You will have to take a hard look at many things, such as the type of friends you have, how much TV you watch, your motivation level, how much of your creativity you use, your hard-core beliefs, your chosen career, your passions, and whether you suffer from the world-owes-me-a-living syndrome. To some degree, you will need to make some effort to either work more, change your line of work, or work smarter.

Some people get very angry when I try to challenge or shake up their money beliefs. One erroneous belief they hang on to is money can buy happiness. They also hold on to the erroneous belief that they can't make more money, even when they desperately want more. Sadly, self-limiting beliefs about money become self-fulfilling prophecies. You can succeed financially if no one else believes in you. But it is practically impossible to succeed financially if you don't believe in yourself — even if a million others do.

So again, the best way for you to attain financial freedom is to earn more and save more of what you earn. Pretty easy, isn't it? There is one major problem, of course: If you have been working at a corporate job for years, you don't have much control over your income. Sure, you can choose to work some overtime if it is offered to you, but this can be quite limiting.

The point is that if you are not controlling your income, someone else is. The problem with the corporate world is that most employees are at the mercy of their employers, dependent on what is given to them in the way of their salaries and raises. In the United States, some employers don't even provide healthcare coverage to their employees. If you want to increase your income, you have to look outside of your current job for a better source of income. This takes an entrepreneurial mindset instead of a typical employee's mindset.

> He who buys what he does not need steals from himself.
>
> — Unknown wise person

The late Joe Karbo, author of *The Lazy Man's Way to Riches* (F. P. Publishing Co., 1973) stated it best: "Most people are too busy earning a living to make [real] money." In this regard, one important benefit of what I do for a living is the opportunity to make a great deal of money in a relatively short period of time. One of my books appearing on *The New York Times* bestseller list, for

> All right, let's not panic. I'll make the money by selling one of my livers. I can get by with one.
>
> — Homer Simpson

instance, could end up earning hundreds of thousands of dollars for me.

A few years ago author Tom Clancy signed a record-breaking contract for a $45 million advance to write two books. This was encouraging to me because it meant that at least one author could make as much as the best-paid professional baseball or football players. The news for me got even better. Author J. K. Rowling, former welfare recipient and creator of the *Harry Potter* series, in 2003 actually made more money than the entire New York Yankees baseball team with a payroll of about $185 million ($205 million in 2005). *The Sunday Times* of London reported that Rowling earned £125 million (or about $215 million). "She is a money-making machine," declared Philip Berresford, compiler of the pay list. "She could be the first billionaire author."

Of course, I realize that I don't have much chance of ever matching the income of Tom Clancy or J. K. Rowling. But given that I am in a position to make $100,000 either this year or the next, I feel that it is possible for me to make $250,000, even $500,000 a year some time in the future. This is a privileged position in which to be, given that this income is much more than the large majority of corporate employees can ever expect to make in a year, even after forty-five years of service. What's more, I have my freedom and work at something I truly love.

You can enjoy a similar position in life simply because you have the talent to earn money without a real job. How do I know? Allowing for the fact that some people are mentally handicapped, almost everyone has. You didn't fall off a turnip truck and hurt your brain, did you? Given that you are reading this book, you undoubtedly have multiple talents. How many are you using in a positive way? Multiple talents can bring you multiple sources of income, if one source of income is not sufficient for you.

No doubt you can't make a great living without a real job if you don't have products or services that enrich people. You have to do something important, sell something important, or start something important in order to succeed financially. You have to see opportunities for profit all around you where other people see obstacles.

Be known as a world-class innovator in your field. Be all about big ideas and bold action. Over the next few days write out ten ideas on how you can improve your product or service so that more people will be able to benefit from it and want to buy it. Big ideas lead to big results; small ideas lead to small results, sometimes no results at all.

Once you have at least one great product or service, the number one enemy is procrastination. Many people have great ideas and plans, but few ever do whatever they claim they are going to do. If they want to succeed at developing and marketing their service or product, they may have to stop watching TV entirely, stop going for drinks with acquaintances from work, stop going to sports events, and stop shopping for junk — regardless of the name brand on it — that doesn't enhance their lives one bit. They must use the extra time and the money they save to get serious about their dream business.

You don't necessarily need blockbuster projects such as the pet rock or Paul Hartunian's Brooklyn Bridge idea to make good money. A series of small, profitable ones will suffice. It has been my experience that sometimes it's the small things, going the extra inch and not necessarily the mile, that can end up making you some real money.

> It doesn't matter if you're rich or poor, as long as you've got money.
>
> — Joe E. Lewis

Several years ago, I started writing a book called *The Lazy Person's Guide to Success*. Two or three months later, I did the title proud by quitting when the book was half completed. I gave up on the book entirely, thinking that no publisher would be interested. When a Spanish publisher requested a copy of another book, on a whim I decided to send half the manuscript to her as well, even though she hadn't asked for it. My devious, "reasonable" mind told me it was a waste of time and money to send the half manuscript, but my creative, "unreasonable" mind told me to send it anyway.

Surprisingly — to my reasonable mind, anyway — several months later this publisher made me an offer to publish the book in Spanish (she thought that the half-manuscript was the complete book). The opportunity to get another book published and an advance of $3,000 were sufficient motivation for me to finish the book. Later, I sold American and other foreign rights to a total of ten publishers.

The Lazy Person's Guide to Success has now made me over $70,000 in pretax income. Had I not sent the half-manuscript to the Spanish publisher, this book would never have been published and would not have added to my real success without a real job. This example shows the value of extra effort. A little can go a long way. In other words, it's the little things that count — many little things make it a big thing.

If you are afraid of leaving your corporate job without a proven source of income, then start small. Start a part-time business while you hold down a real job. When the business has proven to be successful, you can make the big leap and get your own "Corporate Employment Is So Last Year" T-shirt to wear with pride.

Again, there is no secret to attaining financial freedom. Financial freedom does not have to be a dream. You must search for ways to increase your income that are consistent with your purpose, health, and integrity. Then you must exchange the life energy that you are presently putting into your corporate job for the highest pay that you can extract from a dream job or unconventional business.

> If you want to sell 'em fish, sell 'em big fish. That's the secret to success.
>
> — Jack Solomons

When you are doing what you want to do, the things you enjoy, and the things that you are good at, life becomes much easier. There are at least four reasons for this: First, you get satisfaction in life. Second, you get to be very good at what you do. Third, money comes easier. Fourth, you feel good about how you earned your money.

No doubt many readers will want more information on how to earn more money and save more. I could write a 500-page book on this topic alone, but there are already a number of great books written by financial gurus such as Suze Orman, Robert Kiyosaki, and David Bach. These gurus all recommend proven basics — spend less, save more, and invest what you save — along with their own ideas on how to apply these basics. Any of the books by these authors can help you handle money and place you in a much better position to leave corporate life for good.

Based on my own evaluation and the reviews on Amazon.com, likely the best book for attaining financial freedom that provides a proven method for getting there is *Your Money or Your Life* (Penguin Books, 1999) by Joe Dominguez and Vicki Robin. Unlike a lot of get-rich-quick books, this tome is all about redefining your relationship with money and, as a result, your life's work. This will help change the way you use your time and make you more effective in creating a satisfying life that is rich on multiple levels.

Individuals such as Derek Foster, mentioned earlier, prove that financial freedom doesn't have to be just a dream. If you want to attain your financial goals, however, you have to do it all by yourself, regardless of how many books you read. Let me repeat this just in case you didn't get it! You have to do it all by yourself.

Derek Foster has done it by himself, I have done it by myself, millions of others have done it by themselves, and you have to do it by yourself. It's that simple. Otherwise, you won't get to experience the extraordinary lifestyle that is available to people who work at unreal jobs or operate unconventional businesses.

Your Prosperity Will Grow to the Extent That You Do

Now let's talk about prosperity, because freedom and prosperity go hand in hand. Regardless of how much money you make, it's pretty hard to feel prosperous if you work at a job that imprisons you. A recent British Social Attitudes (BSA) survey reveals that six in ten British workers are unhappy in their jobs. The survey also showed a majority of workers reporting:

- The feeling that their work is not useful to society
- Feelings of insecurity
- Exhaustion by the time they get home
- Work-related stress
- Worry over inadequate income

If the BSA findings are anything to go by, it appears that most jobs are spiritually devastating and corporate employment, by itself, is no cure for the above ills. This is why so many people plan to leave the corporate world for good. Interestingly, more than half of all female workers in Britain have already left or are seriously considering escaping the conventional nine-to-five working world in a bid to create their own dream job and reclaim their freedom.

According to a 2005 survey by global recruitment and human resource consulting firm Hudson, 73 percent of female professionals in Britain are disappointed with their career progress to date. What's more, 47 percent of all female professionals do not expect to be working full-time five years into the future. Preferring to follow a career path that offers flexibility, rather than fit in with the demands of the corporate world, British female professionals plan to set up their own businesses, work flexibly, or pursue a freelance career.

Of course, many people who appear to be on top of the world in their careers are terribly unhappy, not only these

> My outlook is that little things are the trip. I'm very happy with very little. Maybe that's why I have so much.
> — Linda McCartney

professional women in Britain. Although many people may have dreams to live a prosperous life similar to mine, my estimate is that only a small fraction of those who intend to do so will succeed. The ones that will eventually succeed will be the ones who are truly committed to their dreams. They must also feel prosperous enough to leave the corporate world for good. This, however, doesn't mean that they must have a big nest egg saved.

> To be without some of the things you want is an indispensable part of happiness.
>
> — Bertrand Russell

In a materialistic world, prosperity is unfortunately and invariably associated with hoards of money and countless possessions. To the truly prosperous people of this world, prosperity is prosperity in its purest and original sense. Prosperity comes from the Latin word *spes*, which means "hope and vigor." To the truly prosperous person, being prosperous means being positive and happy in the moment, regardless of the level of wealth one has acquired.

In another book, I indicated that money maintains its own rules. As a general rule, money doesn't seem to like people who are desperate for it. To experience more prosperity, you must pay heed to the following:

Six Little-Known, But Important Spiritual Rules of Money

1. If money becomes your primary focus in life, then money is all that you will get.
2. Spending a lot of money can get you trapped into thinking you are prosperous and having a good time when all you are doing is spending a lot of money.
3. The person with no money may be poor; however, not as poor as the person who has nothing but money.
4. Prosperity isn't a matter of acquiring how much money you desire; it's a matter of being happy with how much you presently have.
5. It is better to be out of money than out of new creative ideas on how to make money.
6. Above all, the value of money lies in the creative and spiritual uses to which it can be put and not in how many possessions it can buy.

Clearly, true prosperity is living easily and happily in the real world whether you have lots of money or not. I have had the fortune of being on both sides of the fence. I've been broke, over $30,000 in debt and having to borrow money to pay the rent. At one time I even had the sobering experience of sleeping in my car for two cold winter nights when the temperature was -21°F. Extremely cold, of course, but this is still far from the bottom. As Mike Todd said, "I've never been poor, only broke. Being poor is a state of mind. Being broke is a temporary situation."

Many years later I am fortunate enough to have a good income, be spending substantially less money than I earn, and investing a nice surplus each year. Having been broke on more than one occasion makes me a lot more grateful for the financial position I enjoy today. Yet I sometimes felt just as prosperous when I was broke as I do today.

> If you want to know how rich you really are, find out what would be left of you tomorrow if you should lose every dollar you own tonight.
> — William J. H. Boetcker

For instance, the year I wrote *The Joy of Not Working* I was in debt big time, but I was filled with hope and vigor, the true feeling of prosperity. I recall telling a few people that I had a good sense about the book and "it may just make me a million dollars." For the record, to date the book has earned me about half that amount and it still gives me a nice residual income whether I am awake or asleep. This would not have been possible if I hadn't felt prosperous enough to take up writing and self-publishing when I had no savings and little income.

Spiritual leaders say that as a matter of course prosperity will come when you are pursuing the right things with your life. To feel truly prosperous, you may have to leave the corporate world for good simply because prosperity and freedom go hand in hand. For some people this means having to give up a substantial amount of their income, at least for a certain period of time.

Most people are too afraid to give up a secure job because they don't think that they have what it takes to leave the corporate world. False beliefs about your limitations will hold you back from gaining freedom. No complaining and no victim stuff. Okay? The more loving your personality and the more love you have for life and your work, the more money you will attract and the more you will enjoy spending the money.

To make my point about the victim stuff, let me ask you this: How far do you think a young black woman, from a poor family, with a weight problem, and who was sexually molested as a kid can go in life? Most people with the victim mentality will likely respond, "Not very far. She has everything going against her, particularly being poor, having been sexually molested, and being black."

Now, if someone told you that this young, black, overweight woman from a poor family, who was molested as a kid, would become the most powerful woman in television, what would you say? I am not sure what you would reply but I am sure that "No way" is what a lot of people with the victim mentality would utter defiantly.

In fact, the woman I described is none other than Oprah Winfrey. Look where she is today. Arguably, she is the most powerful woman in television. Unarguably, she is also the highest paid. Her income is continually in the tens of millions per year. When *Forbes* magazine published its list of America's billionaires for 2003, it disclosed that Oprah Winfrey was the first African-American woman to become a billionaire. How do you think she arrived at her present position? I can assure you that it was not by adopting the victim stance that is so popular in North America today.

> I was going to buy a copy of *The Power of Positive Thinking*, and then I thought: What the damn good would that do?
>
> — Ronnie Shakes

Many people will argue that Oprah must have had a lot of good luck and big breaks along the way that other people don't get. At an early age I would also have attributed Oprah's success mainly to great luck and big breaks. Over the years, however, I have come to the conclusion that most of us experience great opportunities throughout our lives. The problem is that most of us don't take advantage of them.

Oprah was able to get to where she is because she didn't waste her time being fascinated by her disadvantages, like many people are. Again, extraordinary things are accomplished by ordinary people. Oprah is just one of many examples. There are many significant things in life that we all can accomplish. It takes getting above excuses. This is what Oprah had to say about her early life: "I knew there was a way out. I knew there was another kind of life because I had read about it. I knew there were other places, and there was another way of being."

So, as long as you believe, without doubt as Oprah did, in your prosperity, then you will experience a world in which you are prosperous and free of money worries. Consciously worrying about money or being subconsciously motivated by the fear of running out of money hardly ever produces great wealth. Trust that you will always have enough money to get by, even if you quit your job and pursue your dream career.

Indeed, your prosperity will grow to the extent that you do. Your personal growth may require that you overcome the fear of leaving a secure job for a less secure job, with less pay, but a lot more freedom. Not so long ago I received a letter from Dan Karpf of Andover, New Jersey. As I have said before, I am surprised by the number of interesting characters who have quit their full-time jobs after reading *The Joy of Not Working* to pursue a freer and more prosperous life. Dan Karpf was one of them.

> Every noble work is, at first, impossible.
> — Thomas Carlyle

> Dear Mr. Zelinski,
>
> I've wanted to write to you since I finished reading your book almost two months ago.
>
> After working for various companies for the past 17 years, I got fed up with the long hours and long commutes and wished for an easier life. Thinking about quitting the company I was working for after being cut down to three days a week, I came across your book.
>
> You have written down what I was feeling. Although I am too young to retire, why should I push and stress myself to come home to sleep and start all over again the next day? I had purchased a house by a lake two years ago and didn't have any free time to enjoy the country life I wanted to. By working three days a week, I found that I am able to pay my bills and survive.
>
> Cutting back useless expenses, and doing part-time consulting, I quit my job and never looked back. I am relaxing more, resting on my hammock, and cooking dinner for my wife who is still doing the commute. Although I am back at work, I set my own hours, and am home by 5:00. The summer is coming and I am looking forward to living in relaxation.
>
> Thank you for teaching me that life is worth living and is more than work! I recommend your book to everyone who is looking for a better life.
>
> Sincerely,
>
> Dan Karpf

You may be able to feel a lot more prosperous by making significant changes in your life as Dan Karpf did and millions of corporate employees do every year. Feeling more prosperous doesn't necessarily mean earning more money. Sometimes it means earning less money as Karpf now does. But he feels much more prosperous as you can tell from his letter.

The feeling of prosperity is available to you whenever you want it. Contrary to popular belief, it is an emotional state that has little to do with your wealth or the state of the economy. You can feel more prosperous in a one-room cottage than most wealthy people feel in a twenty-room mansion. Misers will hoard a lot of money and spendthrifts will spend whatever they have; you don't have to do either to feel prosperous. You may have to give up your secure, high-paying corporate job, however, and grow spiritually in the process.

To Acquire the Golden Touch with Money, Hang around People with the Golden Touch

Although money can't buy happiness, sooner or later you will likely want a measure of financial freedom that adds to your feeling of overall freedom and the feeling of prosperity that comes with it. What will help you acquire a great measure of financial freedom is the golden touch with money. Mastery of money is not something with which we are born. Like creativity, it is something we can learn.

> I make money using my brains and lose money listening to my heart. But in the long run my books balance pretty well.
>
> — Kate Seredy

People who are good with money are respectful of themselves and respectful of their money. A long time ago they learned the basics of earning money, spending it wisely, and investing the remainder to attain financial freedom. Most important, they don't spend their money before they earn it. These people also don't brag about their money and don't use their money to intimidate others.

People with the golden touch with money buy luxuries last whereas people who can't handle money buy luxuries first. To most of today's North Americans, having the latest trendy possession is almost more important than being alive. Indeed, instant gratification takes too long! With all the possessions they have acquired on credit, these people may portray the image of being well-off, but they get deeper in debt the longer they collect a corporate paycheck. Their preference for possessions is not the problem; their attachment to them is.

According to Thomas J. Stanley and William D. Danko, coauthors of *The Millionaire Next Door* (Pocket Books, 1998), most self-made millionaires are masters at handling money. They are not driving this year's model of car, they are not wearing designer clothing and Rolex watches, and they are living in a modest home. Indeed, most millionaires say that building financial independence is far more a priority than impressing others. These people who have the golden touch with money are more likely than the average person to have clothing mended or altered, wear a pair of shoes for eight to ten years, reupholster furniture instead of buying new stuff, and buy items in bulk and redeem coupons.

> The only reason a great many American families don't own an elephant is that they have never been offered an elephant for a dollar down and easy weekly payments.
>
> — *Mad* magazine

It behooves us to review the main discoveries of Thomas J. Stanley and William D. Danko in *The Millionaire Next Door*. According to Stanley and Danko, wealth attained by most self-made American millionaires is the result of a lifestyle of satisfying work, motivation, perseverance, planning, and, above all, self-discipline. Keep in mind that most of these individuals reached millionaire status before they were forty-five. There were seven common denominators among the 1,115 millionaires studied for the book:

- They choose the right occupation.
- They are creative in marketing their products and services.
- They live well below their means.
- They efficiently utilize their time, energy, and money in ways that support wealth-building.
- They put much greater value on attaining financial independence than displaying high social status.
- Their parents did not provide financial assistance to them.
- They encourage their adult children to be economically self-sufficient.

Although all of the above factors are important for attaining wealth, pay particular attention to the first two. Choosing the right occupation is a main premise of this book. Another premise of this book is that you must be creative in marketing your product or service, regardless of the unreal job or unconventional business you choose for leaving the madness of the corporate world.

One of the best ways to acquire the golden touch with money is to hang around with people who have attained financial prominence. Smart people learn from their own mistakes and really smart people learn from other people's mistakes! People with the golden touch with money have certain experience, ideas, beliefs, and behaviors that allow them to create and maintain their wealth. It is in your best interest to find out from the masters of money how to be a master of money yourself.

Some people will claim that money-wise friends are hard to find. Where do you look? Not necessarily at the pub with the fanciest cars outside. Remember the famous Texas saying: "Big hat, no cattle." One way to find money-wise friends is to attend courses on investments. People normally have money if they are learning how to be better investors.

If you know a millionaire, take him or her for lunch. Ensure that you pay for the meal. Don't cheap out! Go to a decent restaurant where the millionaire can tell you a few secrets of his or her financial success. An investment of one hundred dollars for lunch will bring you back a return of thousands of dollars of advice if you pay attention and utilize whatever you learn from the millionaire.

If the millionaire has experience and success in your field of business, don't be afraid to ask for his or her trade secrets. Successful individuals actually like to help others who are trying to make it in their field. They feel flattered that someone would ask them for advice. Successful people get a lot out of helping someone else succeed, including feeling needed, receiving praise, the fun of teaching, and feeling good about helping someone else. The more successful humans are, the less of a threat they will see in you, and the more likely they will be happy to give you advice.

> Always try to rub up against money, for if you rub up against money long enough, some of it may rub off on you.
>
> — Damon Runyon

On three occasions I have called millionaire David Chilton, author and self-publisher of *The Wealthy Barber* (Stoddart Publishing, 2002), which has sold approximately two million copies. Chilton was most helpful and gracious in giving me advice on the telephone. I know that I can phone Chilton anytime, but I also know that I shouldn't abuse the privilege. Chilton is a busy person and I try to ensure that I don't take more than ten minutes of his time. Anything over that and I should be paying him at least $100 an hour for his advice or flying to Ontario where he lives and treating him to an expensive dinner at a fine restaurant.

Wealth consciousness means having respect and admiration for accomplished individuals when you meet them. Several people I know constantly criticize all rich people with comments such as "Anyone who is rich has shafted other people to get to where they are today." Of course, this may be true of a small percentage of rich people, but it is certainly not true of all. Moreover, people who constantly criticize rich people will never become rich themselves because they would have to become someone whom they resent.

One of the most important elements for successfully hanging around accomplished individuals is not being envious or resentful of their success. When you encounter wealthy people enjoying their money, bless them and say, "Isn't it wonderful that they have attained so much wealth and are enjoying some of it?" There can't be any pretending on your behalf. Deep down you have to truly admire and be happy for wealthy people. Take delight in their success and you will be further on the road to real financial success yourself.

Try to Spend More on Your Career Training and Personal Development than on Your Next Hairstyle

If you have never done this, attend a two- or three-day motivational event sometime soon. One thing will stand out among the array of successful and polished speakers: They all will say that their success and polish is due to the self-help books they have read, the seminars they have taken, and the mentors with whom they have worked. Surprisingly, most will also admit that they were miserable failures early in their lives.

Take, for example, John Assaraf. He was the leader of a street gang when he was nineteen. Assaraf wanted to change his life but he didn't know how. "I got a job selling real estate," says Assaraf, "and fortunately someone took me to a sales training seminar." He has spent over $500,000 on seminars and coaching in the twenty-five years since then. It seems like a fortune — and it is until you learn that his current net worth is over $1 billion! The return on Assaraf's investment in education has been

> To make headway, improve your head.
> — B. C. Forbes

> You may be a redneck if . . . you have spent more on your pickup truck than on your education.
>
> — Jeff Foxworthy

approximately 2,000 percent.

Harv Eker, author of *Secrets of the Millionaire Mind* (Collins, 2005), advises placing money in different bank accounts, or jars if you don't have a bank account, for different purposes. One of the most important jars is the education jar. Eker states that you should allocate 10 percent of your after-tax income on education. My take on the 10-percent figure is this could be a touch high, particularly if you already earn over $5 million a year. I have allocated 5 percent of my after-tax income for my personal and business education.

The key is not to cheap out when buying information that can help you market your products, learn the latest trade secrets, and be a better person. If you borrowed this book from the library — particularly if you are a well-paid professional — then you are not really committed to real success without a real job. Being cheap will not help you feel prosperous and successful.

You may protest that borrowing a book from the library is a form of economizing. True, it can be if you can't afford the book. But economizing can create a "poor me" attitude toward money as well as all other areas of your life. You are likely feeding your subconscious mind poverty messages that will prevent you from ever becoming truly prosperous and successful.

I have particularly designated well-paid professionals because many are suffering from variations of poverty-consciousness. Several years ago, for example, a schoolteacher, who happened to recognize me from a newspaper article, approached me and asked me for a free copy of *The Joy of Not Working*. Go figure: A schoolteacher earning between $50,000 and $75,000 a year has the gall to ask me for a free book. For all this guy knew, I was making less than $15,000 a year — which was not far from the truth for the first several years of my self-employment.

Surely, if I had the attitude of this schoolteacher, I would never have achieved the success that I enjoy today. Most importantly, I don't cheap out when it comes to acquiring educational products that may help me be more successful and earn more money.

What's more, as already mentioned in chapter 5, I am generous with my books, not just for marketing purposes, but also for the sake of giving. I have donated over 12,000 copies — but I make a point not to give a copy to people who ask for one. Fact is, I would be doing them a terrible disfavor because it would help promote their poverty-consciousness.

Besides spending a lot of money on educational and motivational books, seminars, and CDs, I subscribe to both *Publishers Weekly* and *Book Marketing Update*. These two publications cost me about $650 a year. The subscriptions have more than paid for themselves. Indeed, the leads I have found and followed, along with several subsequent chains of events that resulted, have generated over $100,000 in extra revenue for me.

I am always dismayed by people who want to get into the writing or publishing businesses and have no problem spending money on the latest expensive material goods. But will they spend money on important subscriptions or products that could help them become successful in an exciting career? It has been my experience that over 95 percent won't. Luckily for me and other successful people in my line of business, these wannabes pose no extra competition to us because they are not truly committed to achievement and success.

If you want to be a success at an unreal job, try to spend more on your career training and personal development than on your next hairstyle. One of your best investments from your education account may be hiring a life coach. Coaching will help you get to your ideal lifestyle more quickly and elegantly. Surprisingly, even many of the most successful people have life coaches. As indicated earlier, several Fortune 500 corporate executives pay Tony Robbins a retainer of one million dollars a year so that they can call him anytime for inspiration and advice.

> When I get a little money I buy books; and if any is left I buy food and clothes.
>
> — Erasmus

Pay heed to Jelaluddin Rumi's poetic words written over 800 years ago, "Sell your cleverness, and purchase bewilderment," if you want to have more prosperity come into your life. Whether through a book, a magazine article, a seminar, travel to another country, or a conversation with a truly successful person, whatever it is that you undertake, always look to broaden your experiences and your education.

It should go without saying that education in itself is meaningless. You must put it to good use. Many people — usually the lazy, unmotivated, unsuccessful, and broke in this world — claim that self-help products don't work. Every time I hear someone say that self-help materials don't work, I am somewhat mystified. Underlying this statement is a belief that the materials are all bogus and that whoever created any self-help material is doing it strictly for the money. This is tantamount to saying that college professors and schoolteachers prepare all their lesson plans strictly for their wages and their students should view everything that is taught to them as being bogus.

I have no doubt — none at all — that skeptics who say self-help materials don't work are absolutely wrong. These products have worked for me; this is proof enough. What's more, do you think Oprah would have become as successful as she is if she had the same false beliefs about self-help material? Oprah apparently used a great deal of self-help material to help her get to where she is today. Here is her quote again: "I knew there was a way out. I knew there was another kind of life because I had read about it. I knew there were other places, and there was another way of being."

If you believe that self-help material doesn't work, no doubt it's hard to admit this belief is false and you should give it up for good. The problem is that if you don't give up your false beliefs, they will continue to bring you exactly what you have been getting in your life so far. Oh sure, by keeping your beliefs you get to be right about it. Unfortunately, being right at all costs is like being a dead hero — there is no payoff!

Then there are people who know that the principles in self-help material are useful but they don't ever get around to using them. In this regard, the Buddhists say, "To know and not to do is not yet to know." If you are like many people who have taken motivational and inspirational seminars and not put the material you learned to any use at all, then by all means, quit going. Spend your money on useless trinkets, booze, and VLTs instead. Just don't blame anyone when the Porsche Cayman S or BMW Z8 sports car you would like is driven by someone who has recently taken Harv Eker's "The Millionaire Mind Intensive" course.

> 'It's what you learn after you know it all that counts.
> — John Wooden

It has been my experience that the right educational products such as motivational books, seminars, and CDs can be much more valuable than an MBA for achieving real success without a real job. I should know. I have an MBA and have found virtually no material worth reviewing from the courses I took in the program. Yet I find motivational books, seminars, and CDs great resources for reminding me what helped me become successful at what I do for a living.

The book *Living the 80/20 Way* (Nicholas Brealey Publishing, 2005) by Richard Koch, for instance, serves as a valuable reminder how I can continue to work fewer hours than most people and still be more successful than they are. In my view, on a scale of one to ten, this great book rates an off-the-chart fifteen. My testimonial alone should be sufficient motivation for you to purchase Koch's book and not worry about the price. The $17.95 you spend on the book can bring you back a hundred times your original investment in extra time, money, and enjoyment of life.

Of course, you should not take all career and personal development advice as gospel. You do not need to take the techniques to extremes nor do you have to do everything suggested. Advice reflects one particular person's truth and view of the world. Take whatever useful ideas you need from career and personal development material. Every book, seminar, or coaching session should have at least one important tool, strategy, or insight. Take what appeals to you and discard what doesn't work for you. This applies to this book as well.

> Formal education will make you a living; self-education will make you a fortune.
>
> — Jim Rohn

Your creative mind is your greatest asset and you should be spending money to enhance it. Regardless of the amount you allocate for your career and personal development, this overall point is important. The money you put in your education account is an investment in yourself that can reap unbelievable returns. Search out the best tools available to open up your creative side, get you focused, and direct you toward attaining real success without a real job. These tools may cost you a tidy sum at the outset, but they will save you time and make you a lot more money in the long run.

Prosperity Spending Is Good for Your Financial Soul

Paradoxically, the most important thing that money can help provide is personal freedom, but earning or having a lot of money is not necessarily liberating to everyone. Although not a problem for most people, particularly today's North Americans, it is all too easy for some of us to fall into the trap of spending too little money. Once we have worked hard or smart for many years to create an independent income, it follows that we should be enjoying a portion of it.

Earlier in the book I mentioned my celebration to honor my twenty-five years without a real job. Before I committed myself to having it, I had talked about this event for months. Yet I almost decided not to have it. I feared it would be a flop. Worse, I also feared that the event would cost too much and deplete financial resources that I could use some time in the future.

Fortunately, I decided the purpose of the event was bigger than me; it was to reward all the individuals who had helped and supported me over the years. Virtually everything worked out. Indeed, because of synchronistic events, some things worked out much better than I expected. Instead of a small TV set to show tapes of my appearances on national television, a friend arranged to have his friend come in and set up a DVD imager and a big screen. Twice as many people showed up as I had estimated. Much to my pleasant surprise, three of my friends flew in from Toronto, 3,500 miles from my hometown.

Every person who attended, including the owner and staff at the restaurant where it was held, thought that my celebration was a blast. This event ended up costing me a princely sum but it was worth every cent I spent on it. One of the most important results was that I felt prosperous enough to have spent the money. What's more, I felt motivated to create other ways to earn more money in the future so that I could spend it on other fulfilling experiences.

The lesson I had to relearn from spending a tidy sum on this celebration was that having a good grasp of money means being good at spending a portion, not only being good at saving a portion. This is the only way money can add to the feeling of prosperity. Sadly, the misers of this world have proven that financial independence doesn't necessarily mean prosperity. Many people have put together a great fortune and have not experienced one bit of pleasure out of spending a portion. No doubt some millionaires would have difficulty spending $2,000 or $3,000 to celebrate an important personal milestone.

> Misers aren't fun to live with, but they make wonderful ancestors.
>
> — David Brenner

If you can afford it, but still feel afraid to spend money for something you truly want, you must learn that money is a means and not an end. Prosperity spending is good for your financial soul. Enjoying your money, provided you have truly earned it and haven't borrowed it, will motivate you to produce more. You will also have learned how to appreciate your money so that you can really enjoy yourself when you acquire much more money from one of your creative projects.

If you haven't learned how to enjoy your money, then give me a call. I can help liberate your money and show you how to enjoy it.

No amount will be too large for me. Granted, this is not exactly a project worthy of my receiving the Nobel Prize in Economics, but heck, this is one of the things I can be very good at — particularly when someone else is paying the tab. In the event I am overbooked, give Elton John or Michael Jackson a call. Either one will show you how to feel prosperous and enjoy money like never before.

If it's a crushing experience to spend money for something you would like and can easily afford, you haven't gained freedom — you have psychologically imprisoned yourself. What good is having a lot of money if you still do tasks that you hate? In fact, living ridiculously below your means is just as bad as living way above your means. Staying in a dive by choice, and no longer by necessity, doesn't make much sense. This is definitely a sign of poverty-consciousness and not prosperity-consciousness.

Feeling prosperous means paying your utility bills on time and with a smile on your face. Prosperity means not only giving to the homeless person, but having a smile on your face when you do it. Prosperity also means buying fresh produce with a smile on your face instead of buying day-old bread or bargain overripe fruit with a scowl on your face. Still more, being prosperous means tipping generously with a smile on your face when the waiter has given you great service instead of trying to stiff him with a mere 5 percent, or worse, no tip at all.

Even when you aren't earning a great deal of money, it's important to at least once a week do something to reward yourself — to feel prosperous and deserving of money. While I was earning an income under the government's so-called poverty line, and over $30,000 in the red due to my student loans, I would still have at least one dinner in a good restaurant each week. This was my declaration of my prosperity and of my forthcoming wealth. The weekly dinner was also a

Buying this new Porsche Cayman S with money from my prosperity account is the best thing I ever did. I used to get migraine headaches when I drove a Ford Escort!

reward for my being committed to my creative projects. Now that I can afford it, I have lunch at a restaurant or coffee bar every day, and I usually have dinner at a decent restaurant two to three times a week.

> No matter how rich you become, how famous or powerful, when you die the size of your funeral will still pretty much depend on the weather.
>
> — Michael Pritchard

Keep in mind that you have to put some money back into the economy if you want a healthy economy. If everyone became miserly, there is no telling how bad the economy could get and the discomfort it would cause many people. If you would like others to buy your company's products or services, you have an obligation to buy something yourself. This applies to downturns in the economy as well. During one recession I was dismayed to hear people with high-paying jobs talk about how they had cut their pleasurable spending and then complain about how their adult children could not find work.

With a healthy and balanced attitude towards spending and saving, enjoying your money and life in the present will help you accumulate more money in the future. Sacrificing all your disposable money for savings, and not enjoying at least a portion of it today on pleasure, is actually an act of stealing from yourself. It is unlikely that you will enjoy your money even if you become a multimillionaire.

Although I save a much greater proportion of my net income than most North Americans, I also have made a commitment to spend 5 percent of my net income on things that I don't need but would like to have. This money is placed in a separate "prosperity account" and is designated for things such as travel, music, books, and celebrations.

I would advise that you also create a prosperity account that is separate from your financial independence account. Allot 5 to 10 percent of your net income for things that you want but don't need. Ensure that you deplete your prosperity account every six months or so and spend every penny in this account for your pleasure. Don't be afraid to spend this money frivolously. When you can afford it, the money you enjoy spending frivolously is well spent.

Summing up, although money can't buy happiness, it can add to your enjoyment of life, which is the reason for having financial independence in the first place. Prosperity in itself will come when you are pursuing the right things in your life. Doing the right things in your life includes not only being in the right career, but also spending money on the right things and saving enough to accumulate a nest egg for sabbaticals, retirement, and emergencies. Along with the personal freedom that comes from not having a real job, financial independence will add to your sense of overall freedom.

7

Real Success Means Having Real Friends

The Richest Person Is the One with the Most Real Friends

"People report being happier when they are with friends than when they're with a spouse or child," according to research cited in a recent cover story in *Psychology Today* magazine. Think about this. People experience greater joy while spending time with their friends than while spending time with their children or with their mates. This should give you an idea of the value of friendship.

Interestingly, friendship is one of the most researched items on the Internet. Based on my field work, "friendship" is typed into search engines such as Google and Yahoo much more than "happiness." This indicates that hundreds of thousands of people are interested in making new friendships and enhancing old ones.

Given how important friendship is in our lives, have you ever noticed how little has been written on the subject? Compare, for example, the number of books written on how to handle money to the number of books on how to create and maintain great friends. Yet in many ways friendship is much more valuable than money. Indeed, our human interactions, particularly those with close friends, provide most of the joys or disappointments we have in life.

> If you can't make money, make friends.
>
> — Mezz Mezzrow

In my opinion you can't experience real success unless you have real friends. Therefore, I am devoting a whole chapter to friendship. About a year before starting this book I wrote a gift book called *Life's Secret Handbook for Having Great Friends*, which was turned down by a number of American and British publishers. I am confident it is a great book, nonetheless, given that it is being translated and published by major French and Spanish publishers. As a bonus to my English-speaking readers, I have adapted almost half of the content from *Life's Secret Handbook for Having Great Friends* along with some additional new material about friendship for this book. This is in keeping with one of the most important principles for achieving success in any unreal job or unconventional business — give your customers more than they expect.

Of course, the more success I end up having with this book, the more time I will have for friendship. It has been my experience that one of the great benefits of not working in a corporate setting is having the freedom to spend time with my friends virtually any time I want. Just as important, I have more time available to make new friends and don't have to spend time with workplace colleagues, who seldom turn out to be real friends.

> The richest man in the world is not the one who still has the first dollar he ever earned. It's the man who still has his best friend.
>
> — Martha Mason

Given that passing time with friends provides us with so much joy and happiness, the question you have to ask yourself is, "Am I seeing my friends as much as I should?" According to a recent study, Americans spend 8.9 hours a week with their friends. Canadians spend slightly less time than Americans with 8.7 hours and Britons spend more time with 11.1 hours. Interestingly, American men spend 10.4 hours weekly and American women spend 7.6 hours weekly.

Unfortunately, the modern work world makes our individual lives busier and more fragmented. The result is that many people neglect to devote time to making close friends. "Friendship seems to be the last thing that anyone's getting to," says Jan Yager, an American sociologist and author of several books on friendship. Yager adds, "Friendship is not something that you get to when everything else in your life is taken care of. It's an important relationship even after the school years for emotional health, for career advancement, for physical well-being."

For anyone who has left corporate life for retirement or self-employment, making and maintaining great friendships are keys to creating a new sense of community that translates into social, emotional, and physical well-being. Several research studies conclude that people who have intimate relationships with others live happier, healthier, and longer. On the other hand, lonely people who have few or no friends stand a greater chance of becoming ill and dying an early death.

> Winning has always meant much to me, but winning friends has meant the most.
>
> — Babe Didrikson Zaharias

Friendship should be a universal and all-encompassing topic for each and every one of us. Companionship is essential to a full and rich life. It ranks right up there with fulfilling work and good health. A 2005 study reported in the *Journal of Epidemiology and Community Health* concluded that having a strong network of great friends is even more important than relatives and children for a long and healthy life. When the research team began to study what types of social networks were key later in life, lead researcher Lynne Giles admitted she hadn't anticipated that friends would be so much more important, in terms of longevity, than children and relatives.

People in our society likely do not speak often to their yearning for friendship, as important as it is, because they do not want to appear needy and desperate. Not many people care to admit how lonely they are or can be at times in their lives. Surveys reveal that loneliness is one of the biggest problems humans face. To many people, it is the biggest.

Of this you should be certain: Life can be a really lonely experience without great friends. Above all, great friends can provide you with things that you can't. The reverse is also true.

So what is a friend exactly? A typical dictionary defines a friend as:

1. A person whom one knows, likes, and trusts
2. A person with whom one is allied in a struggle or cause
3. One who supports, sympathizes with, or patronizes a group, cause, or movement
4. A person whom one knows; an acquaintance

The typical dictionary, however, is not only vague, but a little confusing because it defines an acquaintance as:

1. Knowledge of a person acquired by a relationship less intimate than friendship
2. A person whom one knows

Oddly enough, the dictionary seems to say that a friend is an acquaintance but an acquaintance is not necessarily a friend. If there is more to a friend than merely being an acquaintance, what

> With money and wine, you will have many friends, but when you are in trouble, will you see even one?
>
> — Chinese proverb

is it? A confidant? A shoulder to cry on? An ear to listen when no other will? Someone to whom to talk nonsense and have the nonsense liked and honored? Someone to call at 3:00 o'clock in the morning? Indeed, a friend is all of these — and much more!

At this time it's important to touch on one major difference between friends and acquaintances. Acquaintances are like big Mack trucks — cumbersome, dull, and low maintenance. They lose much of their warmth and appeal soon after you first encounter them. Friends are like Ferraris — sleek, exciting, and high maintenance. Provided you look after them, friends keep their warmth and appeal forever.

Plautus, the Roman playwright whose works influenced Shakespeare and Molière, proclaimed, "Your wealth is where your friends are." Put another way, the more people who truly care whether you get up in the morning, the richer you will feel. You will find this to be true whether you are wealthy or broke. Indeed, given the importance of great friendship in our lives, the richest person is the one with the most real friends and not the one with the most money.

Ten Million Dollars Cannot Buy What Great Friendship Can

Although we may not realize it at the time, a chief event in our lives is the day in which we first encounter one of our best friends. If by chance you still don't precisely know why you need great friends, let's get you started: After you work hard or smart to achieve real success without a real job, it's important to enjoy your success and your freedom. Celebrations by yourself, you may have noticed, aren't much fun. They actually tend to be on the quiet side. Even if you have a dog or cat, sharing good news with it isn't quite the same as sharing good news with a great friend.

> Lots of people want to ride with you in the limo, but what you want is someone who will take the bus with you when the limo breaks down.
>
> — Oprah Winfrey

All things considered, happiness is one of the cheapest things in the world when we secure a good part of it through friendship. Portland resident Lenny Dee told an *Utne Reader* reporter, "I have always thought you could invest your energies in making money or making friends. And they achieve much the same ends — security, new experiences, personal options, travel, and so forth. I have always found it more fulfilling to make friends."

Money contributes to our lives, without doubt, but it's just that friendship contributes a lot more. At this point it is worth asking: Can true friends be bought? Not with money — luckily so for the happy poor and unfortunately for the lonely rich. Even so, friends have to be bought. To be sure, friendship carries a price tag — a big one at that. Hey, it should — it is one of life's greatest joys!

To find, win, and keep great friends, you must continually be paying a price. Although many people are not wild about having to continually pay a price for anything, that's just the way it is. The Universe has declared that this is how the friendship game is played.

The price you have to pay for friendship varies in substance and form. Most important, as will be expanded on later, you buy great friendship with intangible substance. You buy great friendship with the inspiration, advice, joy, support, and good feelings that friends expect from you. The major friendship maxim is that the best friends that money can buy will never even come close in quality to the friends that your character, integrity, and compassion will get you.

To be sure, friendship is not always easy — you may have to put in a lot of time and effort for it to work. To have a true friend is one of the highest prizes of life. To be a true friend in return is one of the most formidable tasks of life. In this regard, always remember that friendship is a verb and not a noun. Put another way, friendship is an active element that requires constant input for it to develop, survive, and thrive.

> A friend you have to buy won't be worth what you pay for him.
>
> — George D. Prentice

Whatever you do, don't expect something for nothing. Friendship doesn't work that way. At times, particularly when growing new friendships, you may even have to put more into them than you get out. But the rewards of paying the price to develop great friends can bring prizes that you never dream of.

If you have been paying attention in your journey through life, the following shouldn't be news to you: In many aspects of life, where money and other forms of wealth fail, friendship often comes in handy. Here is a real-life example.

This is a terrific story about friendship and how powerful friendship can be. It involves two long-time friends, Peter Elzinga and Tom Shields, in Alberta, Canada. Tom had been suffering from kidney problems for some time. Like many other patients, Tom was waiting for a transplant, and particularly a match, which is extremely hard to find. As in many countries, people in Canada are not allowed to buy or sell kidneys. They can donate them, however.

Peter offered to help if his kidneys were a match for his friend. In March 2004, after discovering he was a suitable donor, Peter gave one of his kidneys to Tom. Peter even fast-tracked his retirement from a government job so he could make the donation more quickly.

It was not only an incredible act of kindness, but one of courage, since Peter had to spend two to three weeks in the hospital, and could have suffered long-term side effects from his operation. What's more, a kidney-transfer operation is psychologically harder on the donor than the recipient; it's easier on the recipient because the donation will likely save his or her life.

> It pays to know who your friends are but it also pays to know you ain't got any friends.
>
> — Bob Dylan

Happily, both Tom and Peter have been doing fine since the transplant. Many people who know Peter Elzinga said that it was a typical unselfish act that he would do for any of his friends. It should set an example for you and me. What's more, it proves that even though ten million dollars may not be able to buy a new kidney, real friendship can. This leads us into some of the many more remarkable benefits to having a remarkable friend:

Things That a Great Friend Will Do for You But a Million Dollars Won't

- Give you a sincere compliment
- Provide great conversation
- Point out when you are doing something that is not contributing to real success in your life
- Help you deal with the pressures of life
- Vouch for your integrity and honesty
- Give you support and inspiration to do something that makes a real difference in this world
- Phone you when you are down and out
- Say to you, "You're a jerk and a cynic but I like you a lot anyway — that's why you're my friend."

Clearly, there are millionaires who don't have even one friend from whom they can receive any of the above. If you have one friend who does even one or two of these priceless acts for you, you are indeed richer than these millionaires.

Here is another cool real-life story about friendship: When U Tin Oo, a Buddhist monk, was asked how he was able to handle eleven years of imprisonment under the most unimaginable conditions, including solitary confinement, he replied that mindfulness meditation was helpful.

> My father and he had one of those English friendships which begin by avoiding intimacies and eventually eliminate speech altogether.
>
> — Jorge Luis Borges

"But most importantly," stated U Tin Oo, "I would reflect on the preciousness of my friendships. So in moments of difficulty, I would envision their faces one by one and talk to them a bit. I would recall our moments of laughter and the joys we shared. It's the love that you feel [for your friends] that keeps your sanity."

Perhaps you have noticed that attention and kindness from a true friend will warm your heart a lot more when you are sick than receiving $1,000 from a distant or crabby relative. To be sure, your best support during troubled times will always be a dear friend. According to an old Greek proverb, "It is better in times of need to have a friend rather than money." In fact, a great friend is someone with whom you can have fun even when neither of you has any money.

At this point it is worth remembering that friendship isn't important only when you are in dire need. Without great friends, a journey to an exotic foreign land can be really boring; a million dollars will not have much use; Christmas Day will be lousy; the most important of your accomplishments may appear worthless; and life, in itself, will not even come close to being as precious and fulfilling.

It's Not the Quantity; It's the Quality That Counts

"Friends should be few but good," advises another Greek proverb. Put another way, it's the quality and not the quantity that matters in the friendship game. The problem for many corporate workers, particularly men, is that they count time at work around the water cooler as time spent with friends. Clearly, casual acquaintances are not real friends, but to some people acquaintances

> There are plenty of acquaintances in the world, but very few real friends.
>
> — Chinese proverb

are counted as friends because they don't have any real friends.

As a matter of course, the only companionship and socializing many people get while zealously pursuing their careers is at the workplace. Generally speaking, what are known as "work friends" are acquaintances with whom employees are forced to spend a lot of time. What is commonly called friendship in workplaces is merely association among individuals who don't know what true friendship is. This is particularly true for workaholics who have no interpersonal contact outside of where they are employed.

In fact, over the years some workers become totally reliant on the company for social intercourse, so much so that they eventually lose the skills necessary to develop new relationships away from the workplace. Upon retirement, these ex-workers become social misfits. They no longer have the corporate social haven that provided them with familiarity, security, and community.

After twenty years of research in the area of friendship, sociologist Jan Yager (first mentioned earlier in this chapter) recommends that you tread carefully when making friends at work. Yager, author of *Who's That Sitting at My Desk?: Workship, Friendship, or Foe?* (Hannacroix Creek Books, 2004), says that it takes an average of three years to know whether or not someone is a tried and true friend. Yager uses the term "workship" to describe the typical work relationship, which is less intimate than a friendship but more than an acquaintanceship.

> Truly great friends are hard to find, difficult to leave, and impossible to forget.
> — G. Randolf

It has been my experience that what are known as "work friends" generally tend to not be real friends. If you are still fully engaged in corporate life and have no real friends outside your workplace, now is the time to make some. The fellow worker with whom you share a perverse interest in the weather and the fortunes of the New York Yankees is not likely to maintain any sort of relationship with you once you retire. Even if he or she wanted to, why should you bother? There is a lot more to friendship than talking about unpredictable things and superficial events.

There is also a lot more to friendship than talking about work. This may remind you of what Roger Rosenblatt expressed so eloquently: "Do not keep company with people who speak of careers. Not only are such people uninteresting in themselves; they also have no interest in anything interesting. Keep company with people who are interested in the world outside themselves. The one who never asks you what you are working on; who never inquires as to the success of your latest project; who never uses the word career as a noun — he is your friend."

Chances are that we won't ever experience true friendship with casual acquaintances that we encounter from time to time or those with whom we spend a lot of time for ulterior reasons. If social status is your basis for making friends, your friendships are not on sound footing. This is equally true if workplace association is the basis of your friendship. Generally speaking, we should not count on true friendship from colleagues.

Even if you feel that the workplace is a good place to make friends, having developed all your friends in a corporate setting limits your variety of friends and leads to an unhealthy balance in your life. It also makes it more difficult to separate yourself from your job. For a healthy balance in your life, you should be developing some independence and disassociating yourself from the workplace as much as possible.

Business associates or golfing buddies seldom turn out to be close friends. These relationships are normally based on goal orientation and competitiveness, which don't lead to true friendship. Work is where people are fighting for approval, raises, and promotions. People will be friends as long as you are not a hindrance to these desires. If you are, you won't be a friend for long. Friends at work can and do become enemies overnight.

Fact is, friendship at work is fleeting. When transfers and layoffs happen, such superficial friendship proves to be transient at best. Most people are surprised to find that when they retire their former work colleagues don't want anything to do with them, whether the former colleagues are still working or also retired.

> My mother used to say that there are no strangers, only friends you haven't met yet. She's now in a maximum security twilight home in Australia.
>
> — Dame Edna Everage

This can also be true if you are forcefully downsized from your job. After I was fired from Edmonton Power, I had virtually no contact with my ex-colleagues simply because they didn't want to associate with someone who was fired and who no longer worked in their field. Worse yet, I remained unemployed for quite some time so I was considered a total loser by these people. It was no surprise to me that three ex-colleagues whom I invited to my important celebration twenty-five years later didn't bother to show up.

On the other hand, Mike and Rob, two salesmen who used to

call on me at Edmonton Power and with whom I had only casual relationships at the time of my firing, became great friends. Twenty-five years after we met we are still in constant contact. In fact, I see Mike at least five times a year even though he and his family now live in Toronto. Recently, I was happy to take two days out of my routine and utilize $700 from my "prosperity bank account" to fly to Toronto for Mike's surprise birthday party arranged by his wife, Wilma, and his daughter, Sheri. Eight months later, Mike and Sheri flew to Edmonton to attend the event to celebrate my twenty-five years without a real job.

The nearer you are to leaving corporate life for an unreal job or for retirement, the more important it is that the majority of your friends not be associated with your job. As a minimum, you should have at least two or three friends who are close to you and to whom you can relate on a deeper level. These should be individuals whose company you enjoy and with whom you share a number of interests unrelated to your career. They should care about you deeply enough to want to spend a lot of time with you once you leave corporate life for good.

Friends developed through marriage can be just as fleeting as friends developed in the workplace. If you are married, regardless of how intimate you are with your partner, you still require close friends — not your spouse's friends, but your own. Clearly, they aren't real friends if your spouse has chosen them. Relying on your spouse's friends for companionship is not anywhere as fulfilling as having your own friends.

> The good fellow to everyone is a good friend to no one.
> — Jewish proverb

What's more, the older you get, the greater the chance that your spouse will die. This applies particularly to women, who tend to outlive their husbands. In the event that this happens to you, your own true friends can be counted on for support and continued companionship. In contrast, your spouse's friends are likely to drift away soon after your spouse dies.

The key to optimizing happiness is to cultivate quality friendships with a few happy and interesting individuals. Again, quality is more important than quantity. These should be individuals whose company you enjoy and with whom you share a number of interests unrelated to your career or your spouse.

As in many areas of life, less can be more in the friendship game. Although it's nice to have a lot of friends, too many will complicate your life. Succumbing to the temptation to have as many friends as possible will hinder your overall happiness, since it depletes your time, energy, money, and creativity, resources that can be better utilized in getting whatever else you want out of life. What's more, it's unlikely that you will develop many real friends if you spread yourself too thin among too many individuals.

Being popular — if that is what you desire — will not contribute much to how many true friends you acquire in your lifetime. In the truest sense, friendship is based on relationships that are held together by trust, respect, and mutual admiration. If you feel the need to be one of the girls or boys just to be popular, it's best that you head back to junior high and play the superficial games that teenyboppers play. Clearly, you need to be more developed and mature to play the adult friendship game.

Never feel bad being unpopular with a lot of people. This doesn't mean that you can't have friends. Socrates was unpopular. Freud was unpopular. Jesus was unpopular. Get the point? (If you didn't, the point is that all of them still had friends.)

It's just as important to put popularity in its proper place when you are looking for a friend. The fact that a person is popular doesn't mean that he or she will make a great friend. "A friend to all," warned Aristotle, "is a friend to none." Some individuals are not popular because they are different and don't fit in with the "me-too" crowd, whose members tend to imitate each other and aren't quite sure whom it is exactly they are trying to imitate.

> If you want to really know what your friends and family think of you — die broke, and then see who shows up for the funeral.
>
> — Gregory Nunn

The fact is that many genuine, but different, people are unpopular because peculiarity breeds contempt in our society. Yet it has been my experience that some of these unpopular people can make great friends. I would rather hang around genuine, different individuals who offend a lot of people than trendy me-too people who all talk and look alike and don't seem to offend anyone but me. My contention is that it is better to wind up with three or four true and genuine friends than twenty-five pseudo friends who are phonier than a tree full of elephants.

So what exactly is a "true friend"? "True," according to the dictionary, refers to someone who is "faithful, loyal, and sincere." Thus, a true friendship is a matter of degree. One friend may be more loyal and faithful than another. And yet both may be classified as true friends — versus the acquaintance who will take delight in criticizing you when others aren't around.

> If you have one true
> friend you have more
> than your share.
>
> — Thomas Fuller

All things considered, true friends add to your happiness and seldom, if ever, subtract from it. As Alice Walker concluded, "No person is your friend (or kin) who demands your silence, or denies your right to grow and be perceived as fully blossomed as you were intended."

Try surrounding yourself with people who radiate warmth, kindness, and a fresh perspective on life in general. You are likely to wind up with at least one true friend. In my view, a true friend is also someone with whom you can do something boring — and still enjoy it. Following are my favorite qualities that other people have indicated they cherish in a real friend:

Signs of a True Friend

- Goes out of his or her way to make time for you
- Will not abuse you in any way
- Will not take advantage of you in times of weakness
- Will get you to laugh when you get too serious about life
- Continues to be your friend even if you are unemployed or wind up bankrupt
- Still likes you despite your achievements
- Will defend you in your absence when someone says something nasty about you
- Helps you become a better person
- Will say when you have spinach stuck in your teeth

Most important, a true friend should remind you of the person you would like to be. Perhaps you haven't found "the real thing" in the way of friends. Thus the words of Ralph Waldo Emerson: "The only way to have a friend, is to be one."

> Friends are God's way of
> taking care of us.
>
> — Unknown wise person

This brings up an important question: Just what kind of friend are you? Review the above list to see how you measure up. Not only are the above qualities ones that you should look for in a friend, these are the same ones that you should develop and maintain if you want to attract quality friends into your life. Thus, do the things that will make you the sort of person you yourself would really want to hang out with.

If You Want to Soar with the Eagles, Don't Hang around with the Chickens

To be happy, virtually every one of us needs friends with whom we can interact personally, philosophically, and spiritually. Particularly if you can fit all of your good friends and yourself in a phone booth — and still have plenty of room to spare — you may want to expand your circle of friends. You may also want an extra friend or two to support you in your quest for real success without a real job.

But you know that it is not easy to go shopping for friends, regardless of how much money you have. This may well remind you of something you read in the wonderful fable called *The Little Prince*. "Men have no more time to understand anything," the fox said to the little prince. "They buy things all ready made at the shops. But there is no shop anywhere where one can buy friendship, and so men have no friends any more."

You may also be reminded of the song "You've Got a Friend," in which Carole King promises: "Winter, spring, summer, or fall — all you've got to do is call — and I'll be there." The problem is that you don't have Carole's phone number. Worse yet, you don't even know her. So where do you look for great friends like Carole? No doubt you realize by now that if you want new friends, you must go somewhere and create them. You can't wait at home to be discovered.

Put another way, it's time to hit the streets! But which streets? Where you go — and don't go — to meet others is just as important as how often you go. For instance, there's a lot to be said for raunchy night clubs, seedy barrooms, corporate functions, and possibly even bingo halls. These places attract and remove from other places a lot of people whom you wouldn't want to associate with anyway.

> You can always tell a real friend: When you make a fool of yourself, he doesn't feel you've done a permanent job.
>
> — Laurence Peter

On a slightly more serious note, if you have been looking for true friendship for a long time and haven't found it, you have been looking in the wrong places — or not enough places. Ann Landers advised us, "If you want to catch a trout, don't fish in a herring barrel." The same applies to friends. If you want to meet a great friend or two, don't hang out where idiots and ax-murderers hang out.

Assuming that you want to meet interesting people, you must

go where interesting people hang out. Don't expect to meet many artists where Hell's Angels are known to hang out — and vice versa. Similarly, if discussing philosophy is important to you, you probably won't experience this with a group of customers at a Tim Hortons donut shop, who normally discuss sports, TV shows, and little else. Perhaps visiting art galleries, museums, or planetariums doesn't seem like a good way to meet others; nonetheless, you are more likely to meet a like-minded person at one of these places than at the local pub.

Why don't you hang out at country clubs if you want to meet some new male friends?

Country clubs attract corporate executives and other riffraff I have no desire to meet or to get to know any better.

One key way to make new friends is to hang around people who have the same passions and interests as you. Common interests constitute one of the basic foundations for genuine and meaningful friendships. Pursue your interests that involve a social setting and you are bound to make new friends sooner or later. Whether your personal passion is chess, golf, tennis, dancing, paper-airplane making, pen bouncing, beer-can crushing, or generating false symptoms of severe physical self-abuse, get out of your home to where people congregate to pursue these same interests.

Meeting interesting people will depend not only on where you go, but also on how you present yourself. Taking a risk by extending yourself is one way to form a bond with someone else. The dynamics of social interaction and the foundation of friendships are based on the ability of the participants to give as well as to receive.

So, in the words of Abbott and Costello, "Who's on first?" Once you encounter people, someone has to initiate a relationship for a friendship to develop. Like it or not — and most people don't — you have to get to first base on your own if you're serious about playing the friendship game.

As always, start at the beginning. Be the first to say, "Hi." Put another way, instead of waiting for others to be friendly, take matters into your own hands and show them how. You shouldn't wait to be introduced to someone or expect someone else to initiate a conversation. Make your move and worry about the details later.

In her recently published book, *The Fine Art of Small Talk* (Hyperion, 2005), Debra Fine has several lists of conversation openers. These include "What was your best job ever?", "What was your worst job ever?", and "What advice would you give someone just starting in your business?" These three are not only great ice-breakers; they may also help you learn something valuable that will help you choose and become more successful in an unreal job or unconventional business.

Clearly, you will make ten times more acquaintances in a month by being interested in people than you will in a year by trying to get people interested in you. When you were a child, practically everyone you met had the potential to tell you something new and help you learn interesting things about the world. Refuse to be like most adults, who think they know practically everything they need to know and have nothing interesting to learn from someone new.

The Law of the Farm applies to friendship: "You reap what you sow." Clearly, if you want more friends in your world, you must take responsibility for meeting them, then growing them — and not someone else. How great your friends turn out will depend mainly on how great you are to your friends.

Your essence does matter! What do you stand for? What is your true character — behind your facade and your promises? Why would anyone want to hang out with you? Probably because you can make a difference in their lives, as you would like them to be able to make a difference in yours.

> A friend is like a four-leaf clover, hard to find but lucky to have.
>
> — Samantha Rosales

The more complete person you become, the more complete friends you will hook up with. To ensure that you show up as a complete person to others, stop being boring. Some people like to talk about weird stuff. Others like to talk about weirder stuff. Still others like to talk about the truly weird. If you are any one of these people, ensure that someone is really interested in your particular brand of weirdness before you spend an hour talking about it.

Clearly, being boring is one of the biggest obstacles to making new friends — and great friends. Being boring is the lack of adventure, passion, energy, humor, and charisma. The friendship game doesn't care what you have to do to stop being boring. As the

> If I don't have friends, then I ain't nothing.
>
> — Billie Holiday

Nike ad used to say: Just do it!

Here's a start: To avoid being boring, be different: Different looking! Different acting! Different talking! You may appear to be from a different planet — but this will make you interesting. What's more, it will give you charisma!

"Charisma, moi?" you may protest. Yes, you! According to experts on charisma, this elusive quality can actually be developed by anyone. There are certain principles that apply. Here are a few:

To-Do List for Developing Charisma

1. Look like a winner and act like one.
2. Have big dreams.
3. Build a bit of a mystique around yourself.
4. Be genuinely interested in others.
5. Have a great sense of humor.
6. Be known for your integrity.
7. Be patient and graceful under pressure.
8. At times be spontaneous instead of always predictable — predictable is boring!
9. Be kind and generous.
10. Regardless of your success, be modest.

Most important in the friendship game: Winners do what losers don't do. Just as telling — winners don't do what losers do! Put another way, it is just as important to know what not to do as what to do. So, after you have a To-Do List for developing charisma, it's just as important to have a To-Don't List! Here is a starter To-Don't List to help you make more friends:

To-Don't List for Developing Charisma

1. Don't walk around with that weird, always-take-me-seriously look.
2. Don't bore people with long stories that go nowhere; move on to something mutually interesting instead of beating the crap out of a boring topic.
3. Don't boast when you win in chess or other games; don't make excuses when you lose either.
4. Refrain from egotistical stories about yourself. When it comes to friendship, a big ego is its own revenge.

5. Don't make a point of trying to show people how much knowledge you have while declaring to people that you are no fool — they may develop deep suspicions that you are one.

6. Don't insist on being right all the time — particularly if you are afraid of being alone.

7. Don't be a victim of your over-education. When given a choice to be intellectual or pleasant, leave the intellectual to others.

8. If you earn a high income or have great success, don't look down on people who don't.

9. Don't judge people too much. It's tedious and won't make you many friends. Besides, judging other people is still God's job.

10. Don't become a me-too person. When you become like everyone else, you may as well be no one. When you become a me-different person, you become an interesting person.

Everyone has an interesting story to tell if you ask them for it. Being eager to learn new things is one of the best qualities to help you make many new acquaintances. Of course, the tangible rewards of meeting new acquaintances go far beyond the opportunity to learn something new. Some of your new acquaintances may develop into great friends.

Regular and close contact with others is a must if you want to develop new and close companionship. Take the initiative to call someone who is just a good acquaintance. More frequent meetings with a good acquaintance can result in a deeper relationship. Of course, having just one new companion can lead to others. Friends often develop in twos or threes or more. Mixing with your new-found friend's group of friends and acquaintances gives you the opportunity to develop your own circle of friends.

Although you don't want to associate with obnoxious people, you can't be too picky when choosing new acquaintances. Don't let your mind trick you into

I am beginning to like hanging around you. Can we be friends?

Only if you aren't rich. The richer my friends, the more they tend to cost me.

Perhaps the most delightful friendships are those in which there is much agreement, much disputation, and yet more personal liking.

— George Eliot

rejecting someone who may be good for you. It's best to suspend judgment for at least a short while. This will make a world of difference regarding how fast you create new acquaintances, as well as how many friends you ultimately create.

Given that even the most social of people usually don't meet more than twenty to fifty new people each year, you must give individuals a chance to show their essential qualities. No doubt there has been at least one person in your life for whom you didn't particularly care at your first encounter, but who turned out to be a great friend. People have a tendency to surprise us if we give them a chance.

In the same vein, never force or hurry a person to become your friend. Like the redwoods of California, great companionship takes time to grow. It must withstand the shocks of bad weather, many seasons, and unexpected adversity before it blossoms and matures. "We cannot tell the precise moment when friendship is formed," mused Samuel Johnson. "As in filling a vessel drop by drop, there is at last a drop which makes it run over; so in a series of kindnesses there is at last one which makes the heart run over."

Whatever number of friends you choose to bring into your life, the ideal is to have a variety — male and female and from all walks of life. What's more, let age play no part in your choice of companionship; try to have friends from all age groups. Particularly, try to have close relationships with individuals younger than you. They will influence you to renew your energy and have a fresh outlook on life. While older friends will help you grow old gracefully, young ones will help you think young — and stay young.

Don't overlook where many fear to go in search of friendship. Often the places most people don't want to visit conceal the biggest opportunities. The unknown and unexpected can add immensely to your experience of life and to the number of friends you have.

I don't need a friend who changes when I change and who nods when I nod; my shadow does that much better.

— Plutarch

Look for friends who think differently from you. Do keep in mind that it takes all kinds of people to make an interesting world. Just think how boring the world would be if everyone was exactly like you.

Be sure to seek out new people, new places, and new points of view. Talk to the young and the old, the sailors and the painters, and the waiters and the writers. Communicate with them, express yourself to them, and listen carefully, particularly if they have a different viewpoint from your own.

My thirst for power, riches, and success was unquenchable until I discovered whiskey.

Sounds like you are the type of male friend most women like me are looking for.

You live on a planet with over 6.5 billion human beings. Surely, you can find a good friend or two in this bunch of characters. Think how much harder it would be to find a friend on Mars. You would have to settle for a rock as your best friend. Luckily, on Earth finding the right people to create friendship with is a numbers game.

To get the most out of your companionship, choose your friends well! One of the greatest time-wasters and obstacles to success in all areas of life is associating with the wrong people. Yet surprisingly many people spend time with others whom they don't even like. Associating with the wrong people can cost you your time, energy, creativity, and money. They can even cost you your health — mainly mental.

For achieving real success without a real job, it helps to have friends who are going to inspire you to greater heights. "Keep away from people who try to belittle your ambitions," advised Mark Twain. "Small people always do that, but the really great make you feel that you, too, can become great." You want to hang around a group of motivated people with whom you can trade ideas, find inspiration, and not end up dejected every time you meet with them.

It is a terrible mistake to befriend a bunch of misfits solely because it makes you look like a genius when you are around them. After all is said — and mostly left undone — there is no glory in outdoing a bunch of muddleheads and blunderers. If you hang around with a bunch of misfits, you are likely to become one yourself. Just like them, you will come back from the Burger King with ketchup on your shirt after eating two more hamburgers than you should have.

Sure, negative people can come in handy if you are negative yourself. If you consult enough negative people, you can confirm any negative opinion you have of something or someone else. But being a skeptic is not in itself a virtue. What good is it to hang around with negative people who are going to pump you up with negative energy and negative beliefs? If you are like me, you already have enough of your own that you have to continually conquer.

The best strategy is to avoid endarkened people at all costs — hang around with enlightened people instead. Avoid people who set low personal standards that they constantly fail to achieve. Make friends, instead, with individuals who have big dreams for themselves. Hang around people who are making it in life, not ones who are barely hanging on. The former are much harder to find than the latter, but when you find them, the price you will have paid will be well worth it. Keep searching.

Generally speaking, birds of a feather flock together. So if you want to soar with the eagles, don't hang around with the chickens. Make no mistake about it. The degree of your happiness will be determined by the company you keep. So will the success that you attain without a real job. Keep good company and you shall become like them. Keep bad company and the same applies.

> Be careful with the environment you choose for it will shape you; be careful with the friends you choose for you will become like them.
>
> — W. Clement Stone

If we force ourselves into constant contact with "cool and creative," the odds are sky high that cool and creative will wear off on us. Hang out with cool and creative Web designers, for instance, and you will end up cool and creative. Ditto: Cool and creative life coaches. Ditto: Cool and creative janitors. Ditto: Cool and creative engineers (granted, having been an engineer in a former life, I realize that I may be stretching it here).

Interestingly, most people earn within 20 percent of the average income of their closest friends. I am not suggesting that you hang around wealthy people just because they have money. Keeping up with them could drive you into bankruptcy. Hang around people who can make a difference in your energy field. Successful people hang around other successful people to be motivated by them. They say, "If they can do it, I can do it too." Try to model yourself on their inner and outer strengths.

All too often, people admire successful individuals just because of the degree of money, status, or fame they have acquired. The key is to admire them, instead, for the obstacles they had to overcome to be successful and how generous they are with their money and advice in helping others less fortunate than themselves. Of course, these are signs that they can make a good friend.

The point is that a part of you becomes whom you hang around with. Drink coffee only with positive, focused people whom you can learn from and who will not drain your valuable energy with their constant complaining and lousy attitudes. By developing relationships with those committed to constant improvement and the pursuit of the best that life has to offer, you will have plenty of company on your path to the top of whatever mountain you seek to climb.

No Matter Which Way You Look at It, Flat Out — Great Friends Rule!

All things considered, friendship is truly one of the best gifts we can give ourselves. Great friends enrich our minds, inspire our imaginations, and enlighten our spirits. To be happy, we require friends in our lives because we have needs. It's rather tricky — probably impossible — for us as individuals to fulfill all our needs by ourselves. One friend may satisfy a certain need and another friend may satisfy a different need.

For a friendship to succeed, however, it must work both ways in all respects. You must trust your friends, and they must trust you. You must be getting something of value from them, and they must be receiving something of equal value from you. You must find them pleasant to be around, and they must find you just as pleasant.

> Don't make friends who are comfortable to be with. Make friends who will force you to lever yourself up.
>
> — Thomas J. Watson Sr.

You can have different friends for different reasons and different occasions. Apple friends are for when you want to experience the apple feeling. Orange friends are for when you want to experience the orange feeling. You can have many types of friends: Male friends. Female friends. Casual friends. Good friends. Great friends. Best of all, you can have one person whom you consider your overall best friend.

The great thing about friends is that you get to choose them, unlike relatives and colleagues you have to put up with in a workplace. Another great thing about friends is that you can dump them much easier than relatives or work colleagues when you no longer want them around. Of course, people get to choose you as a friend — and they can dump you pretty fast if they no longer want you around. After all, the friendship game is full of surprises — some good and some not so good.

While it may appear accidental, it's possible to dramatically increase the chances of meeting a new friend or two — and keeping them as friends forever. This is the really cool part: Once you understand the fundamentals of friendship, you may never have to be without any true friends. Ever again! Best of all, real friends will support you in your pursuit of real success without a real job much more than colleagues in a typical workplace will support you in advancing a workplace career.

Real success means that you have a lot of time to spend with your friends, and are in fact doing so. This leads to an important reminder: If you are working hard to attain whatever success means to you, but don't have time to make any real friends, or spend time with ones you already have, you ain't no success! After all, isn't having good times with great friends what life is ultimately all about? The truth is that you may go broke, become divorced, and get fired — but as long as you have real friends to spend time with, you still have life and happiness.

Above all, great friends make life complete. Have you ever noticed that when you have dinner at a restaurant with a good friend, a lousy meal will end up tasting a lot better? Good friends will also make a long journey seem a lot shorter. They will be there to make you feel better if you get into a fight with a spouse, work colleague, or relative. Best of all, even ten minutes in the company of a good friend will make any lousy day — even with a little bit of hell in it — worth living. Ultimately, great friendship doubles your joys and expels most of your sorrows.

> Parents start you off on life but friends get you through it.
> — Dee Chou

At this time it is worth remembering something else worth remembering: With a great friend by your side, nothing is ever so good that it can't get better — including having attained real success without a real job. This is what makes the difficult task in growing great friends so worthwhile.

EPILOGUE: Pets. Spouses. Kids. These are all worth having in life. Even careers, money, and possessions are okay in their own ways. But, flat out — great friends rule!

8

It's All in How You Play the Game, Isn't It?

It's Never Too Late to Be What You Might Have Been

Over the last few years, whenever working on a new project, I have reflected upon the words of Thomas Carlyle: "The best effect of any book is that it excites the reader to self-activity." In this regard, I hope that this book will infect you with the motivation and commitment that you require to pursue some of your dreams.

Whether it's making new friends or having a more fulfilling career, a dream not acted upon will remain just a dream. The strongest single factor for attaining any one of your dreams is self-esteem — believing you have talent and creativity, believing you deserve your dream, and believing that it is possible for you to attain the dream.

It's important to contemplate the wisdom of this Chinese adage as it relates to your dreams: "If you get on the train today, you'll overpay your fare. But if you don't, you'll be left behind in the dust." In other words, you can pay the high price today that has to be paid for you to pursue your dreams, or you can keep waiting for the perfect moment when you don't have to pay the price, and end up never getting to where you want to go.

> The cost of a thing is the amount of what I will call life which is required to be exchanged for it, immediately or in the long run.
>
> — Henry David Thoreau

Most of us, above all, are committed to comfort, low risk, and stability. We don't want to work at anything important in life; on the contrary, we want all the important things in life to come without any obstacles, stress, or difficulty. When we are comfortable, we say we are "feeling no pain." Unfortunately, feeling no pain is not synonymous with the memorable experiences of accomplishment, satisfaction, and creative fulfillment that come from pursuing and attaining our dreams.

It comes back to the issue of commitment: You should constantly challenge yourself as to whether or not you are truly committed to pursuing your dreams. You need to determine what you want in life and do whatever it takes to make it happen. If you don't, you are likely to wake up the day you turn sixty and wonder why you didn't take that vacation, make more real friends, or chase that dream career.

Some time ago a number of individuals, all over sixty years old, were asked what advice they would give themselves if they had life to live over again. It behooves us to pay attention to six of their most important suggestions:

How to Be More of a Person than You Have Been

- Take the time to find out what you really want to do with your life.
- Take more risks.
- Lighten up and don't take life so seriously.
- Be more patient.
- It's best to suffer from the Peter-Pan syndrome — relive your younger days. What were your dreams when you were young?
- Live the moment more.

> The deepest personal defeat suffered by human beings is constituted by the difference between what one was capable of becoming and what one has in fact become.
>
> — Ashley Montagu

That is to say, you don't want to leave this world with songs unsung that you would like to sing. Nor do you want to end up on your death bed pleading, "Lord, give me one more shot and I'll give it all I got." It's best that you start singing these songs today if you want to ever sing them. Instead of spending most of your spare time watching TV or wondering whether there is life after death (sorry, there are no points for this one), spend more time experiencing life after birth by chasing your dreams.

As a kid what was your answer to the question "What do you want to be when you grow up?" At one time we all had dreams of becoming someone we looked up to, such as a musician, a police officer, a bank president, or a train engineer, to name just a few.

When I was in my early teens, for instance, my dream was to be either a schoolteacher or a businessman. Unfortunately, I made the mistake of going into engineering because of a school principal's dubious advice.

Being in prison is punishment; so is work that is not done with joy — as I found out by being an engineer. Perhaps you, like many people, are a firm believer that "work was not meant to be fun — that's why they call it work." More power to you. In fact, congratulations! You don't have to take any action and can continue to get perverse satisfaction from all the suffering and complaining in which you love to immerse yourself.

I hate this job as much as the last one.

Cheer up, Harry! In the afterlife you won't have to look for work!

Just keep in mind this little bit of wisdom that comes from Edmond Bordeaux Székely in his book *Creative Work: Karma Yoga* (Academy Books, 1973): "If you feel that work is a punishment or hardship, or if you have no desire for work, or live in the hope of retiring soon — do not think you are entertaining the thoughts of a wise man; you are merely dancing to mental tunes that savages played ten thousand years ago."

Fact is, work can be fun and satisfying if you are prepared to make it happen. A better way of life is available to you if you are presently trapped in the corporate world. Escaping corporate life can give you the freedom to become more of a person than you have ever been. Why not take advantage of it? Remaining in a lousy job will ensure that you never become the person you have always wanted to be. You have to ask yourself: "How long do I work at a lousy position before I have too much of working in a lousy position?"

> It is better to begin in the evening than not at all.
>
> — English proverb

The good news is that it's never too late — or too early, for that matter — to change direction in your life, to be what you might have been. Of course, those who are resistant to change at thirty will be even more resistant to change at ninety-three. Don't be one of them. If you keep doing what you have been doing, you will keep getting what you have been getting well into infinity and beyond.

Ron Smotherman in his book *Winning Through Enlightenment* (Context Publications, 1979) concluded: "Satisfaction is for a very select group of people: those who are willing to be satisfied. There aren't many around." Do you want to be in the select group of people who are satisfied in their careers? If the answer is yes, then you have to keep making the following personal inquiries:

Important Career Questions

- What am I good at?
- How about my strengths and weaknesses?
- What talents and accomplishments do others give me compliments for?
- Which talents and strengths would I like to use and improve in a career?
- Who does work that I would like to be doing?
- What work would I do for free just for the enjoyment?

Keep asking these questions every day for the next year if you have to. The answers may eventually lead you into work that you can be passionate about. Your true calling will likely appear when you are ready for it. This may not be until you are forty or fifty or even sixty. The good news is that you can trade your corporate job for a real good life at any age provided you have the courage and conviction to make it work.

> You don't get to choose the life you have, but you do get to choose who you are going to be in it.
>
> — Unknown wise person

If you want to be successful working in an unreal job or unconventional business, pay attention to what successful people are doing in similar jobs to what you want to do. While making life-altering changes to create a fulfilling lifestyle is not always easy, millions of dissatisfied employees have shown it is possible. They have gotten their emotional acts together, left the corporate world, and accomplished what the majority have not. It is no wonder that these individuals live happier and fuller lives.

Still another example of a person who left corporate life is Jules Maidoff, who quit the New York rat race to pursue his dream. When he was in his mid-thirties, Maidoff experienced the traditional success to which millions of people aspire. It took him awhile to realize that what the majority aspire to is just mass ignorance in action.

Part of New York's artistic elite, Maidoff owned a hugely successful graphics-design studio in Manhattan and was part of the city's artistic elite. His workday, however, wasn't just an eight-hour affair — a good sign for anyone that he or she is either in the wrong job or is doing it wrong. Maidoff spent long hours at work, later hurrying to socialize with the bigwigs of New York at cultural events and parties well into the night.

"The years raced by," Maidoff told a *CNN/Money* reporter. "I wasn't seeing the seasons. I wasn't seeing my wife. I wasn't watching my children grow up the way I wanted to." So when he was forty, Maidoff bought a farmhouse in a small Tuscan village outside Florence. Three years later, he closed his New York firm and gave up all the trappings of traditional success. He packed up his family and moved them to the farmhouse in Italy.

Maidoff's plan for success without a real job was to make it as an artist. Although he had painted part-time for years, Maidoff made his move with nervousness and reservation. He had no idea how he would do and whether anyone would buy his art.

> It's the people who risk going too far who find out how far they can go.
> — T. S. Elliot

Several years later, Maidoff, sixty-three at the time, was enjoying a lifestyle that is about as good as it gets for an artist. Not only was he living in Tuscany, his paintings were being featured in galleries around the world. Some of his works had already been featured in exhibits along with the likes of Niki de St. Phalle, Cy Twombly, Man Ray, and Alexander Calder. Moreover, Maidoff had been invited to exhibit or received awards from such prestigious centers as the Pennsylvania Academy of Art, the Museum of Modern Art in New York, and the Corcoran Gallery of Art.

Maidoff insisted that his talents hadn't given him any unique advantage to pursue a lifestyle that many others only dream about. I wholeheartedly agree with Maidoff. A similar lifestyle to the one Maidoff is enjoying isn't available only to people who get it as a retirement prize after toiling away at a high-paid job that they hate for several decades. People can create unreal jobs with similar lifestyles at any age.

Sadly, many people — even those with exceptional talent and significant financial resources — continue to toil away at jobs they hate because they are afraid to give up the trappings of traditional success. If you are one of them, no doubt there can be a privileged, cut-above-the-crowd feel to having a high status job with great pay — until you factor in the fact that you have no creative fulfillment and virtually no freedom. Even worse, you are not happy.

If your work doesn't give you personal satisfaction, or you have stopped learning and being challenged, this is a good sign that you should move into another career altogether. Pay attention to what

Jules Maidoff told the *CNN/Money* reporter about what it takes to have a career and lifestyle similar to his: "My advice is take charge of your own life. You have to ask yourself, 'What is success?' I asked [myself], 'Is the American New York dream of success my dream?' My answer was, 'No.'"

All told, Jules Maidoff is experiencing real success without a real job because, like me, he didn't accept society's definition of success. Real success is about commitment, courage, and taking risks, which are all necessary for the kind of personal fulfillment that we all want. As indicated in chapter 1, one of the keys to success is not accepting society's definition of success as our own.

I find you particularly intriguing. You don't have a Ph.D. in literature, political science, or any other unique specialization. You don't even have a master's in philosophy! Why in the world do you want to drive a taxi?

Real success, in my view, is being true to yourself. "If the world is really just a stage and we are all actors," asks Phil Humbert, "what kind of play are you writing with your life?" The way to awaken and create the best script for your life is to examine the lifestyle that you are presently leading. Following are a list of questions you should ask yourself to ensure that the main character in your life does not have to experience the same old worn-out plot and the recurring, boring drama:

- Am I in control of my lifestyle?
- What does success mean to me today?
- Does my career allow me to utilize my best talents and creativity in interesting projects?
- What am I achieving and planning to achieve that makes me proud?
- What more can I do that is creative or unique?
- Am I continually learning something new in the career field I have chosen?
- Am I making as much money as I would like?
- Do I make the most of my money to give me the best quality of life and the financial freedom I would like?
- Do I get all the satisfaction that I want from my job?

- Does my lifestyle complement my partner's?
- Do I spend enough money on my personal education?
- Do I complain too much, particularly about my job?
- Do I criticize people who are successful instead of blessing them?
- Do I take sufficient vacation time?
- Do I have enough real friends in my life and do I devote sufficient time to see them?
- Do my time commitments allow me to make a contribution to making this world a better place?
- Am I grateful for what I already have in my life?
- Do I do something special for myself every day?
- Am I living in the right country or in the right part of the country?
- What will make me feel better about my career?

Above all, ask yourself what would give you true happiness. Listen to your answers carefully. Once you know what will make you happy, you must not wait for destiny to show you the way. Do whatever you have to do to attain it. You cannot afford not to.

> Success is when you don't know if you're working or you're playing.
> — Warren Beatty

Whatever you dream of doing, begin today. "Twenty years from now you will be more disappointed by the things that you didn't do than by the ones you did do," warned Mark Twain. "So throw off the bowlines. Sail away from the safe harbor. Catch the trade winds in your sails. Explore. Dream. Discover."

Look Ma; Life's Easy

Perhaps even after reading this far you are still convinced that it is best that you forget all this nonsense and stick to a real job, for fear that you will find yourself in the poorhouse in no time, with the wolf at your door. Nothing is certain in life so I can't make any guarantees either way. Remember, however, that negative thoughts often create your reality and life ends up sending you pretty much what you expect.

Sometimes the most difficult aspect of adopting a more relaxed and prosperous lifestyle is just beginning it and dealing with the criticism and objections of other people, including friends and relatives. Most people don't want you to succeed at something that they consider unrealistic. They themselves don't want to subject themselves to any risk that being without a real job entails and certainly would not like to see someone thrive at a lifestyle that they only dream about.

A little over a decade ago my net worth was on the minus side to the tune of $30,000. What's more, the bills were coming in faster than I was able to rip them up. Yet I never had to declare personal bankruptcy and today I have no financial problems.

One of the reasons for my present financial success is that I kept telling myself that sooner or later my risk-taking would pay significant rewards and that I would pay off my debts. This was not merely positive thinking; it was dynamic, productive thinking. Indeed, calculated risk-taking has produced extraordinary results for many ordinary people.

> A positive attitude may not solve all your problems, but it will annoy enough people to make it worth the effort.
> — Herm Albright

If you have had financial worries for a long time, likely you haven't found out how to use your imagination and creativity to turn a passion into a money-generating unreal job. In most Western nations it takes enormous skill and effort to constantly experience a lack of success and a state of poverty-consciousness — in fact, more than it takes to achieve a modest amount of success and wealth. Real success and wealth do not require hard work and long hours, just creativity, risk-taking, persistence, and enthusiasm for what you do.

Success is a game that is better played when it loses its huge psychological charge — when you realize that you are not desperate for success. Even if you don't have much money, what you do have is overwhelming creativity to generate whatever it takes to achieve something important that eventually generates a substantial amount of money. There is more than enough opportunity to earn money — you don't have to fight or suffer for money, just find an enjoyable way to earn it.

In fact, attaining real success without a real job is relatively simple. "Simple does not mean easy!" you may yell out in protest. You are right — to a degree — because in many ways, even wealth is easier to acquire than real success. You can inherit wealth, for instance, but you can't inherit real success.

Luckily, there is a way to make the game of attaining real

success without a real job much easier. You are about to discover an awesome paradoxical life principle. It is called The Easy Rule of Life. In fact, I wrote a complete book on this life principle; the book is called *Look Ma; Life's Easy* (ironically, one of my best books, which is published in Spanish, French, Korean, Russian, and Chinese but, alas, not English).

Following The Easy Rule of Life can get you from Loserville to Success City in record time. (You may also want to call this principle The Easy Rule of Success.) Once you master it, you will know whenever you are taking a way-too-casual and blasé approach to something that couldn't be more serious and important to you. This is a diagram of The Easy Rule of Life:

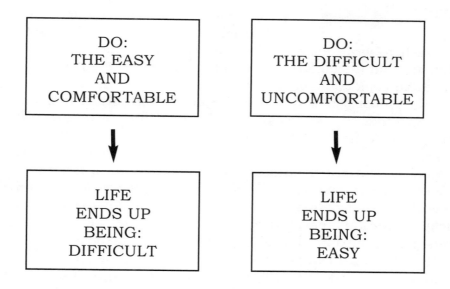

The premise of the Easy Rule of Life is that when you always do the easy and comfortable, life turns out difficult. When you regularly do the difficult and uncomfortable, however, life turns out easy. Think about it carefully, and you will see how this rule applies to all areas of your life.

In particular, think about how this awesome paradoxical life principle applies to attaining real success without a real job. To be sure, real success without a real job will not always be easy — you may have to do many difficult and uncomfortable things to attain success. But once you attain success, life will be much easier.

Moreover, life will be much more satisfying because you have accomplished something extraordinary. Indeed, you could win the biggest lottery in the history of lotteries and you wouldn't get the satisfaction that comes from attaining true success on your own.

Be clear that The Easy Rule of Life is unforgiving, especially to those with the victim mentality. Self-proclaimed victims seldom accomplish anything worthwhile, to say nothing of the disappointment and grief they put themselves through. Being a victim may make you feel secure and comfortable, because it's familiar territory. There are no real payoffs, however.

> The biggest sin is sitting on your ass.
>
> — Florynce Kennedy

The Easy Rule of Life tells you that each day you should be doing something difficult and uncomfortable. If you have always wanted to write a book, for instance, but have resisted doing so, you should force yourself to write for an hour each day. This may continue to be difficult and uncomfortable for a long time, but eventually you will have the book completed.

Alas, most people would rather be comfortable, which just goes to prove that real success is not for everyone. In this regard, you must be different from the masses — be willing to be uncomfortable! If you want to become a professional speaker, but would be scared half to death to speak in front of more than two people, then choose to be terribly uncomfortable. Make your first speech in front of one hundred people. What's more, be willing to deliver your first speech wrong, but at least do it. You will feel great because you will know that you have done your best.

If you want to be truly alive and experience a sense of achievement and satisfaction, you have to concentrate on doing many difficult and uncomfortable things, not just one. It's difficult and uncomfortable to be highly organized; it's difficult and uncomfortable to pay attention to the important things in life; it's difficult and uncomfortable to save money; and it's difficult and uncomfortable to keep agreements. Regardless of how difficult and uncomfortable these things are, give up your comfort zones and start doing them.

Throughout this book I have recommended a lot of great career books. If you immerse yourself in these books, if you let these books work their magic on you, you can have a career you love. How many have you decided to read? If you haven't given these books more than a passing thought because it would be way too much work to read them, then you are not all that committed to changing your life.

It's easy to wring your hands and whine about the lack of opportunity in today's world. It's much harder and more uncomfortable to acknowledge that there is a lot of opportunity, spot it, and capitalize on it. If you are not doing something risky and uncomfortable every day, you are stagnating as a human being. There are probably at least one hundred different areas in your life in which you are taking the easy and comfortable way at this time.

Most humans believe that anything which is extremely difficult shouldn't be attempted. This is, of course, pure nonsense. On the contrary, the idea that something is extremely difficult is a good reason for tackling it. Every extraordinary achievement was once considered not only extremely difficult, but impossible by the experts. Yet this did not stop the people who pulled off these achievements. Think Thomas Edison! Think Albert Einstein! Think Mother Teresa! Think Richard Branson!

> The greater the difficulty, the more glory in surmounting it.
> — Epicurus

"But my life is already difficult and I don't want it to be more difficult," you may vehemently protest. "I am sure my abilities don't match Edison's, Einstein's, Mother Teresa's, or Branson's. Because I have had a tough life already, I am afraid of doing anything new on my own. I don't like making mistakes and most of my family and friends will likely make fun of me if I fail."

Let me try to put this as delicately as I can: So what? In case you haven't heard about him yet, let me introduce you to an amazing individual from Vancouver, B.C., in order that you can put your own life and your own circumstances in proper perspective. When he was only nineteen, Sam Sullivan sustained a broken neck in a skiing accident. The accident that fateful day paralyzed him from the neck down and confined him to a wheelchair for the rest of his life.

During the first two years after the accident, Sullivan lived with his parents; then he moved into a rehabilitation facility and went on welfare. Each year he became more dejected about being a quadriplegic, and his life in general. Seven years after the fateful day, at the age of twenty-six, Sullivan realized that he had lost his youth and his life was wasting away.

Sullivan became even more depressed because his life wasn't going to get any better, given the hopelessness of his situation — or so he thought. At this point he seriously considered cashing in his chips — in other words, putting a gun to his head and pulling

> No matter how qualified or deserving we are, we will never reach a better life until we can imagine it for ourselves and allow ourselves to have it.
>
> — Richard Bach

the trigger — instead of carrying on with life.

In fact, Sullivan did kill himself. Ouch! Well, fortunately not in the literal sense, but "figuratively," Sullivan told a reporter with *The Globe and Mail*. "I actually went through with the whole thing in my mind, saw it actually happening, and after I did I said to myself, 'Okay, it's over. I just killed Sam, now what?' I imagined my soul leaving my body and someone else's soul taking its place."

That day, Sullivan saw the incredible opportunity that life had to offer, even for a quadriplegic with minimal use of his hands. He realized that he still had his most precious resource — his creative brain — and with that he could make every day a gift for the rest of his life.

"After that I lost all the baggage I'd been dragging around with me," Sullivan told the reporter with *The Globe and Mail*. "All those expectations, all my dreams and hopes that I had before the accident, they no longer plagued me. It was all I used to think about for a long time. After that day I never thought about them again."

Indeed, Sam Sullivan came back to life that day and took on new dreams with courage and zest that puts most of us to shame. He started several nonprofit companies and took classes at Simon Fraser University, where he earned a degree in business administration. Here are just a few of this remarkable character's many other incredible accomplishments: He learned how to drive a car fitted with special hand pedals, taught himself Cantonese, and mastered the art of flying an ultra-light aircraft.

One day Grace McCarthy, the former deputy premier of British Columbia, suggested Sullivan enter politics. So he ran for city council, got elected, and spent twelve years serving his city. This gets much better, however! In November 2005, twenty-six years after the skiing accident, Sam Sullivan, forty-five at the time, was elected mayor of Vancouver, the third largest city in Canada, one of the most beautiful cities in the world, and the designated host of the 2010 Winter Olympics.

Three months later, the Vancouver mayor traveled to Turin, Italy, where the 2006 Winter Olympics were being held. Sergio Chiamparino, the mayor of Turin, was to complete the ceremonial task of handing the giant sixteen-foot Olympic flag to the mayor of the next Winter Olympics venue. By tradition, each mayor was supposed to wave the flag as he clutched it. This presented a problem for Sullivan, given that he had limited use of his hands. Grabbing the flag was out of the question, let alone waving it.

Someone suggested that Sullivan could have an assistant take the flag while he sat alongside in his wheelchair. This would have been the easy and comfortable way out for him but he would have no part of it. "That symbolism doesn't work for me or my life," said Sullivan. He attacked the problem with his creative mind and had the Vancouver city engineers design a special device to fit on the side of his automated chair so that he could wave the flag himself.

Sullivan has likely never specifically read about The Easy Rule of Life in one of my books, but he certainly knows about the way it works and its merits. Notwithstanding that his days before traveling to Turin, Italy, were filled with budget meetings and feuding politicians, he spent some time secretly learning how to speak Italian. He then astonished the Vancouver media, *The Washington Post* reported, as he rolled around the Turin airport speaking perfect Italian to the employees who helped him into a specially fitted van that accommodated his electric wheelchair.

If you were fortunate enough to see the closing ceremonies of the Turin Winter Olympics, which I went out of my way to see on TV because of Sullivan, you will have to agree that it was a sight to behold. Sullivan made Olympic history gliding on to the central stage in his electric wheelchair. Turin Mayor Sergio Chiamparino passed the Olympic

> Do just once what others say you can't do, and you will never pay attention to their limitations again.
>
> — James R. Cook

flag to Jacques Rogge, president of the International Olympic Committee, who inserted the flag into the special pole holder attached to Sullivan's wheelchair. Sullivan obviously enjoyed being under the spotlight as he moved his wheelchair back and forth with a hand control and waved the flag eight times as is the custom in the closing ceremonies.

After his return from Turin, Sullivan was inundated with fan mail from people around the world who had learned a few things about him and had seen him wave the Olympic flag at the closing ceremonies. Sullivan received more than 1,000 letters and e-mails; among the fan mail were personal stories from individuals struggling with personal tragedy or disability, who claimed Sullivan inspired them to seek a much better life — or just better live the one they already have.

Politicians use a rule of thumb that for every letter they receive,

> If you aren't living on the edge, you're taking up too much space.
> — Unknown wise person

there are one hundred other people who feel likewise. It follows that Sullivan probably inspired tens of thousands of others around the globe, who did not bother contacting him, to seek a better life, too. It is my hope that placing his story in this book will inspire another ten thousand individuals — including you and me — to much greater heights.

The crux of the matter is that if Sam Sullivan — as a quadriplegic — can accomplish all the things he has, you can certainly create a rewarding lifestyle if corporate life is not for you. Deep down, practically every one of us is aware that we have talent and potential that we are squandering. We also know that we can make a big difference and improve this world if we use this talent and potential. Unfortunately, it's much easier to subconsciously suppress our talent and potential and fit in with the mediocrity of the masses, who claim it's only the privileged who can achieve anything significant in this world.

Yet greatness — as exemplified by Sam Sullivan — has never been determined by luck, status, power, possessions, or exceptional ability. The foundation of greatness is good character, comprising such things as risk-taking, individuality, courage, and overcoming major obstacles and opposition in accomplishing something extraordinary that is of service to others. Contrary to popular belief, it's not because the successful people of this world get all the breaks; the most successful people play the success game in a completely different way than most people do. They simply follow The Easy Rule of Life and say, "Look Ma; life's easy."

Whether you like it or not — and it has been my experience that most people don't — the degree to which you follow The Easy Rule of Life will determine how much satisfaction and happiness you achieve throughout your whole life. Start using The Easy Rule of Life and your life will change remarkably. You will want to kick yourself for having taken so much time to implement it, but at least you will have gotten your life to work at this time, and you can go forward from here.

How long does it take to change your ways and start using The Easy Rule of Life to your advantage? But a second or two. Then the uncomfortable work begins to keep changed. One day at a time — forever! Repetition makes the master. When you eventually achieve true success in your life, you will pat yourself on the back and exclaim, "It's all in how you play the game, isn't it?"

Failure Is the Universe's Way of Ensuring That Too Much Success Doesn't Happen All at Once

Although this book is about pursuing your dream career via an unreal job or operating an unconventional business, remember that there is no such thing as a perfect job or business. Regardless of the route you take to real success, you will always have to overcome barriers and adversity. What's more, you will have to experience failure.

> You miss 100 percent of the shots you never take.
>
> — Wayne Gretzky

But failure, put in proper perspective, can have its positive aspects. For instance, I first self-published my international best-selling book *The Joy of Not Working* because I was quite sure no major publisher would be interested. Surprisingly, I still failed to get an American publisher after the book had sold 10,000 copies in Canada the first year, which is the equivalent of selling 100,000 copies in a year in the United States. In fact, twenty-five American publishers still rejected my Canadian bestseller. Talk about getting no respect! Following is a form rejection letter that I received from one of the publishers:

Dear Colleague,

Thank you for sending us the proposal/manuscript. We regret that we are unable to use your material. As you know there are many reasons to decline a manuscript, so please do not consider this to be a judgment on the value of the work. We just don't see this particular piece fitting into our list at this time.

We wish we could respond to each proposal with a personal note, but the heavy volume of submissions we receive makes it impossible to do so. Please be assured that your proposal was given careful and thoughtful consideration.

Thank you for your interest in Ten Speed Press.

Sincerely,

The Editors

Perhaps you have noticed that the publisher that sent me the above letter was none other than Ten Speed Press, whose imprint is on this book, and that distributes it for me. This gets even better. Ten Speed Press now actually publishes *The Joy of Not Working*, which it agreed to undertake five years after it rejected the book, because by that time the book had sold 50,000 copies in Canada.

Note that I am finding value in reminiscing about the failure that I experienced some time ago, and even having fun with it. I now get to place the rejection letter that my publisher sent me well over a decade ago in another book that I have had published in association with it. Be clear that I am not doing this out of spite for Ten Speed Press. I am deeply honored to have had this prestigious publisher release several of my books and I have great respect for Phil Wood, the owner.

The core of the matter is that my success would not have been attained if I hadn't been willing to continue promoting and marketing *The Joy of Not Working* in the face of all the rejection and failure I endured — and I endured a lot. Yet today many authors and wannabe writers say how "lucky" I am to have Ten Speed Press publish and distribute my books. I agree there's also a certain element of "luck" associated with being successful at anything. The point, however, is that no luck will come your way unless you keep taking some form of positive action when a lot of failure shows up in your life.

> If at first you do succeed —
> try to hide your astonishment.
> — Harry F. Banks

Anything worthwhile requires risk and in virtually all arenas of life risk is directly proportionate to reward. Generally speaking, the higher the risk, the higher the reward. Whether you want conventional success or real success as you define it, you must be willing to take risks. As indicated in chapter 4, one of the greatest risks is failure.

Failure plays a big part in every success story, but not everyone appreciates how big of part it plays. Failure, in fact, turns losers into winners. Every winner knows that you must be willing to lose a few battles in order to win the war. "A [real] failure is a man who has blundered," stated Elbert Hubbard, "but is not able to cash in the experience."

Truth be known, all truly successful people are creative and take calculated risks, expecting that they will experience a good measure of failure. They know that the journey to real success will always require a lot of failure, which, contrary to public belief, is good for us. "We live in an age of publicity and hype. There's something about success that dehumanizes you," claims award-winning film producer Norman Jewison, "whereas failure reminds you of who you really are."

It has been my experience that the key to real success without a real job is to fail more than the average person is willing to endure. If at first you don't succeed, you are about average. Never overlook the power of the law of averages, which says that if you try enough times, you are likely to succeed sooner or later. It follows that if you double your failure rate, you are also likely to double your success rate. Thus, you should be eager to fail if you want to succeed.

> Many of life's failures are people who did not realize how close they were to success when they gave up.
>
> — Thomas Edison

I am not saying that you will necessarily succeed in every area of life that you attempt. You may, in fact, try one field of endeavor, fail at it, wind up in another field, and succeed wildly at it. Perhaps you didn't know that Mark Twain had to endure his share of failures. He lost considerable money on patents that he thought held great promise. Twain registered three patents under the moniker Samuel Clemens, which was his real name.

One patent was for Mark Twain's Memory-Builder, a pegboard game to help people learn the history of the world. His other two patents were for an adjustable strap on the back of a vest and a scrapbook with preglued pages. None of these patents ever made Twain any money. Yet he was able to adapt to these flops and not have them interfere with his being a successful author.

Above all, failure must be taken in stride and with humor. After having lost over $40,000 on one of his patents, Mark Twain declared, "I gave it away to a man whom I had long detested and whose family I desired to ruin."

Viewed from a spiritual point of view, failure is the universe's way of ensuring that too much success doesn't happen all at once. Failure is also the universe's way of ensuring that you enjoy your success once you attain it. In short, a life without failure won't get you anywhere worth going — a life with a lot of failure will, however. Again, it's all in how you play the game, isn't it?

Do Your Best and the Best of Things Will Come Your Way

Leaving corporate life would be more appealing for some people if I told them that attaining real success without a real job was easy for me, but I can't — because it wasn't. The good news, however, is that it was a heck of a lot easier than it would have been for me to work at a real job for the twenty-five years that I have been without one. One of the keys to achieving what success means to me was doing my best.

> People forget how fast you did a job — but they remember how well you did it.
>
> — Howard Newton

Real success without a real job requires motivation, effort, and excellence on many levels — as it should; otherwise there would be no satisfaction from attaining this success. In simple terms, the object is to operate out of excellence as you pursue your dreams. Choose a reasonable amount of time you would like to work. It can be eight hours a day, or it can be as little as two or three. Then ensure that you give it your best within that time frame — no more and no less.

Generally speaking, I choose not to work more than five hours a day; I am intense when I work, however. And I always try to do my best. At least one reputable publisher has published or will publish every one of my fourteen manuscripts, including this one. Yet book experts estimate that only one out of ten manuscripts written in North America ever gets published. How do I attain my success rate of 100 percent while writers as a whole attain 10 percent? I simply do what has to be done. Five of my books were originally rejected by publishers; therefore, I self-published them first to prove their worth in the marketplace.

As I mentioned earlier, even my international best-selling book *The Joy of Not Working* was originally self-published because I felt no publisher would be willing to publish it. Since then it has been published, not only by Ten Speed Press, but also by sixteen foreign publishers. Moreover, the book has sold over 200,000 copies worldwide. You can well imagine that this gives me a great sense of accomplishment. Plain and simple, I would not have been able to claim this success if I had not done my best in the four or five hours I work each day.

To experience similar success in any field of endeavor, you must also take risks and do your personal best. Just for the record, shortly after I began writing this book I happened to look at *The Art of Seeing Double or Better in Business*, the first book that I ever wrote. After skimming through a few pages, I realized how badly written it was. The fear that I wasn't good enough to write this book soon gripped my mind. But I soon realized that the fear was irrational (in bleak moments there is often a ray of sunshine).

The fact is, I did my best while writing my first book, and I have done my personal best ever since, improving my writing ability over the years. All I have to do is keep doing my best. There is no more that I can ask of myself. I will still attain much more success than millions of North Americans who have much greater talent and ability than me, but seldom, if ever, do their best.

Doing your best should be a lifelong journey. The measure of your success is not how well you have done relative to anyone else in society. Instead, the measure of your success should be how well you have used your creativity and ability to achieve worthy goals, regardless of how humble these goals are.

Doing your best means rising above the mediocrity so prevalent in society today. Being average just won't do. Indeed, most people are so mediocre that it is not necessarily a great compliment to say that someone in particular is above average.

If you don't want, as George Thorogood sang in his famous song, to "Get a Haircut [and get a real job]," then you must do your best and pay whatever price it takes to become a success without a real job. Avoid clinging desperately to the concept of traditional success and doing your best will come more naturally.

> If you don't want to work, you have to work to earn enough money so that you won't have to work.
> — Ogden Nash

Most people don't do their best because they don't enjoy what they do. They are working primarily for the reward of the paycheck, at the same time resisting the jobs they don't like. As a result they don't know the definition of excellence and never do their best. If you ask them how they are doing, they will reply, "Average." They even think that being slightly above average is quite a remarkable accomplishment.

Take a little time and list the things that promote your being average, including the people with whom you hang around. To rise above mediocrity you must remove everything in your life that represents mediocrity. Surround yourself with people and things that represent excellence and you will be inspired to do your best so that you, too, represent excellence.

"If you don't do it excellently, don't do it at all," advised Avis President Robert Townsend. "Because if it's not excellent, it won't be profitable or fun, and if you're not in business for fun or profit, what the hell are you doing here?"

Fact is, real success in our chosen careers comes from excellence, which requires that we constantly produce results beyond the ordinary. We must always try to go past the psychological limits we impose upon ourselves. This starts with the commitment to excellence, which is the commitment to do our absolute best regardless of the circumstances that we encounter.

For instance, if you are going to go broke, do your best at it. As the Texans advise, "Go broke big!" You don't want to declare personal bankruptcy due to a mere $5,000 personal investment. Declare personal bankruptcy because you have given it your best in a business venture where you have lost $500,000 or more. There is not one self-made millionaire or billionaire who has never lost money big time. You have to do the same if you want to become filthy rich some day.

Truly successful people know that we cannot forecast or know everything before we act. To get in the game, we have to get in with what we have. As emphasized in chapter 3, extraordinary things are accomplished by ordinary individuals — the only difference between the extraordinary and the ordinary is the "extra." The most successful, in the end, are those who define their own goals and do their best in trying to achieve these goals. They also do their best with the time they have available to them.

> I owe my success to having listened respectfully to the very best advice, and then going away and doing the exact opposite.
>
> — G. K. Chesterton

In chapter 4 we discussed the importance of using your time where it gives you the best results. Following are, in my view, the top ten worst and top ten best uses of your time. If you want to attain the freedom that comes not having a real job, I would strongly suggest that you adopt the latter.

The Top Ten Worst Uses of Your Time

1. Doing what everyone else is doing
2. Complaining about your situation in life and arguing why you are a victim
3. Criticizing others, particularly those who are rich and successful
4. Watching television
5. Gossiping and talking on the telephone
6. Doing things other people want you to do but you don't really want to do
7. Regretting the past and worrying about the future
8. Shopping and buying things that you can't afford
9. Working at things you hate or are not good at
10. Working at a lousy real job

The Top Ten Best Uses of Your Time

1. Attempting different things that hardly anyone else is doing
2. Utilizing inspirational books and tapes to educate yourself about your unreal job or unconventional business
3. Developing intellectual property
4. Meditating and exercising
5. Laughing and playing and celebrating life with your friends
6. Doing things that relate to your overall purpose in life and that bring you real success without a real job
7. Enjoying the present moment for all it is worth
8. Saving and investing your money in optimum ways
9. Doing things that you love and are good at
10. Working at a great unreal job

At the heart of using your time well is not to indulge in any blaming and any complaining. You must take absolute responsibility for your career and the rest of your life. You will do your best when you want to do something, not because you have to do it, and not because you are trying to please somebody. No one will ever expect you to achieve the impossible. You must not hope to be more than you can. It is not always possible to achieve as you want, but only as you can. Only in knowing your limitations, and doing your best, will you come closest to perfection.

> Read something every day that no else is reading. Think something no one else is thinking. It is bad for the mind to be always a part of unanimity.
>
> — Christopher Morley

If you enjoy what you do, and you always do your best, you will have no regrets. If other people try to criticize you for your lack of traditional success, you won't have to accept the poison they are trying to inflict on you. In your heart you will know "I have done my best at what I love and I have no regrets."

Another key to achieving real success is the suppression of resentment toward successful people who represent excellence. Spend more time in the presence of masters instead of resenting them. Bless the masters and learn from them. The way to become a smarter person is to find a really smart person and pay close attention to what he or she has to say.

In the same vein, never wish deprivation or unhappiness unto others. What you would like to deny others, you will eventually deny yourself. Your thoughts won't affect people who operate out of excellence; these thoughts will negatively affect what you attain in your life, however. Therefore, be happy for others who experience the success and joy that you would like for yourself.

> Perfection is our goal, excellence will be tolerated.
>
> — J. Yahl

Enjoy the company of masters and be receptive to their wisdom and any advice they give you on how you too can be a master in your field. Allow the experience to inspire you to greater heights so that miracles start happening in your life. Again, by miracles I refer to personal achievements that are out of the ordinary and that you once thought impossible.

Write down the ten best qualities of individuals whom you admire and who represent excellence to you. For instance, the quality of punctuality represents excellence. To people who operate out of excellence, punctuality is being there early or on time. Excuses for tardiness — none whatsoever — just don't cut it in the realm of excellence.

Each day when you rise, read the list of qualities that represent excellence and focus on these qualities. Strive to embed these ten qualities within yourself throughout the day. Soon you will notice small differences in yourself. After a month or two, at least a few of these important qualities will have become truly yours.

Above all, doing your best at working toward your dreams takes constant effort even if it's only four hours a day. Just as telling, you have to be incredibly determined to make these dreams happen. Do your research, follow up, and, most important, don't give up. Trust me on this one: Do your best at the things that are important to you and the best of things will come your way.

Ah, Real Success Without a Real Job — There Is No Life Like It!

The goal of this book has been to raise your consciousness about what it takes to escape the corporate world and make a better life for yourself. Besides those cited in this book, thousands upon thousands of individuals have successfully changed their work so that it better matches their personalities and preferences. You can also make the great escape from corporate life by adopting the success principles in this book. Here is a summary of what it takes, in my view, to make your dream of having a remarkable and satisfying lifestyle come true:

Ten Golden Rules for Attaining Real Success Without a Real Job

1. Choose work that you truly enjoy.
2. Choose an area that allows you great freedom.
3. Don't make your main purpose earning a lot of money.
4. Create an unreal job or start an unconventional business.
5. Choose an area that you can expand to multiple streams of income.
6. Identify your target markets and serve them well.
7. Be creative, particularly in generating new ideas and in marketing your products and services.
8. Spend big bucks on your career development and learn from the best in your field.
9. Contract out anything that you dislike or are not good at.
10. Work as hard as you have to for a good living — and as little as you can get away with!

Now is the time to take all the important material in this book that is relevant to your life and run with it. It is my wish that you will be motivated enough to undertake the difficult things that have to be done in the short term, so that your life becomes easier in the long term. As you should have learned by now, life isn't always easy.

> Success follows doing what you want to do. There is no other way to be successful.
>
> — Malcolm S. Forbes

In fact, as I approach the completion of this book, I am glad that life is not as easy as many people would like it to be. Writing intently for at least three or four hours a day, instead of taking it easy for the last four months, has reminded me of the great satisfaction and other rewards that come from undertaking difficult, challenging, and sometimes frustrating projects. Of course, I still have other challenges ahead; the major one is marketing the book so that it doesn't fade away into the land of nowhere as happens to the vast majority of the 200,000 books published in the United States and Canada every year.

> Freedom comes from seeing the ignorance of your critics and discovering the emptiness of their virtue.
>
> — Ayn Rand

No doubt there will be at least a few critics and complainers of this world who will trash anything and everything I have written. Regardless of what they say, however, I know in my heart that I have done my best and at the same time accomplished something significant — in fact, my best work ever. So if anyone suggests that I make significant changes, I will likely respond with a line I occasionally borrow from a famous playwright: "Who am I to tamper with a masterpiece?"

Masterpiece or no masterpiece, I have been transformed by writing it. On page 36 I recommended that you ask yourself twelve questions that will help identify your major purpose or important calling in life. The question I had yet to clearly answer myself was the last one: "What sort of legacy or gift would I like to leave to the world?"

Giving some serious thought to this question made me realize that I would like to leave a charitable legacy after I check out of this world for good. My dream is to make a million or two from my books and other sources of income that will fund a course at either the community college or the university in my hometown. The course will be called "Real Success Without a Real Job" and will be taught by a part-time instructor who has attained a measure of real success without a traditional job. Students taking the course will learn the success principles that they must follow if they want to work outside the corporate world at an unreal job.

I admit that my idea for eventually sponsoring a course to teach these principles is a rather quirky dream and a large one to attain. Even so, I am making this dream public. In doing so, I will be more committed to achieving it. I would suggest that you also make your goals public. You must have big goals and believe that you can attain most of them. If you set big goals, as Vancouver mayor Sam Sullivan does, you will be inspired to achieve more. Moreover, if you tell the world about your huge goals, other successful people will be attracted to you and be inspired to help you achieve these goals.

Most successful people in unreal jobs or unconventional businesses have their stories about miraculous incidents that helped them achieve real success without a real job. These chance encounters and synchronistic events did not start happening, however, until these people had made a commitment to their dream job and actually started working toward it. Then the magic began.

With your high intention and commitment, something magical can also start happening in your life. You must allow yourself the experience of letting go of corporate life and jumping into the flow of an unreal job, however. Only then can the magic begin in your life! What will help the magic even more is your having a purpose bigger than making a lot of money just to spend or hoard. You must have a purpose that is bigger than you, in other words.

Once you are totally committed to your purpose, the "how you get there" will eventually show up just in the process of your putting the effort, energy, and persistence into getting there. Meaningful relationships between causally unconnected events and people will start to happen. You will receive money out of the blue when you need it most, and sometimes when you don't need it except to remind you that you are doing the right thing in your career. Facts or figures that you need for your website or a book will appear in today's or tomorrow's newspaper. One obstacle after another will disappear, sometimes suddenly, sometimes after some time. Many unconnected events will converge in fortuitous ways.

> The future belongs to those who believe in the beauty of their dreams.
> — Eleanor Roosevelt

Taking responsibility for your dreams and goals is important. Let's say that on some mystical level you already took responsibility and utilized your tremendous mental powers to create me writing this book for you. In other words, if it weren't for you, for the five months that it took me to write the manuscript I could have been in Vancouver relaxing, cycling, wining and dining at great restaurants, and having coffee at my favorite coffee bars. I trust, however, that you will allow me to spend some time marketing this book and doing a host of other enjoyable things before you again create me writing another book for you.

In the interval, use the principles given herein that best apply to your life situation. The concepts are simple, but profound changes can be made in your life if you apply them. How do I know? All of these success principles have been used by thousands of people worldwide to transform their lives and achieve real success without a real job. If you accept these principles, and follow them religiously, they will transform your life, too.

Always keep in mind that success ultimately is a mode of

> Never work before breakfast; if you have to work before breakfast, eat your breakfast first.
>
> — Josh Billings

traveling and not the destination itself. If you experience real success without a real job long enough, however, you will reach the point of no return. Indeed, there will be no going back to a real job. You will have likely passed the point of no return when you experience the majority or all of the following symptoms:

Irrefutable Signs That You Have Achieved Real Success Without a Real Job

- You no longer know how to prepare for job interviews and don't care that you don't know.
- You wonder why people get up before 9:30 A.M.
- Most people with real jobs criticize or envy you.
- You rely on job ads rather than the Dilbert cartoon for your laugh of the day.
- You are always the last one to know when there is a holiday for working people and you happily work your usual four to five hours anyway.
- You don't ever need any job references.
- You no longer have a Daytimer because you forget to look in it after making an entry.
- Multitasking means working on your laptop in a coffee bar for two hours and watching attractive members of the opposite sex at the same time.
- You know what resume means but have completely forgotten what résumé means.
- You are confident that you will have no problem adjusting to retirement.
- You forget to set your clocks ahead or behind one hour and there are no consequences.
- You realize that prosperity does not require hard work or having lots of material possessions — just creativity, personal freedom, and work that enriches you.
- You have no financial problems because you save more money than most people who earn twice as much as you.
- You can go a whole year without having to set an alarm clock.

- You feel sorry for people who have to work at a real job — even those who earn a million a year.
- You have great friends and spend a lot of time with them, even dropping your work entirely for two or three days when a friend from out of town comes to visit.
- Working at your unreal job connects you to all that is bigger than you.
- You enjoy your unreal job; thus, you can be both at work and not at work simultaneously.
- You get much more enjoyment out of the work you do than from the monetary rewards.
- You know you are no longer employable in a real job and don't care.
- You try to keep an open mind about hard-working lawyers, executives, and doctors but you still can't help feeling just a bit superior.
- You wouldn't trade your present livelihood for anything else — bar none!

Ah, real success without a real job — there is no life like it! Real success without a real job is adventure, satisfaction, riches, and happiness all on your own terms! I can sing its praises as well as anyone. I have earned it, I am living it, and I am enjoying it.

> It doesn't matter who you are, where you come from. The ability to triumph begins with you. Always.
> — Oprah Winfrey

You can, too. My wish is that there will be thousands of ordinary people who read this book, are inspired by it, and eventually achieve extraordinary accomplishments working at an unreal job or operating an unconventional business. With your intention, commitment, eccentricity, dedication, and creativity, you can be one of them!

All things considered, attaining real success without a real job is a game in many ways. It's important to play the game here and now, in the present. Of utmost importance is to find a version of the game worth playing, a version that you truly enjoy. Ensure that you laugh and have fun, even when the score is not in your favor. You have to play the real success game with gutso, and if you get really good at it, you will miraculously transform your life — forever! After all, it's all in how you play the game, isn't it?

About the Author

Ernie Zelinski is best known as the author of *The Joy of Not Working,* an international bestseller that has sold over 200,000 copies and has been published in sixteen languages. He has negotiated eighty-seven book deals with key publishers in twenty-four countries for his fifteen books.

Photograph by Greg Gazin

Feature articles about Ernie and his books have appeared in major newspapers including *USA TODAY, Oakland Tribune, Boston Herald, The Washington Post, Toronto Star,* and *Vancouver Sun.* He has been interviewed by over 100 radio stations and has appeared on CNN TV's Financial News and CBC TV's National News.

Ernie has an Engineering degree and an MBA from the University of Alberta. Because he is truly organizationally averse, he has not had a real job for over twenty-five years. Ernie speaks professionally on the subjects of real· success, retirement, and applying creativity to business and leisure. You can e-mail Ernie at vip-books@telus.net or write to him at Visions International Publishing, P.O. Box 4072, Edmonton, AB, Canada, T6E 4S8.

Irresistible Websites by Ernie Zelinski

Ernie's two websites (listed on the bottom of this page) will further challenge and/or inspire you with cool stuff such as:

- The free e-book *1001 Best Things Ever Said about Work (and the Workplace)*
- Other free e-books including a fine slice of *The Joy of Not Working,* seven volumes in the *Graffiti for the Soul* Series, and over half of *How to Retire Happy, Wild, and Free*
- Resources to help you escape corporate life
- Real life success stories from readers
- What's new to help you attain real success without a real job
- News about Ernie's latest projects

www.Real-Success.ca

www.thejoyofnotworking.com

Irresistible Books by Ernie Zelinski

THE JOY OF NOT WORKING: A Book for the Retired, Unemployed, and Overworked — 21st Century Edition

Ernie Zelinski could change your view of the world forever. Ernie has already taught more than 200,000 people what *The Joy of Not Working* is all about: learning to live every part of your life — employment, unemployment, retirement, and leisure time alike — to the fullest. With this revised and expanded edition, you too can join the thousands of converts and learn to thrive at both work and play. Illustrated by eye-opening exercises, thought-provoking diagrams, and lively cartoons and quotations, *The Joy of Not Working* will guide you to enjoy life like never before.

HOW TO RETIRE HAPPY, WILD, AND FREE: Retirement Wisdom That You Won't Get from Your Financial Advisor

With its friendly format, positive tone, and lively cartoons, *How to Retire Happy, Wild, and Free* is for those individuals who absolutely, positively want to read The World's Best Retirement Book. Above all, retirees are granted the knowledge, freedom, and opportunity to live life like never before. Nancy Conroy of the Association of Pre-Retirement Planners raves: "*How to Retire Happy, Wild, and Free* is optimistic, practical, humorous, and provocative AND comprehensively addresses the many issues impacting individuals as they think about their retirement." The World's Best Retirement Book has already sold over 40,000 copies through word of mouth alone.

Available at fine bookstores throughout the universe, or by ordering directly from the publisher.

Ten Speed Press

P.O. Box 7123, Berkeley, CA 94707

800-841-2665 / www.tenspeed.com